Contact

*50 Verified Encounters with the Virgin Mary
Across 2000 Years and Around the World*

R.A. Varghese

TESTAMENT Book House

228 Park Ave S
PMB 19611
New York, New York 10003-1502

ISBN 978-1-7364447-3-3

Published May 2021

R.A. Varghese is the author and/or editor of sixteen books on the interface of science, philosophy, and religion. His *Cosmos, Bios, Theos*, included contributions from 24 Nobel Prize-winning scientists. *Time* magazine called *Cosmos* "the year's most intriguing book about God." *Cosmic Beginnings and Human Ends*, a subsequent work, won a Templeton Book Prize for "*Outstanding Books in Science and Natural Theology*." Varghese's *The Wonder of the World* was endorsed by leading thinkers including two Nobelists and was the subject of an Associated Press story. He co-authored *There is a God—How the World's Most Notorious Atheist Changed His Mind* with Antony Flew. His most recent work, *The Missing Link*, a study of consciousness, thought and the human self, includes contributions from three Nobel Prize winners and scientists from Oxford, Cambridge, Harvard, and Yale.

For
Rachel – "Little Lamb"
Mary – "Exalted of God"
Michael – "Who is like God"
and our grandson

May the Virgin extend her maternal mantle over their lives and
lead them to the Triune God

Contact!

50 Verified Encounters with the Virgin Mary Across 2000 Years and Around the World

"If I saw an angel come down to teach us good, and I was convinced from others seeing him that I was not mad, I should believe in design."

- **Charles Darwin**, Letter to Asa Gray in "The Life and Letters of Charles Darwin"

"I do not think our cures can compete with those at Lourdes. There are so many more people who believe in the miracle of the Blessed Virgin than in the existence of the unconscious."

- **Sigmund Freud**, *New Introductory Lectures on Psycho-Analysis*

"I had read a lot about the fashions and frivolity of Paris. These were in evidence in every street, but the churches stood noticeably apart from these scenes. A man would forget the outside noise and bustle as soon as he entered one of these churches. His manner would change, he would behave with dignity and reverence as he passed someone kneeling before the image of the Virgin. The feeling I had then has since been growing on me, that all this kneeling and prayer could not be mere superstition; the devout souls kneeling before the Virgin could not be worshipping mere marble. I have an impression that I felt then that by this worship they were not detracting from, but increasing, the glory of God."

- **Mahatma Gandhi**, *My Experiments with Truth: An Autobiography*

"I had some stunning thoughts last night, the result of studying Tolstoi, Spengler, New Testament and also the result of praying to St. Mary to intercede for me to make me stop being a maniacal drunkard ... So far, every prayer addressed to the Holy Mother has been answered ... But I do want to point out, the reason I think she intercedes so well for us, is because she too is a human being." - **Jack Kerouac**, Letter to Bob Giroux, February 1963

"Is Christ only to be adored? Or is the holy Mother of God rather not to be honored? This is the woman who crushed the Serpent's head. Hear us. For your Son denies you nothing."

- **Martin Luther**, Last Sermon at Wittenberg, January 1546

"Love gave her a thousand names" - Flemish hymn on the titles of Mary

"The Lord, the apostles and the prophets have taught us that we must venerate in the first place the Holy Mother of God, who is above all the heavenly powers. If any one does not confess that the holy, ever virgin Mary, really and truly the Mother of God, is higher than all creatures visible and invisible, and does not implore with a sincere faith, her intercession, given her powerful access to our God born of her, let him be anathema."

- **Seventh Ecumenical Council** (accepted by Protestants, Catholics and Orthodox) of the undivided Church, [Second Council of Nicaea]

"It is not every spirit, my dear people, that you can trust; test them, to see if they come from God; ... you can tell the spirits that come from God by this: every spirit which acknowledges that Jesus the Christ has come in the flesh is from God." 1 John 4:1-3.

"Then the dragon was enraged with the woman and went away to make war on the rest of her children, that is, all who obey God's commandments and bear witness for Jesus." Revelation 12:17.

Foreword

Most Rev. David L. Ricken, DD, JCL, Bishop of Green Bay, Wisconsin

Bishop Ricken declared the apparition of Our Lady of Good Help as worthy of belief making it the only Marian apparition approved in the United States of America

Greetings in the Lord Jesus!

I am very pleased to write this forward to *Contact!*, Roy Varghese's most recent book which tells the story of fifty verified encounters of the Blessed Virgin Mary throughout history. This book is an excellent resource for those who wish to hear what Mary is saying to us and to see how she always leads us closer to her divine Son Jesus.

One of the highlights of my life and ministry as a bishop was the small part I played in bringing the apparition of Our Lady of Good Help, also known as Our Lady of Champion to its current status as the only ecclesiastically approved site of Marian apparition in the United States. Building upon the work of my predecessor bishops in northeastern Wisconsin, and after a thorough examination by three Mariological experts, in 2010 I officially declared that the apparitions near the small town of Champion were worthy of belief. And that it is reasonable to believe that in1859 Mary had appeared to a young Belgian American woman named Adele Brise. Furthermore that from that humble experience lives were changed and saved. This declaration was easy for me to make, since it only served to confirm what was already a deeply held and long lasting belief of the People of God living in the Diocese of Green Bay. Mary had indeed appeared here.

How fitting and reasonable it is for us to believe these things. If Mary was preserved from the stain of sin by her Immaculate Conception, and if consequently she was kept from the pain and decay of death and Assumed into Heaven, then it is altogether fitting that she in her glorified body can appear. And appear she does, throughout the world, at different times and places, yet always with the same message of faith, hope and charity. And she often warns us to turn back to our faith in Jesus Christ and to seek his salvation before it is too late.

Mary always points to Jesus. This is her whole task as the Theotokos, or God bearer. Her example of saying yes to God when he called and her Motherly tenderness in interceding for the Church is a powerful example for us on how to live the Christian life. Mary indeed is the highest honor of our race! And she has appeared amongst us.

When you read **Contact!**, I urge you to ponder the fact that these apparitions actually did happen. The veil of heaven was pulled back for a brief moment and the Mother of God spoke to us. Let us follow Mary's example of faith, and always do the will of her divine Son Jesus.

Sincerely Yours in Christ,

Most Rev. David L. Ricken, DD, JCL
Bishop of Green Bay

One "Appearance", Many Encounters

The Once and Future Queen

Hic iacet Arthurus, rex quondam, rexque futurus "Here lies Arthur, king once, and king to be".

Sir Thomas Malory, Le Morte d'Arthur 21:7

> "Then the angel said to her, "Do not be afraid, Mary, for you have found favor with God. Behold, you will conceive in your womb and **bear a son** ... the Lord God will give him **the throne** of David his father". (*Luke* 1:30-32)

> "A great sign **appeared** in the sky, **a woman** clothed with the sun, with the moon under her feet, and on her head a crown of twelve stars. She was **with child**". (*Revelation* 12:1-2)

> "Then the dragon became angry with the woman and went off to wage war against the rest of **her offspring**". (*Revelation* 12:17)

This is the story of "contact", of the terrestrial touching the celestial. The point of Contact is the Virgin Mary, the Mother of Jesus of Nazareth. Jesus said of her to his disciple, "Behold, your mother." She is the "contact" person sent by her Son, her heavenly Father and her Spouse the Holy Spirit. She is the one who "makes contact" with us.

The Contact, by which we mean the act of "making contact," is one and many at the same time. The fundamental manifestation of the Contact is the Appearance in the Sky that we see in Chapter 12 of the biblical *Book of Revelation*. Here we see the Appearance of the Woman Clothed with

1

the Sun, the Bearer of the King of Creation, the Mother sent to protect her other progeny from their Adversary, the Devil.

But this Appearance of *Revelation* 12 unveils itself in a multitude of locales and eras, in hearts and minds, in healings and conversions, prophecies and promises. Above all, these manifest the Contact made by a Mother who constantly hastens to the rescue of her children beset by travails and threats to their safety, sanctity and salvation.

The salvific Death of her Son took place once in history. But it manifests itself continually. "Saul, Saul, why do you persecute me?" "Those who ... have fallen away ... are recrucifying the Son of God for themselves and holding him up to contempt." (*Hebrews* 6:4,6.) "A Lamb that seemed to have been slain." (*Revelation* 5:6).

In like manner, the Appearance of *Revelation* 12 is a continual appearance mirrored in multiple channels and vehicles and settings.

For clarity's sake, we have focused on fifty global channels of the Contact, fifty encounters with the Appearance, that span every era from the first century to the present. Each one of them, like the thousands of others reported through every century, tell us the same tale of maternal protection. "Am I not here who am your Mother," she said in 16th century Mexico to a fearful native of that land.

The Mother of *Revelation* 12 is not simply Our Lady of Fatima or Our Lady of Lourdes, a European phenomenon. She is the Virgin of Guadalupe (Mexico, 1531), the Healing Mother of Vailankanni (India, 1500s and 1600s), Our Lady of Kazan (Russia, 1579), Our Lady of La Vang (Vietnam, 1798), Our Lady of China (1900), Our Lady of Akita (Japan, 1973), and Our Lady of the Word (Kibeho, Rwanda, 1981). Neither are all her "verified encounters" recent. She came to St. James the Greater in Spain in 40 A.D. and to the ancient Christian community of India in 335 A.D.; as Our Lady of the Snows in Rome in 352; as the Theotokos of Protection (Pokrov) in Constantinople in 912 A.D.; as Our Lady of Walsingham in England circa 1061 and as Our Lady of Mount Carmel (again in England) in 1251.

In modern times, the "verified encounters" with the Virgin Mother have been collectively witnessed by tens of thousands and sometimes hundreds of thousands of witnesses. This was the case at Fatima (Portugal, 1917) where the Miracle of the Sun was witnessed by 70,000 people; at Zeitoun, (Egypt, 1968) where she was seen (and photographed) by several hundred thousand people of every religion; and Hrushiv (1987, Ukraine) where she was seen not only by hundreds of thousands of people but on national TV. In Akita (Japan, 1973), the statue of the Virgin was seen shedding tears on TV by 12 million Japanese viewers.

The encounters documented here barely scratch the surface of the accounts of the Contact. Ralph McInerny notes that there are two thousand such stories of ancient encounters with the Virgin in Latin; another five hundred in verse and six hundred in prose in old French; and numerous others in Anglo-Norman, English, German, Norse and Spanish. In *Miracles of Mary*, Michael S. Durham writes that "the Virgin Mary has appeared more than 21,000 times in the past ten centuries." The French paper *Le Monde* even said there were 21,000 claims of apparitions between 1976 and 1986!

The stories told here, we claim, are "verified encounters." But who does the verifying? Scientific "verification" in the strictest sense applies only to the world of quantities (from quarks to genes) and their measurement; this is the true nature of modern science as astutely explained in the recent book *The Knowledge Machine* by Michael Strevens. Such quantitative measurement procedures are impossible to apply in the world of persons, encounters, testimonies and nature-transcending phenomena attesting to the Contact.

Nevertheless, the verification applied to the encounters with the Virgin is analogous to the "rules" of science.

First, there is the phenomenon, the appearance of the Virgin. It is this phenomenon that has to be explained. In science, we start with a specific phenomenon as well and try to explain it. For instance, we observe matter in motion and try to explain why and how this happens.

Second, in scientific practice, a theory is proposed to explain the phenomenon and the theory is analyzed by peers. In the case of the claimed appearance, Church-appointed committees critically study the credibility of the witness and the consistency and coherence of their claims. In this situation, the Church plays the role of judge, jury and prosecutor. The witness is considered guilty until proven innocent. It may be asked if the Church can be relied on to play this role.

In almost all instances of such claims, Church authorities have been skeptical. At the best of times, the Church is reluctant to share its authority with any other source. Neither does it want to be a party to something that turns out to be fraudulent or a diabolic deception. Hence its default position has been critical. The historian David Blackbourn notes that, "For all historians of the subject, clerical approval has created superior documentation." Likewise, Yale historian Jaroslav Pelikan writes that, "The miraculous powers of the Virgin of Lourdes and the Virgin of Fatima have received certification at the highest level of authority."

The veracity of all the encounters chronicled here have been "certified" by Church authorities.

Thirdly, and most importantly, for a theory to pass scientific muster it must make successful predictions and be repeatable by anyone. Newton's laws of motion made predictions which can and have been verified; and experiments that assume the truth of the theory can be repeated by anyone (as shown by the success of space flight for instance). In the case of encounters with the Virgin, there is prediction and repeatability of a certain kind, namely, continuing phenomena that transcend the laws of nature. These include the enduring signs/"smoking guns" documented in many of the encounters listed here, such as the miraculous images of Guadalupe or las Lajas, that cannot be explained from the standpoint of science. In addition, there are the miracles experienced in the various encounter sites to this day. The only explanation of the "smoking guns" and the continuing miracles lies in the existence of a supernatural order of being of which the Contact is a witness.

It is these three "confirmation" principles that in one way or another underlie the fifty encounters reviewed here.

But first some questions: who is the Virgin and why was she sent? How do we know if her mission is of God? And do we know if any of this is true?

The questions have clear and cogent answers. We treat these in more detail in the Reference section. For now we present a few quick responses before turning to the hard data that testify to the Contact.

The Jewish Queen-Mother in Scripture and Ancient Christianity

Our first glimpse of the Virgin Mary is in the Gospels. Mary of Nazareth is Jewish like her Son and his disciples and the earliest leaders of the new Faith. Too often, we have forgotten this in the case of both the Virgin and her Son.

Perhaps the greatest breakthrough in biblical studies over the last three decades has been the discovery of the Jewish Jesus. A May 2008 *Time* story described this as one of the "ten ideas that are changing the world." To understand what Jesus of Nazareth said and did and how he was perceived we must understand first the theological thought-world and symbol-universe in which he lived, spoke and acted. He was Jewish and lived in the world of Second Temple Judaism. Now this might seem obvious but incredibly most of the leading lights in the history of New Testament criticism seemed entirely oblivious to it. As a result they created a Jesus of their own imagination and in their image – a German Jesus or a hippie Jesus, to give two examples, instead of the Jewish Jesus of first century Palestine. They missed the meaning of his affirmations, teachings and actions as understood by his contemporaries. Fortunately, a re-discovery of the Jewish Jesus is now in progress.

In like manner, many Christians today have also ignored the Jewish identity of the Mother of Jesus, Mary of Nazareth. Of central importance here is the understanding of the first Christians – formed by their Jewish legacy – that she was the New Eve, the Ark of the Covenant and the Queen-Mother. All three dimensions are important in understanding the Contact.

The process of re-discovering the Jewish Mary has finally begun. *Jesus and the Jewish Roots of Mary* by the New Testament scholar Brante Pitre is a pioneering work in this area. Pitre says, "Judaism is especially important for understanding Mary.... Every book on Mary that rejected Catholic

5

beliefs as unbiblical invariably ignored the Old Testament background of what the New Testament says about Mary.... The reason so many people can't see how biblical Catholic beliefs about Mary really are is because they are only looking at what the New Testament says about her, and ignoring the prefigurations of Mary in the Old Testament. Keep looking at the New Testament in isolation, and you'll never understand who Mary really is. Start looking at Mary through ancient Jewish eyes, and everything becomes clear."[1]

Among other things, in his writings, Pitre highlights the importance for the first Christians of the Virgin's status as Queen-Mother:

> The first Christians did not get their beliefs about Mary from the celestial goddesses of paganism. "It got them from Judaism. In order to see this clearly, you have to look at Mary through ancient Jewish eyes. You have to look at Mary in light of what the Old Testament says about the Jewish Queen.
>
> In ancient Israel, the king did not rule alone. There was also a queen. However, the queen was not the king's wife, but his mother. She was known as the "Queen Mother"—in Hebrew, the gebirah.
>
> To get an idea of just how important the Queen Mother was, consider what the Bible says about Bathsheba, the wife of King David and mother of King Solomon.
>
> When Bathsheba comes into David's presence, she bows to him as her king (1 Kings 1:15-16). But after David dies and Solomon her son becomes king, the tables are turned. Now, when Bathsheba comes into Solomon's presence, he bows to her (1 Kings 2:19)! The king himself honors his mother because she is queen.
>
> But it doesn't stop there. King Solomon also has a "throne" brought in, so that his mother can sit at his "right" hand (1 Kings 2:19). Everyone knew what this meant. The Queen Mother was the most powerful person in the kingdom—second only to the king himself.
>
> That's why when the Queen Mother asks a favor of Solomon, he answers: "Make your request, my mother, for I will not refuse you" (1 Kings 2:20).

What does all this mean for who Mary was, and how Christians see her today?

First, if Jesus really was the long-awaited Jewish King—the Messiah—then his mother was the Jewish Queen.

That's what it would have meant to a Jewish girl like Mary when the angel Gabriel told her that her son would "sit on the throne of his father David" (Luke 1:33). As mother of the new King, Mary would be the new Queen Mother.

It's also why the book of Revelation describes the mother of the Messiah as a woman "in heaven" wearing "a crown of twelve stars" (Revelation 12:1-2). The crown shows she is a queen, and the twelve stars symbolize the people of Israel.

Second, if Mary is the new Queen Mother, then it makes sense to honor her. After all, "Honor your father and your mother" is one of the Ten Commandments (Exodus 20:12).

It isn't idolatry to honor the queen. If the queens of earthly kingdoms are honored and loved by their people, then how much more the Queen Mother of the Kingdom of God?

Finally, if Mary is the Queen Mother of Jesus' Kingdom, then she is certainly no ordinary woman. She is, quite literally, the most powerful woman in the universe. She is the true Queen of Heaven.

And Mary is still alive in heaven. (After all, we call it "eternal life"— not death.). As Queen Mother, Mary sits at Jesus' right hand. And, like King Solomon, Jesus will not refuse her requests.

That's why, since ancient times, Christians have asked Mary to pray for them. Consider the words of the most ancient Christian prayer to Mary we possess, written in Greek and discovered in the early 20th century on a scrap of papyrus:

"Under your mercy, we take refuge, O Mother of God. Do not disregard our prayers in time of trouble, but deliver us from danger,

O only pure one, only blessed one." (Anonymous Christian Prayer, 3rd-4th century)

If Jesus really is the King he claimed to be, and Mary really is the Queen Mother, then it makes sense to ask her to intercede with her Son for us and for a world in need. [2]

The consolidation of the canon of the New Testament took place only in the fourth century and was, in fact, guided by a body of truth that came before it. This body of truth, held by the faithful from the very beginning, included the doctrines and devotions relating to the Mother of Jesus. Even a critic of Marian devotion like the Baptist Albert Mohler acknowledged that "forms of Marian devotion can be traced to the earliest periods of church history."[3]

The catacombs of the Christian martyrs of the second and third centuries not only show images representing the scriptural stories but also images of the Virgin in which her mediation is invoked for protection and defense. We get some idea of what the early Christians thought about the Virgin Mary from prayers like the famous *Sub Tuum Praesidium*, found in an Egyptian papyrus from approximately 250 A.D., that formed part of the Coptic Christmas liturgy: "We fly to thy patronage, O holy Mother of God; despise not our petitions in our necessities, but deliver us always from all dangers, O glorious and blessed Virgin. Amen." Churches in ancient Israel highlighted the connection between Jesus and Mary: "Archaeologists have unearthed a 1,500-year-old inscribed Christian blessing that begins, 'Christ, born of Mary,' the Israel Antiquities Authority reported Wednesday (Jan. 20, 2021).... The church itself dates to the late fifth century A.D.... The opening line, "Christ born of Mary," was likely intended to protect the reader of the inscription from evil forces."[4] The *Jerusalem Post* notes that "The words "Christ born of Mary" were widely used at the beginning of documents or other forms of text, serving as a blessing and protection from evil."[5]

Collectively, the teachings of the earliest Fathers, Councils and liturgies show us a historic Christian consensus about the Virgin Mary that emerged from the very beginning and extended over the first fifteen hundred years of Christendom. It was a consensus that the New Testament reveals a Mary who was the Immaculate (Council of Constantinople III), All-holy (Nicaea II), Perpetually Virgin (Constantinople III) Mother of God (Ephesus, Chalcedon), Mother of Humanity and Intercessor before the Trinity (Nicaea II); she was the New Eve with Jesus the New Adam and, as New Eve, Mother of all Christians.

The historic Christian consensus on Marian doctrine and devotion, therefore, is the scriptural understanding of Mary proclaimed by the Fathers, ancient liturgies and Councils. If we reject that understanding then consistency demands that we also reject their understanding of such doctrines as the Blessed Trinity or the two natures and one Person in Christ. These latter doctrines are not taught in so many words by Scripture but the people who were closest to the human authors of Scripture understood these authors to be teaching certain doctrines about the Triune God, the incarnate Son of God and the Blessed Virgin. These doctrines stand or fall together: picking and choosing is neither logically nor historically defensible.

The historic Christian consensus on Mary as Mother of God, perpetually virgin and personally holy was inherited and accepted by the architects of the Protestant Reformation, Martin Luther, John Calvin and Ulrich Zwingli. (We will be considering their views of mediation in the Reference section.)

But the ancient veneration of the Virgin has been lost in modern times. Did this loss come about from a re-discovery of what the Bible teaches? The answer is "No" since the faithful in ancient times were familiar not just with the New Testament narratives but, sometimes, with the authors of these narratives. Moreover, if the Christian community had been wrong for all these centuries in its fundamental beliefs about the Virgin Mary, then there is no reason to believe it was right on any other doctrine including the doctrine of the Trinity. The doctrines and devotions relating to the Virgin Mary, then, are inextricably intertwined with Christianity as a whole.

Affirmation of the appearances of the Virgin Mary in history was also ancient. The Protestant Evangelical magazine *Christianity Today* called the claim of an apparition witnessed in Asia Minor in 238 A.D. the "first Marian apparition" (strictly speaking, it was preceded by a 40 A.D. apparition in Spain).

In the Reference section, we will review the historical understanding of the Virgin as the New Eve and the contemporary renaissance of Marian studies among Christians of every background.

We turn now to the rationale for the Contact.

The Virgin Commissioned as Mother of the Faithful

"Mary is the Mother of Jesus and the mother of us all. If Christ is ours, we must be where he is; and all that he has must be ours, and his mother is therefore also ours."[6] Martin Luther

"When Jesus saw his mother and the disciple there whom he loved, he said to his mother, "Woman, behold, your son." Then he said to the disciple, "Behold, your mother." And from that hour the disciple took her into his home." *John* 19:26-7

"A great sign appeared in the sky, a woman clothed with the sun, with the moon under her feet, and on her head a crown of twelve stars. She was with child ... Then the dragon stood before the woman about to give birth, to devour her child when she gave birth. She gave birth to a son, a male child, destined to rule all the nations with an iron rod. Her child was caught up to God and his throne.... The huge dragon, the ancient serpent, who is called the Devil and Satan, who deceived the whole world, was thrown down to earth, and its angels were thrown down with it. Then I heard a loud voice in heaven say ... "The Devil has come down to you in great fury, for he knows he has but a short time." When the dragon saw that it had been thrown down to the earth, it pursued the woman who had given birth to the male child..... Then the dragon became angry with the woman and went off to wage war against the rest of her offspring, those who keep God's commandments and bear witness to Jesus." *Revelation* 1-2,4-5, 9-10,12-13, 17

The Gospels spotlight the role played by the Virgin in the earthly mission of her Son. The Gospel of *John* and the *Book of Revelation* tell us that this role takes on a new dimension in the work of salvation through the rest of history. We learn in the Epistles that those who accept the divine offer of salvation become adopted brothers and sisters of Jesus filled with the Holy Spirit and thereby children of the Abba Father. But to become an adopted brother or sister of Jesus is to become a child of his Mother. This last feature tells us why her Son tells his beloved disciple, "Behold, your mother." As Brant Pitre and other New Testament scholars have pointed out, the "beloved disciple" in John represents all disciples. "The Beloved Disciple represents every disciple" and so "Jesus is also giving Mary to all who believe in him—all his "beloved disciples."[7]

The *Book of Revelation* consolidates the understanding that all the followers of Jesus become children of his Mother.

In fact, *Revelation* 12 spells out the reason for the Contact. She makes contact because her Son gives her to us. This is her divinely appointed role – to be our Mother.

Taken as it stands, there can be little doubt that the Woman Clothed with the Sun is the Virgin Mary. For the text says earlier that she is the mother of "a son ... destined to rule all the nations with an iron rod.". This is a reference to Psalm 2 with its prophecy of the Messiah who will rule all nations with an iron rod. From the reference to the Messianic Psalm 2 and to the account of his ascension to Heaven (*Revelation* 12:5), it is apparent that the son of the Woman is Jesus.

Strangely, many of today's most ardent defenders of the literal reading of Scripture have suddenly developed cold feet concerning the literal truth of this passage. Yes, they say, the text shows that she is the Mother of the Messiah but we should interpret "Mother" to mean the People of Israel or, if that does not work, as the Christian Church. Neither of these allegorical interpretations "work" for various reasons. You cannot justify a collective interpretation of one of the figures (the Woman) and an individual interpretation for the other (the Son). Second, the people of Israel have never been represented as the Mother of an individual who is the Messiah anywhere else in Scripture. In fact, the writer of this book is painfully aware of the persecution of Christians by the Pharisees, et al, and it is unimaginable that he would represent them playing a maternal role! Third, the Christian Church cannot seriously be thought of as the "mother" of Christ when the Church emerges *from* Christ. In fact, the Woman is shown as Mother of all Christians. So the Marian interpretation is the only plausible one.

Of course, the Virgin Mary in her own being represents both the People of Israel and the Church and thus, in a secondary allegorical sense, the "Woman" can be seen as representing both Israel and the Church. For an example, think of the references to the Daughter of Zion in the Old Testament that parallel texts about the Mary of the New Testament. At a primary level, "Daughter of Zion" referred to Israel but in a secondary sense, it has been seen as a prophecy of the Virgin Mary who embodies Israel receiving her Savior.

Pitre points out that since both the Child (Jesus) and the Dragon (the Devil) are concrete individuals, the woman too has to be seen as an individual. And since she is shown to be the Mother of the Child, she is none other than the Virgin Mary. He notes too that, since she is wearing a crown, the Woman is a queen and, in view of the practice in ancient Israel, she has to be seen as the Queen-Mother. The Mother who is thereby Queen.[8]

At its close, *Revelation* 12 has more to tell us about the Woman: "Then the dragon became angry with the woman and went off to wage war against the rest of her offspring, those who keep God's commandments and bear witness to Jesus."

As the text makes clear, all those who "bear witness for Jesus", then, are children of the Woman. As we have seen, the Woman is the Mother of Jesus. The dragon is referenced (12:9) to "the primeval serpent known as the devil or Satan" of *Genesis* 3. *Revelation* 12 is thus linked to *Genesis* 3 which refers to the future conflict between the serpent and the Woman and her Son. Historically, Christians (including Martin Luther) have seen *Genesis* 3 as a prophecy of the coming of Christ and his Mother and their war with Satan. This dovetails with the *Revelation* 12 account of the war between Christ and his Mother on the one side and Satan on the other (the International Ecumenical Bible Commentary notes that *Revelation* 12:17 is a clear reference to the messianic text of *Genesis* 3:15).

The Virgin's Motherhood as manifested in *Revelation* 12 shows her mediation on behalf of her children. This maternal mediation is the reason for the Contact. The Contact is continual and multifarious but it is always the Contact of *Revelation* 12:17.

The Virgin Mother in History

Revelation 12 shows us the Woman, her Son the King, the Devil and the other "offspring" of the Woman. Her offspring are those "who keep God's commandments and bear witness to Jesus." The Devil is "angry" with the Woman and wages war on "the rest of her offspring". As their Mother she provides

> Protection and encouragement and healing
> Exhortations to keep the commandments of God
> Exhortations to witness to Jesus
> Exhortations to turn away from the Devil and damnation

Every one of the encounters described in the present work, every encounter with the Virgin in human experience and history, falls under one or more of these categories. Most importantly, every one of them is the Appearance of a Mother.

The most eloquent formulation of her motherhood came at Guadalupe where she told Juan Diego: "Am I not here who am your mother?"

Every other encounter is just as much the Appearance of the Mother. Once we recognize this, everything falls into place. Everything about the encounters, astoundingly diverse as they are, makes sense. They are many but one as we shall see. A mother exercises her maternal role in many respects: meeting physical, spiritual, emotional and many other kinds of needs. So it is with the Virgin Mother.

The understanding of this mother among the first Christians was of her as the Sorrowful Mother. She is both Sorrowful (Calvary) and Merciful (Cana). This is central to her relationship with her children as exemplified in the encounters.

When we speak of encounter here, we are speaking of the manifestation of the Contact in one form or other. Most of the instances discussed involve appearances of the Virgin to one or more witnesses. Some of these appearances involve messages, some involve signs and wonders and some are just visions intended to show her presence. Other manifestations of the Contact involve icons of the Mother – whether images or statues – that localize and "broadcast" the loving presence and activity of the Mother for the faithful.

As we have said, the encounters cannot be scientifically "verified" because science deals only with what can be measured. The Contact is not quantifiable in this manner. The Church, on the other hand, deals with the kind of non-quantifiable spiritual realities associated with the Contact. The Church "believes" what cannot be seen but only if the right kind of evidence is produced (as will be illustrated). To be sure, many details of the ancient encounters are lost in the murky mists of time. But the evidence for them rests on two foundations: first and foremost, the contemporary miracles associated with them and, second, the existence of a community continuously testifying to their essential truth.

Many encounters, one Contact. Concretely speaking, we see below how the diversity of these encounters can be classified under one or more dimensions of the Contact.

Protection against sickness
Guadalupe, Mexico, 1531; Lourdes, France, 1858; La Vang, Vietnam, 1798; Vailankanni, India, 1500s-1600s; Kuravilangad, India, 335; Genoa, Italy 1490; Ocotlan, Mexico, 1541; Las Lajas, Colombia, 1754; Lichen, Poland, 1813, 1850; Fillipsdorf, Czech Republic, 1866; Knock, Ireland, 1879; Beauraing, Belgium, 1932; Banneux, Belgium, 1933; San Nicolas, Argentina, 1983-1990.

Protection and Encouragement in the Midst of travails
Fatima, Portugal, 1917; La Vang, Vietnam, 1798; Dong Lu, China, 1900, 1995; Kazan, Russia, 1579; Czestochowa, Poland, 1382; Kuravilangad, India, 335; Constantinople (Istanbul), Turkey, 912; Walsingham, England, 1061; Kibeho, Rwanda, 1981-1989; Vallarpadam, India, 1752; Rue de Bac, France, 1830; Pontmain, France, 1870; Hrushiv, Ukraine, 1914, 1987;

Caacupé, Paraguay, 1500s; Sao Paulo, Brazil, 1717; Tra Kieu, Vietnam, 1885; Zeitoun, Egypt, 1968; Jerusalem, Israel 1954

Exhortations to keep the commandments of God
Lourdes, France, 1858; Fatima, Portugal, 1917; Genazzano, Italy, 1467; Akita, Japan, 1973; Damascus, Syria, 1982-1990; Cuapa, Nicaragua, 1980; Wisconsin, USA, 1859

Exhortations to undergo conversion and witness to Jesus
Guadalupe, Mexico, 1531; Zaragoza, Spain, 40; Rome, Italy, 352; Walsingham, England, 1061; Genazzano, Italy, 1467; Lezajsk, Poland, 1578; Champion, US, 1859; Damascus, Syria, 1982-1990; Venezuela, 1651; San Nicolas, Argentina, 1983-1990; Šiluva, Lithuania, 1608; Rome, Italy, 1842; Laus, France, 1664; Querrien, France, 1652; Hungary, 1960

Exhortations to turn away from the Devil and damnation
Fatima, Portugal, 1917; England, 1251; Quito, 1594; Akita, Japan, 1973; Kibeho, Rwanda, 1981-1983; La Salette, France, 1846; Rome, Italy, 1947

It is not a coincidence that the Virgin appears often to children who instinctively recognize her to be their Mother. Children also happen to be reliable witnesses who are less likely to be misled by preconceptions. Even when she appears to adults, such as with Juan Diego, she speaks to them as her children.

Although the best-known encounters with the Virgin Mother have shaped entire populations, their ultimate objective is individual and personal. They are meant to lead each human person to a personal relationship with the Mother given to them by their Savior. As a Mother, her interest is primarily in their salvation and secondarily in meeting all their other needs.

The Evidence is In – "Case Closed"

We turn now to a totally different issue – one which is of decisive importance. Why should we believe any of this? What "proof" is there that any of it happened?

The answer lies in the enduring signs, the "smoking guns", scattered all through the various encounters. How do we explain the dizzying variety of phenomena across the world and across centuries that somehow still form a unified pattern? How do we explain the mysterious "black boxes" associated with some of these encounters that entirely elude scientific explanation even in the present day – the tilma of Guadalupe or the healing waters of Lourdes (that are made up simply of water!) or the rocks of Las Lajas? How do we explain the continuing power of personal transformation at the sites of these encounters?

Most of the encounters discussed here concern apparitions of the Virgin. The Oxford American Dictionary defines the term "apparition" as "an appearance, something that appears, especially something remarkable or unexpected." This newer definition certainly fits in with its usage in a Marian context.

The very idea of "apparitions" of a human person is peculiar to Christianity. Although there have been claims of appearances of angels in post-Christian religions, reports of a human person sent by God appearing across history with a message for the world is quite simply unique to Marian apparitions. Neither Hinduism nor any of the world religions has any tradition or even concept of such a phenomenon. Thus reports and claims of Marian apparitions stand in a class of their own without analogy or replication in the history of religions.

Apparitions must be distinguished from dreams, illusions and hallucinations (none of these three exist anywhere except in the mind of the subject) on the one hand and visions on the other. In an apparition, the witness sees a three-dimensional person who is really there but who has a glorified body (the resurrected body). Whereas a vision is an internal event, an apparition is external: a person is present at a definite location in space and time and is visible (in many of the great apparitions) to more than one witness. Visions can be imaginative (involving images) or spiritual (imageless) but in a vision a body is not objectively present although an angel who appears in a vision will "assume" a body. The witness to an apparition is commonly called "visionary". This term is somewhat misleading since it suggests that the witness is "unworldly" (most visionaries have been down to earth) or the viewer of a vision. We will continue to use the term "visionary" here with all its handicaps since the only other viable alternative, "seer," has been hijacked by dabblers in the occult.

What is the character of the "seeing" in an apparition? It is perhaps a distinctive perception that occurs when we witness a glorified body. Maybe it is even a foretaste of the kind of "seeing" that we will enjoy in a glorified state. We know it has the character of normal "seeing" to the visionary because all the visionaries report that the Virgin appears to them and converses with them as a three-dimensional flesh-and-blood human being - albeit clothed in heavenly splendor. We know also that this "seeing" is restricted to the visionaries, since nobody else present at an apparition sees the Virgin (except in those apparitions like Hrushiv and Zeitoun where she appeared to thousands of people - in those instances she did not come to entrust specific individuals with a specific mission).

Finally, we know that, in most cases, a visionary is visibly transformed during the apparition and enters into a state of ecstasy in which he or she is oblivious to sensory stimuli (this has been observed not just in modern apparitions like Lourdes, Fatima and Beauraing but also in the cases of mystics through the centuries such as Teresa of Avila). Thus, a third-party observer present at an apparition does not "see" the Virgin but can see the changes to the visionary - the state of ecstasy and the fact that he or she is communicating with someone who is invisible to the observer.

Apparition sites can also be venues of extraordinary phenomena that are visible to all present: the dancing sun at Fatima or such physically miraculous objects as the tilma. Again, spiritual fruits are associated with apparition sites: conversions, renewed fervor and the like.

A glorified body exhibits the properties we observe in the Risen Body of Jesus (although he had not yet ascended to Heaven): it is three-dimensional and yet agile (not limited in its speed of movement), subtle (passing through solid objects), invisible (unless it appears to a chosen soul), immortal and immune to any decay or disease. This body appears only to those who have been specially selected: the Risen Christ did not appear before the Roman or Jewish authorities but only before faithful followers who were entrusted with a mission.

Similarly, the glorified body of the Mother of Jesus only appears to those who have been selected for a mission. The souls of these individuals are elevated in such a manner as to be able to "perceive" the glorified body (although we note that their sensory organs also play a role as evidenced by the movement of their eyes and lips during an apparition). Until the General Judgment only two human beings have their glorified bodies: Jesus who rose from the dead and ascended to Heaven and Mary his Mother who was assumed body and soul into Heaven (as affirmed in the ancient liturgies and in *Revelation* 12). The only true apparitions are appearances of a Risen Body and this is why we hear almost always of apparitions of the Virgin Mary. Jesus will come again in his Risen Body only at the end of history - although he can and has appeared in visions as have saints and angels.

Every visionary has said that the beauty and splendor of the Blessed Virgin was beyond any earthly description - this is only to be expected if we are to go by the description of the template of every Marian apparition, the Woman Clothed by the Sun. In many of the apparitions, the visionaries did not at first know if the Lady they saw was the Virgin – just as Mary Magdalen did not at first recognize the Risen Christ. But once he spoke she knew who he was - and once the Lady spoke the visionaries knew who she was.

Evidence and Explanation

The globe- and history-spanning nature of Marian apparitions is little known. Almost as little-known is the fact that there is a comprehensive body of tangible evidence supporting the historically accepted apparition reports. Moreover, despite repeated attempts to do so by the most determined skeptics, not one of the constituents of this body of evidence has been nullified nor a single visionary (witness of the apparition) discredited. The Prosecution has had every possible opportunity to undermine the veracity of the star witnesses and the credibility of the evidence on the table. And yet it has presented no case. An a priori rejection of supernatural phenomena is irrelevant because it simply begs the question raised by the existence of the evidence. Speculative theories about apparitions as projections of fears and fantasies from the vulnerable visionary's unconscious are not helpful in the courtroom because they cannot begin to account for the tangible evidence. So the Prosecution has built no case. And the jury - here the human race - reached its verdict a long time ago: the visionaries were truthful when they reported the apparitions of the Virgin.

The tangible evidence is extraordinary in its variety. Take the famous tilma of Guadalupe with the miraculous image of the Virgin. Despite decades spent in trying to show it to be a human painting, there is still no scientific explanation for its origin (its colors, for example, do not originate from any animal, vegetable or mineral dye known in this world). Take the spring at Lourdes. Numerous meticulously documented healings have taken place here but the analyses done on the contents of the spring have shown it to be plain water (such healing springs are not uncommon in Marian apparitions, another prominent example being Vailankanni, India). Take the prophecies of Fatima about the second world war and the rise and demise of Communism in Russia (the apparition took place before any of these events).

Or (as highlighted earlier) take the televised apparition of the Virgin in Hrushiv, Ukraine - an apparition that appeared on the television screens of the former Soviet Union - and the photographs of the Lady of Light that were taken during the apparitions in Zeitoun, Eqypt before hundreds of thousands of people. Likewise, the sparkling tears on the wooden statue of Our Lady of Akita appeared on national TV in Japan.

A recurrent motif in Marian apparitions is the Virgin's desire to provide a "sign" for those who do not believe. "Signs" were on occasion demanded by church authorities or family members who wanted evidence that the visionary was indeed witnessing an apparition of the Virgin. The most famous sign of all was the Tilma of Guadalupe but others, such as the miracle of the sun at Fatima, have been almost as remarkable. Here it may be well to note that signs and wonders in Marian apparitions are never performed for sensational purposes but in response to a request for evidence (in contrast to the kind of bizarre phenomena one would expect if these events were diabolically directed). The signs serve the function of giving sufficient ground for belief - and this was the case with the signs and wonders performed by Jesus. Thus the Virgin acknowledges and responds to legitimate demands for evidence.

The case for the authenticity of the apparition claims chronicled here may be summarized as detailed below:

1. The revelation of God in Jesus Christ was truly a revelation of God as he is in himself and of the origin and purpose of human life.

2. God acts in human history through His chosen instruments to bring about conversion to Christ and subsequently sanctification and salvation. But a true conversion cannot be coerced: it must be freely accepted.

3. In God's blueprint of salvation, the Virgin Mary is the New Eve who brings us the New Adam through her free choice, the Spouse of the Holy Spirit (she is the only human person in Scripture who is overshadowed by the Spirit), the Mother of all Christians who are adopted brothers and sisters of her Son Jesus. Her first apparition to the faithful is shown in Scripture in *Revelation* 12. *Revelation* 12:17 shows that she will be present with Christians throughout their battle against Satan. At Cana, we see that her intercession bears fruit in "signs." Many interpretations have been given of the significance of this event but two facts are undeniable: she requested a miracle and her Son performed one in response. We are intrigued also by the curious comment, "My time has not yet come." Does this mean that when his time has come (which it did on Calvary), his Mother can intercede with him for miracles?

4. Numerous credible witnesses across the globe and throughout history have claimed to have seen the Virgin. Some of these witnesses were the holiest people of their time who were later venerated as saints. Most of the witnesses were children who were in many cases very severely questioned but still held to their stories. During an actual apparition, it is quite evident to onlookers that a naturalistically inexplicable change has taken place in the visionary (technically termed a state of ecstasy). In some of the apparitions, the Virgin asked the visionaries to keep certain of her messages as "secrets" that could only be revealed to the appointed person at the appointed time. The tenacity with which the younger visionaries have refused to reveal these "secrets" - from Lourdes to La Salette

to Fatima – despite threats (sometimes to their lives as at Fatima) and bribes is another paradoxical feature of the apparition stories.

5. The ecclesiastical authorities have in most instances been skeptical about apparition claims and visionaries. Fatima, for instance, was approved as worthy of belief only thirteen years after it ended. Thus, the Christian community as a whole did not simply accept claims of apparitions without carefully securing and studying the evidence. Generally, the visionaries themselves were transformed by their experiences and led exemplary lives thereafter.

6. The messages of the various apparitions are remarkably consistent despite the enormous differences of locations and timeframes.

7. The messages received at the various apparitions in one way or another echo the words of the Virgin Mary recorded in Scripture: on the importance of doing God's will; on the divine mandate that all generations are to call her blessed; and on the intercessory role she assumed at the beginning of her Son's ministry.

8. Many of the major apparitions have ended with a "lasting sign" that is not susceptible to natural explanation (the tilma of Guadalupe for instance).

9. There is a correlation between the crises in history and the appearances of the Virgin: she comes whenever her children need her.

10. The apparitions have had a concrete effect on history and on millions of people.

All of the facts above call out for an explanation. Explanation is the fundamental job of both good science and sound philosophy. We start with the assumption that explanations exist for everything (and this is where the quest for an explanation for the existence of the universe leads ultimately to the existence of God). We accept explanations for phenomena that most plausibly fit the evidence. We discount purported explanations that are driven by ideological agendas or mere speculation especially when these refuse to address the evidence in hand.

No serious naturalistic explanation has been offered by the skeptics.

If we look at the global and history-spanning nature of the encounters known as apparitions, the curious consistency of messages from multiple witnesses separated by time and space, the tangible "lasting signs" and the resultant mass conversions continuing to this very day, we are left with no other plausible or viable explanation but that of the witnesses and the masses.

The encounters individually and collectively testify to the Contact made by the Virgin Mother.

NOTES

[1] https://www.catholicworldreport.com/2020/09/07/what-does-the-bible-really-say-about-mary-the-mother-of-the-messiah/

[2] https://aleteia.org/2018/11/01/a-jewish-perspective-on-the-queen-of-all-these-saints-were-celebrating/

[3] http://www.rapturenotes.com/mary.html

[4] https://www.livescience.com/christ-born-of-mary-church-artifact.html

[5] https://www.jpost.com/archaeology/ancient-christ-born-of-mary-inscription-unearthed-in-northern-israel-656071

[6] *Luther's Works*, Weimar, 29:655:26-656:7.

[7] https://www.catholicworldreport.com/2020/09/07/what-does-the-bible-really-say-about-mary-the-mother-of-the-messiah/

[8] https://catholicproductions.com/blogs/blog/revelation-12-and-mary-queen-of-heaven

Everywhere, Every Time

50 Verified Encounters with the Virgin from Around the World

Overview

The Contact manifests itself in apparitions (appearances) and miraculous icons, extraordinary events and transformational messages. It is a global, millennia-spanning phenomenon.

Universal and Perennial

The first ever apparition of the Virgin that is universally recognized took place in Spain in 40 A.D. This apparition was followed by five others that are traditionally accepted. Three of these were reported in Asia and two in Europe – Asia Minor (238 A.D.), France (ca. 250 A.D.), India (335 A.D.), Italy (352 A.D.) and Turkey (912 A.D.).

Through the centuries, many men and women who later generations called saints have reported witnessing apparitions of the Virgin. This pattern goes back to such famous instances as the Asia Minor apparition to St. Gregory the Wonder Worker and to St. John Damascene of Syria in 749. She appeared to the founders of some of the most influential religious orders in history ranging from St. Francis of Assisi (Franciscans) to St. Ignatius of Loyola (Jesuits). Many famous mystics were also favored with apparitions: St. Bernard of Clairvaux, St. Bridget of Sweden, St. Gertrude, St. Catherine of Siena, St. Sergius of Radonezh, St. Teresa of Avila, St. Margaret Mary Alacoque and St. Seraphim of Sarov.

In the second Christian millennium, authenticated encounters with the Virgin continued to take place across the world and not just in Europe as some assume: two in Mexico, two in India, two in Vietnam, two in China, seven in South America, one each in the USA, Egypt, Syria, Israel, Rwanda and Japan. Europe had several "high-impact" apparitions, the two best-known being in France and Portugal. But Guadalupe, Mexico, was the single most influential apparition of all and converted an entire nation to Christianity. Three of the most powerful icons in history were also re-discovered in this period: the Black Madonna in Czestochowa, Poland in 1382, Our Lady of Kazan in Kazan, Russia in 1579 and Our Lady of Aparecida in Brazil in 1717.

House of God

In many of the major and minor apparitions, the Virgin asked the visionary to build a chapel or shrine. This was the case in the French apparition of the third century and, of course, later in Guadalupe. Another instance was the famous apparition to Richeldis de Faverches, Lady of the Manor of Walsingham, England, in 1061. The Lady Richeldes was asked to build a replica of the House of Nazareth in England and was given both the physical specifications for the structure and supernatural assistance in its construction. The Holy House of Walsingham became one of the four greatest shrines of Christendom next to Jerusalem, Rome and Compostella, Spain, and attracted thousands of pilgrims. The popularity of this shrine indicates that the idea of Marian apparitions had been established in the minds of the faithful.

Again, St. William of Vercelli, an Italian hermit, was asked to construct a church on the top of Monte Vergine, Italy. This church was made a basilica and is now a pilgrimage center. In 1233, the Virgin appeared to seven merchants of Florence and asked them to form a religious order in which they dedicated themselves totally to God. They did as she requested and built a monastery on Monte Senario; the order they founded is now called the Order of the Servants of Mary. The apparition took place on August 15 - later to be celebrated as the Feast of Assumption.

Enduring Evidence

In terms of enduring tangible evidence, the Virgin sometimes left behind naturally inexplicable items that continue to testify to her visitation. In Guadalupe, Mexico (1531), the Virgin left behind an image of herself on a cloak made of cactus; in Coromoto, Venezuela (1651), she left an image of herself on a small paper card. Extensive investigation showed that neither of these images derive from any known substance. Likewise, the image of the Virgin and her Infant imprinted in the rock after an apparition in Las Lajas, Colombia (1754) is not made of any pigment or dye. In two of the earliest Indian apparitions, Kuruvilangad and Vailankanni, India, the Virgin directed the young visionaries to springs that became renowned for their healing properties. Lourdes, France, is similarly renowned for the healing spring personally "uncovered" by the Virgin. In these three and numerous similar cases, the "miraculous" liquid is chemically identical with ordinary water. In certain apparitions – Fatima, Poland and Quito, Ecuador, for instance – the Virgin offered previews of the future that were sometimes spectacularly fulfilled.

Barriers

Persecution, church corruption, dogmatic skepticism and internecine conflict often had an effect on the public awareness of apparitions. Between the Protestant Reformation and the end of the Inquisition, Europe went through a dry spell with respect to Marian devotion in general and apparitions in particular, This is not to say apparitions did not occur – but the recipients were unlikely to report them publicly for fear of reprisals. Paradoxically the hostility to apparitions of this period came from both Protestant and Catholic authorities. The post-Reformation Protestant iconoclasts dismissed Marian devotion as an idolatrous superstition and alleged that Marian apparitions came from the Devil. On the Catholic side, there were two forces at work: first, there was the so-called Catholic Enlightenment which had no interest in Marian piety or visions and promoted a "rationalized faith"; second, any claim to a supernatural vision or message was a risky proposition during the Roman and the Spanish Inquisitions. The historian David Blackbourn observes that the Jesuits were suppressed in 1773 partially because they were so closely associated with the Marian revival.

One of the well-known apparitions of the 19th century fell victim to inter-religious and political controversy. This was the reported apparition of the Virgin to three children in the village of Marpingen, Germany. The visionaries claimed to have seen a "woman in white" on July 3, 1876, in the woods near their home. In a subsequent apparition, she is reported to have said that "I am the Immaculately Conceived." Several cures were reported from water brought to the site of the apparitions. Thousands of people converged on the site. The Protestant Prussian Government was alarmed by the sequence of events and detained the children for five weeks and subjected them to severe interrogation. Under pressure from the civil authorities, one of the children retracted the claim of having witnessed the apparitions but later retracted the retraction. The parish priest became a supporter of the apparition and was subsequently harassed by the Government. Soldiers prevented pilgrims from coming near the apparition site. Bishops disagreed amongst themselves on the facticity of the claims. At the time of the reported apparition, the diocese had no bishop because of an ongoing conflict between the Catholic Church and the Prussian Government. The famous German Mariologist Matthias Scheeben investigated the phenomenon and reached a favorable verdict. Once a bishop had been appointed to head the diocese (in 1881), the Church never issued a formal verdict because of the controversy. The first of the visionaries died at the age of 14; the other two became nuns and died at a relatively young age.

Opening the Floodgates

The Spanish Inquisition ceased in 1820 and the Roman Inquisition in 1829. The first of the "modern" apparitions in Europe was reported in 1830. This was the apparition of Our Lady of the Miraculous Medal to a nun at the Rue du Bac in Paris, France. The Virgin made prophecies, later fulfilled, of events that were to take place in the next forty years and asked the visionary to produce and distribute a medal with a portrait of herself as she was seen in the apparition. Many of those who wore the medal reported miracles and it soon became known as the Miraculous Medal; hundreds of millions of these medals have been distributed since the apparition. (Another such miraculous instrument of grace given in an apparition was the scapular that the Virgin passed on through St. Simon

Stock in 1251). The body of the visionary, who died in 1876, remains incorrupt.

Three other major apparitions took place in France in the 19th century. After the French Revolution, France became the center of gravity of skepticism and Christophobia. So the French apparitions may be considered the Virgin's counter-attack.

At La Salette, in 1846, the Virgin appeared to two shepherd children and warned them of chastisements that were to afflict the world in both the immediate future and the end-times because of sin (although these could be averted if people were to convert). A spring was later found at the site of the apparitions and many miraculous cures were reported here. At both Rue du Bac and La Salette, the Virgin had spoken of the present age being evil; and at both she had shed tears. At Lourdes, in 1858, the Virgin appeared to an impoverished young girl at a grotto and asked for penitence. She also asked her to drink the water from a particular spot there: on digging into the ground there, the visionary found a spring which is today the great healing spring of Lourdes. The visionary was also told to request the parish priest to build a chapel. The priest had asked her to find out who she was from the lady and, in one of the final apparitions, the Virgin said, "I am the Immaculate Conception." Over five thousand cures have been reported at Lourdes although only about sixty of them have been thoroughly investigated. In 1871, the Virgin appeared to five children in the village of Pontmain. Although silent, she "spoke" through a scroll that was unfurled before them. Her title in this apparition was "Our Lady of Hope" because of her response to petitions for protection from the advancing Prussian army.

The great Church-approved apparitions of the 20th century are Fatima, Portugal; Beauraing and Banneux, Belgium; Jerusalem, Israel; Zeitoun, Egypt; Akita, Japan; Kibeho, Rwanda; Hrushiv, Ukraine; Dong Lu, China; Rome, Italy; Budapest, Hungary; Cuapa, Nicaragua; San Nicolas, Argentina; and Damascus, Syria.

At Fatima, three shepherd children witnessed six apparitions of the Virgin between May 13 and October 13, 1917. Portugal at the time was ruled by an anti-supernaturalist regime. But thousands of observers witnessed the famous miracle of the sun during the last apparition. Various prophecies made at Fatima were subsequently fulfilled. The Fatima request for prayer, reparation for sin and devotion to the Immaculate Heart of Mary were persistent themes in most subsequent apparitions. To reinforce the terrible consequences of sin, the Virgin gave the visionaries a glimpse of Hell and the fate of unrepentant sinners.

At Beauraing, Belgium, too, where the Virgin appeared to five children in 1932, the emphasis is on the conversion of sinners and on leading good lives. The Virgin appears with a golden heart to emphasize the importance of devotion to the Immaculate Heart. The next year in Banneux, Belgium, the Virgin described herself as the Virgin of the Poor. She took the visionary to a spring and said, "This spring is reserved for all nations - to relieve the sick." Many miraculous cures were reported by those who came to the spring.

"Silent" apparitions were witnessed in Jerusalem, Israel (1954) and Zeitoun, Egypt (1968). The second apparition was witnessed by hundreds of thousands of people of all religions and took place over a church that is believed to have been built over the site where Joseph and Mary stayed with the baby Jesus during their exile in Egypt.

These silent apparitions were followed by an apparition of the Virgin in Akita, Japan, in 1973, where she spoke to a deaf nun, through a statue. This statue of the Virgin, modeled on the image of Our Lady of All Nations from Amsterdam, wept blood on 101 occasions. Like Fatima, the Akita message was prayer, penance, reparation for sins. If Fatima showed the fiery flames of Hell as the ultimate consequence of sin, the warning of Akita is that the sins of the world are going to call down fire from the sky which will destroy much of humanity. The tears of blood are the tears of a Mother lamenting the impending (but not inevitable) loss of her children.

In Cuapa, Nicaragua, in 1980, she repeated the message of conversion while warning that the consequences of sin could be a third world war. She wept at the hardness of heart that prevented so many from converting but promised, "A mother does not forget her children. I have not forgotten you, all you who are suffering. I am your mother, mother of all sinners. Please pray this prayer knowing it is pleasing to my Son: Most holy Virgin, you are my mother, the mother of all sinners."

In Kibeho, Rwanda, in 1981, the Virgin warned that "There is not much time left in preparing for the Last Judgment. We must change our lives, renounce sin. Pray and prepare for our own death and for the end of the world." Solar phenomena and other miracles were witnessed by thousands of the pilgrims. The Virgin predicted the savage bloodshed that was to come to Rwanda.

In San Nicolas, Argentina, from 1983 to 1990, the Virgin delivered 1800 messages. The messages invite the faithful to consecrate themselves again to God. Many conversions and healings have been reported. In Damascus, in 1981, the visionary exuded olive oil from her fingers. The oil was seen to produce miraculous cures. The visionary also suffered the wounds of the stigmata. The messages in Damascus have focused on Church unity.

The Hrushiv apparition which went on from April 27, 1987 to August 15, 1988 was seen by hundreds of thousands of people. The Virgin offered encouragement to the faithful people of Ukraine but said that Russia's failure to convert to Christ could lead to a third world war.

Over the last 100 years, thousands of other apparitions and locutions have been claimed in Asia, Africa, Australia, Europe and the Americas. But none have received the official "certification" characteristic of the encounters studied here.

Preliminary Approval

In an appendix, we consider one of the apparitions that is still under investigation but has received preliminary approval – Medjugorje, Bosnia, the destination of over 30 million pilgrims. After a period of conflict between various Church authorities, a papally appointed commission recommended approval of the first seven apparitions of Medjugorje. Further, the Pope has placed Medjugorje under the jurisdiction of an Apostolic Visitor who is a papal envoy. Pilgrimages are not only permitted but encouraged. Medjugorje has certainly inspired a torrent of polemic mostly directed at individuals and events that are tangential to the only relevant datum: the phenomenon itself. The generation of such polemic will not surprise those who have studied the history of apparitions. For instance, before their approval, Beauraing and La Salette spawned storms of controversy both within and outside the Church and succeeded in confusing many of the faithful. The principals of Lourdes and Fatima were both subjected to abuse.

Fulfilling Revelation 12:17

"Then the dragon became angry with the woman and went off to wage war against the rest of her offspring, those who keep God's commandments and bear witness to Jesus."

Every instance of the Contact serves the objective of bringing the peoples of the world to Jesus and the Law of God. At Guadalupe, the Virgin brought eight million Aztecs to her Son within seven years. Likewise, she drew the indigenous to Christ after the apparitions in Venezuela, Colombia and other "mission fields". Historians say that through her apparitions in 19th century France, she did more to preserve the Faith than any apologist or church authority. She has consoled those who are persecuted for their faith in China, Vietnam and many other countries. She continues to draw millions of people of all religions to her shrines in India.

She is also specially loved in the Islamic world partly because of the great honor she is given in the Quran. Her apparition at Fatima strikes a chord because Fatima was the name of the favorite daughter of the founder of Islam; Lourdes was named after a Moslem commander who became a Catholic; Medjugorje is in the middle of a Moslem-majority country; Zeitoun, Egypt and Damascus, Syria are in Moslem-majority countries. At Zeitoun, she appeared to nearly two million people in all, most of them Moslem. There are good reasons then for the traditional belief that Mary will be Heaven's Ambassador to the Islamic world - a role she has already started fulfilling.

It has also been widely believed that she will bring the peoples of China and Russia to her Son.

At another level, she has had a supernatural impact on the course of history. This impact centers on warnings of impending tragedies sometimes with prescriptions for prevention (usually reparation and prayer) along with manifestations of her intercession in response to the petitions of the faithful.

Prophetic Warnings

In the warning category, we might include the apparitions that have been reported before such great calamities as the French Revolution, the destructive wars of 19th century Europe and the two world wars and other calamities of the 20th century. Some of the most striking supernatural warnings (verifiable as having taken place before the events in question) are listed here. The hundreds of claimed apparitions during these periods that were never formally investigated are not included.

In 1634, in Quito, Ecuador, the Virgin told the nun to whom she appeared that the 20th century would see a flight from faith and morals and that the Church itself would be internally affected by heresy and apostasy; this would be followed by a chastisement and then a renewal.

In the Miraculous Medal apparition of 1830, the Virgin prophesied that the King of France would be overthrown, the Archbishop of Paris would be stripped of his clothes, churches would be desecrated and the streets would run with blood - all over a period of 40 years. All the prophecies came to pass within 40 years of 1830: the King was ousted in a matter of days, churches were desecrated, the then-Archbishop was beaten and stripped of his clothes and two subsequent archbishops were murdered and mobs roamed the streets.

At La Salette in 1846, the Virgin warned of the failure of the potato and walnut crops and famines and the death of children from disease. Within a year the crops failed and over a million people died of famine in Europe; many children died of cholera.

On May 12, 1914, the Virgin appeared to 22 people in the village of Hrushiv, Ukraine, and warned that Russia would become a godless country and would go through two wars; Ukraine would suffer for 80 years and then be free. In 1987, she appeared in the same village and said their freedom was at hand and that Ukraine would soon be an independent state.

At Fatima, Portugal, starting in May 1917, the Virgin made these prophecies: the War would come to an end soon but a greater war would break out after a strange light is seen in the northern sky; Russia would scatter its errors around the world; various nations will be annihilated; Russia will be converted; the Pope will be assassinated; in the end the Immaculate Heart of Mary will triumph and there will be an Era of Peace. The First World War did end soon after. Strange lights were seen in the northern sky (claimed by some to be the aurora borealis) in 1938, prior to the beginning of World War II the next year. Russia did become Communist and scattered its errors around the world and various nations have been annihilated. In fact, on October 13, 1917, on the last day of the Fatima apparitions, Vladimir Lenin walked into Russia. The Communists were removed from power in 1991 (after the requested consecration was carried out). The prophecy of the papal assassination has not been literally fulfilled but some have argued that the prophecy concerns the attempted assassination of Pope John Paul II who was saved by the Virgin's intercession. The prophecies about the Triumph and the Era of Peace lie in the future. Three "secrets" were given to the Fatima visionaries. The first two Secrets were the revelation of Hell and the importance of devotion to the Immaculate Heart. The Third Secret included the assassination of the Pope and the persecution of the Church. In March 1939, the Lord told Sister Lucia, "The time is coming when the reign of my justice will punish the crimes of various nations. Some of them will be annihilated."

The most destructive battle of the Second World War (claiming nearly 200,000 lives), the Battle of the Bulge, took place in the Ardennes where two Belgian towns, Beauraing and Banneux, are located. The battle represented Hitler's final – and ultimately futile – attempt to stop the Allies in their liberation of occupied Europe. These were the two places where the Virgin last appeared (in 1932 and 1933) before the outbreak of the War. She appeared especially grave and sorrowful in her last apparition at Banneux.

At Akita, on October 13, 1973, the Virgin warned that if humanity did not repent the Father would inflict a punishment greater than the Deluge on humanity, that "Fire will plunge from the sky and a large part of humanity will perish." (October 13 was also the anniversary of the last apparition of Fatima in 1917 with its fiery sun miracle; again on October

13, 1884, Pope Leo XIII received a prophetic revelation about the battle between God and Satan in the 20th century.)

In Cuapa, the Virgin said, "If you do not change your ways, you will hasten the arrival of the third world war. Pray, pray, pray my children for the entire world. The world is seriously threatened."

On August 15, 1982, in an eight-hour long apparition, the visionaries in Rwanda, Africa, were warned that the rivers would run with blood; they were shown visions of thousands of corpses and asked to flee the country. During the civil war which broke out in 1991, over a million people were killed; the rivers were choked with bodies.

In Ukraine, in 1987, the Virgin warned, "The times are coming which have been foretold as being those in the end times."

And as the Virgin of Revelation, in Rome she warned in 1947: "The shepherds of the flock are not fulfilling their duty. Too much of the world has entered in their soul to give scandal to the flock ... There will be days of sorrow and mourning. From the east a strong people, but far from God, will launch a terrible attack, and will break the most sacred and holy things.... The world will go into another war, the most ruthless of all.... The wrath of Satan is not being any longer held; the Spirit of God is withdrawing from the earth, the Church will be left a widow; She will be left at the mercy of the world. The most affected will be the Church of Christ to cleanse It from the filth It has inside."

Maternal Interventions

Of the many great interventions of the Virgin in history, two great miracles of the Rosary involve Austria. On October 7, 1571, the ships of Spain, Venice and the papal states, under the leadership of Don Juan of Austria, faced a huge Turkish armada. The Turks had taken over Constantinople, the Balkans and Cyprus and were now poised to conquer Rome and thereafter all of Europe. Pope Pius V had asked the Christians of Europe to pray the Rosary to avert a Turkish triumph. The battle began disastrously for the Christian fleet for the Turks had managed to separate the three squadrons and were now preparing to cut them to pieces. At that time a tremendous wind mysteriously swept through the area throwing the Turkish fleet into disarray and 230 of their 300 galleys were captured or destroyed; the Christians lost 16. This decisive victory is attributed both to the Rosary and to Our Lady of Guadalupe because on board the ship of Prince Andrea Doria, whose squadron had initially been outflanked by the Turks, was an image of Our Lady of Guadalupe (specially sent from Mexico) whose intercession the Prince had sought.

The Austrians did not forget this miraculous rescue when their country was taken over by the Soviet Union in the aftermath of the Second World War. In 1948, three years after the Soviets had taken over, ten percent of all Austrians (700,000 at the time) began a rosary crusade pledging to say the rosary daily until the Soviets left. Seven years later, on May 13, 1955, the Soviets mysteriously left the country. (May 13 was the anniversary of the first Fatima apparition, which was an apparition of Our Lady of the Rosary). This was the first time in history that the Communists had ever peacefully relinquished control over a country they had taken over - and there was no humanly plausible explanation as to why they would have given up such a resource-rich and strategically located country.

There are several other instances of the Virgin's direct intervention in protecting those who seek her help.

In 1900, the Christians of Dong Lu, who numbered less than a thousand, were attacked by an enemy army of over ten thousand who sought to wipe them out. The army came to a halt and then fled when they saw a beautiful lady in the sky and a fiery horseman who charged towards them. A similar incident took place in Tra Kieu, Vietnam in 1885, where a woman in white intercepted the cannon balls and bullets of an anti-Christian army.

In 1871, war had broken out between France and Prussia. The rapidly advancing Prussians had captured the Emperor and were on the verge of taking over Paris. At this time, the devout villagers of Pontmain, France, sought the Virgin's intercession and protection. On January 17, she appeared to five children in the village asking them to pray and giving them two messages, "God will soon grant your request" and "My Son allows Himself to be moved." At the exact time of the apparition (5:30 p.m.), the Prussians stopped their advance for reasons that baffle historians. Some of the Prussians are reported to have seen a lady in the sky and one of their generals said they could go no further because "there is an invisible Madonna barring the way." The Virgin's title in Pontmain (appropriately) is Our Lady of Hope. Her blue robe in Pontmain had 42 stars - 42 years later France would enter the First World War.

In 1938, after repeated requests from Sister Lucia, the Portugese bishops consecrated their country to the Immaculate Heart of Mary. When the Second World War broke out, Portugal was untouched. (Why did the Virgin appear in Fatima, Portugal? Two reasons can be given. First, King John IV of Portugal officially consecrated his country to Our Lady of the Immaculate Conception on October 20, 1646, and gave her his crown. Secondly, on May 5, 1917, Pope Benedict XV asked the faithful to petition the Mother of Mercy to bring peace to a world at war. Eight days later, on May 13, she responded with her "peace plan" for the century.)

Two of the great miracles of the Second World War involved the mysterious protection of devotees of the Rosary in both Hiroshima and Nagasaki, Japan. On August 6, 1945, when the atom bomb was dropped on Hiroshima, four Jesuit priests, Frs. Hugo Lassalle, Hubert Schiffer, Wilhelm Kleinsorge and Hubert Cieslik, were at the hypocenter of the blast. They were living in the rectory of the church of Our Lady of the Assumption which was eight blocks away from the site of the blast. Amazingly, the priests in the rectory were the only survivors within the one-mile radius of the explosion. And their house was undamaged although all the buildings around them were destroyed. Just as astonishing, they suffered none of the after-effects of radiation as confirmed by some 200 medical tests conducted over the years. One of them later said, "We believe that we survived because we were living the message of Fatima. We lived and prayed the Rosary daily in that home." Three days later, another atom bomb was dropped on Nagasaki. The Polish Marian devotee Maximilian Kolbe had built a Franciscan Friary there. The brothers who lived there also prayed the Rosary every day. Again, although Nagasaki was destroyed, the friary and its brothers were unharmed.

The Virgin has often chosen Marian feast days to manifest her intercession. The most famous such event in recent times was the miraculous survival of Pope John Paul II. The attempt on his life took place on May 13, 1981, the anniversary of the first apparition of Fatima - and the Pope attributed his escape to a direct intervention of Our Lady of Fatima. It was during his convalescence after the assassination attempt that the Pope studied all the key documents relating to Fatima. When he left the hospital, he was determined to honor the request of both the Virgin and the Lord that Russia be consecrated to the Immaculate Heart. On June 13, 1929, the Virgin had told Sister Lucia, "The moment has come when God asks the Holy Father in union with the bishops of the world to make the consecration of Russia to My Heart, promising to save it by this means." Several popes had sought to meet these conditions and make the appropriate consecration - but none had performed it as requested and Russia continued to spread its errors.

On March 25, 1984, Pope John Paul II made the requested consecration in union with bishops around the world. In July 1989, Sister Lucia confirmed that the required consecration had been accomplished and accepted and "God will keep his word." By the end of 1989, Communism collapsed throughout Eastern Europe. By the end of 1991, the Soviet Communist state came apart and a free Russia was reborn.

Future Chastisement?

At Fatima, Akita and several of the modern apparitions, the Virgin was looking beyond Communism toward a final chastisement from Heaven. Her messages always affirmed that repentance and reparation could mitigate and even eliminate this chastisement. And beyond the chastisement lies the Era of Peace.

With the thousands of nuclear, chemical and biological weapons stockpiled around the globe, it is not difficult to foresee a terrestrial and even accidental Armageddon not to speak of the potential global chaos that could be triggered off by a breakdown of communication and computer systems or the destruction of satellites.

Even in the Old Testament, the chastisements of God usually came through the natural realm. If Yahweh allowed a heathen army to defeat the Israelites because of their moral laxity, one could see the events as they transpired without seeing the hand of God in them. Likewise the fall of the Berlin Wall and of Communism in Europe could just be seen as inexplicable events - one does not have to relate them to the Fatima prophecy. Similarly, a future divinely directed chastisement may not be recognized as such by those who lack discernment or the benefit of a commentary from the Virgin. In fact, the whole "problem of evil" is really a question of the reality of chastisements: for the doctrine of original sin sees moral evil as the prime cause of the disorder in the world: a chastisement can sometimes be self-inflicted rather than divinely instituted.

It may be said that the prophets of nuclear doom have not only been wrong but consistently wrong. For this we should be thankful. But once a nuclear event or a "natural" worldwide chastisement in some form comes to pass, nothing will ever be the same again - we will not be able to write and read about it as we do now, activities we take for granted. In the previous two world wars, life on the home front could go on with some semblance of normality. Except in heavily damaged areas, newspapers and movie theaters were still operational, food was available.

The viral pandemic of recent times is simply a preview of what kinds of horrors are possible. Today, there are weapons that can destroy every form of life on the planet. There are unstable regimes run by unstable tyrants who possess these weapons. And across the world almost all of us have broken - and continue to break - every law in the Book. If ever the Fatima messages of penance and reparation and prayer were applicable it is today. And that is why the Virgin weeps over the world today as her Son wept over Jerusalem!

Chronology

Year (A.D.)	Place	Witness	Title
ca. 40	Zaragoza, Spain	St. James the Greater	Our Lady of the Pillar
ca. 238	Neocaesarea, Turkey	St. Gregory the Wonder-Worker	
ca. 250	Le Puy, France	Lady named Villa	Virgin of Le Puy
ca. 335	Kuravilangad, India	Three boys	
ca. 352	Rome, Italy	John of Rome, Pope Liberius	Our Lady of the Snows
ca. 912	Constantinople, Turkey	St. Andrew the Blessed and St. Epiphanius	The Theotokos of Protection/ Pokrov
1061	Walsingham, England	Lady Richeldes de Faverches	Our Lady of Walsingham
1251	Aylesford, England	St. Simon Stock	Our Lady of Mount Carmel
1382	Czestochowa, Poland	The people of Poland	Our Lady of Czestochowa, the Black Madonna
1467	Genazzano, Italy	Townspeople	Our Lady of Good Counsel
1490	Genoa, Italy	Benedetto Pareto	Our Lady of the Guard
1531	Guadalupe, Mexico	Juan Diego	Our Lady of Guadalupe
1541	Ocotlan, Mexico	Juan Bernardino	Our Lady of Ocotlan
1578	Lezajsk, Poland	Thomas Michalek	Our Lady of Consolation
1579	Kazan, Russia	Matrona	Our Lady of Kazan
1594	Quito, Ecuador	Mother Mariana de Jesus Torres	Our Lady of Good Event (Buen Suceso) of the Purification
1500s, 1600s	Vailankanni, India	peasant boys. sailors	Our Lady of Good Health

1500s	Caacupé, Paraguay	Indio Jose	Our Lady of the Miracles of Caacupé
1608	Šiluva, Lithuania,	Shepherd children and villagers	Our Lady of Šiluva
1651	Venezuela	Cacique (Chief) of the Cospes Indians	Our Lady of Coromoto
1652	Querrien, France	Jeanne Courtel	Our Lady of All Help
1664	Laus, France	Benoîte Rencurel	Our Lady of Happy Meetings
1717	Sao Paolo, Brazil	Domingos Garcia, Joao Alves and Felipe Ramos	Our Lady of Aparecida
1752	Vallarpadam, India	Meenakshi Amma	Our Lady of Ransom
1754	Las Lajas, Colombia	Maria Mueses de Quiñones and Rosa	Our Lady of the Rosary of las Lajas
1798	Quang Tri, Vietnam	Villagers of Quang Tri	Our Lady of La Vang
1813, 1850	Lichen, Poland	Tomasz Kłossowski and Mikołaj Sikatka	Our Lady of Lichen
1830	France	Sr. Catherine Laboure	Our Lady of the Miraculous Medal
1842	Rome, Italy	Alphonse M. Ratisbonne	Our Lady of Zion
1846	La Salette, France,	Melanie Calvat and Maximin Giraud	Our Lady of La Salette
1858	Lourdes, France,	Bernadette Soubirous	Our Lady of Lourdes
1859	Champion, USA	Adele Brise	Our Lady of Good Help
1866	Fillipsdorf, Czech Republic	Magdalene Kade	Our Lady, Help of Christians,
1871	Pontmain, France,	Eugene Barbedette, Joseph Barbedette, Francoise Richer, Jeanne-Marie Lebosse, Eugene Freiteau	Our Lady of Hope
1879	Knock, Ireland	Eighteen villagers of Cnoc Mhuire	Our Lady of Knock,
1885	Tra Kieu, Vietnam	Enemies of the Christian villagers	The Lady in White of Tra Kieu

1900, 1995	Dong Lu, China	Christians of Dong Lu and their enemies	Our Lady of China
1914, 1987	Hrushiv, Ukraine	Marina Kizyn, then hundreds of thousands of onlookers, Soviet TV	Our Lady of Hrushiv
1917	Fatima, Portugal	Lucia dos Santos, Francisco Marto, Jacinta Marto	Our Lady of Fatima
1932	Beauraing, Belgium	Fernande, Albert and Gilberte Voisin; Andree and Gilberte Degeimbre	Our Lady of the Golden Heart
1933	Banneux, Belgium	Mariette Beco	The Virgin of the Poor
1954	Jerusalem, Israel	Students at the Coptic school of St. Anthony and parishioners of the Coptic Patriarchal Church	
1947	Rome, Italy	Bruno Cornacchiola	The Virgin of Revelation
1960	Budapest, Hungary	Elizabeth Kindleman	Flame of Love of the Immaculate Heart of Mary
1968	Cairo, Egypt	Hundreds of thousands of Moslems, Jews and Christians	Our Lady of Zeitoun
1973	Akita, Japan	Sister Agnes Sasagawa	Our Lady of Akita
1980	Cuapa, Nicaragua	Bernardo Martinez	Our Lady of Cuapa
1981-1983	Kibeho, Rwanda	Alphonsine Mumureke, Nathalie Mukamazimpaka, Marie-Claire Mukanganga	Our Lady of the Word
1982-1990	Damascus, Syria	Myrna Nazzour	Our Lady of Soufanieh
1983-1990	San Nicolas, Argentina	Gladys de Motta	Our Lady of the Rosary of San Nicolas

Note – the Vatican Commission appointed to investigate the apparitions claimed in Medjugorje, Bosnia, has recommended approval of the first seven of the apparitions. The apparitions began in 1981.

In addition to the visitations above, Christian leaders through the centuries have reported their own encounters with the Virgin. Here are some of the better known of these.

Year	Place	Witness
ca. 455	Constantinople	Emperor Leo I
ca. 657	Toledo, Spain	St. Ildefonso, Bishop of Toledo
ca. 708	Evesham, England	Egwin, Bishop of Worcester
948	Einsiedeln, Switzerland	St. Conrad of Constance
1119	Monte Vergine, Italy	St. William of Vercelli
1153	Citeaux, France	St. Bernard of Clairvaux
1214	Clairefontaine, Luxembourg	Princess Ermesinde
1216	Assisi, Italy	St. Francis of Assisi
1233	Florence, Italy	Seven founders of the religious order Servants of Mary
1298	Helfta, Germany	St. Mechtilde
1373	Vadstena, Sweden	St. Bridget
1380	Siena, Italy	St. Catherine
1392	Zagorsk, Russia	St. Sergius of Radonezh
1522	Manresa, Spain	St. Ignatius of Loyola
1536	Savona, near Genoa, Italy	Antonio Botta
1561	Avila, Spain	St. Teresa of Avila
1779	Sarov, Russia	St. Seraphim of Sarov
1861	Turin, Italy	St. John Bosco

Online

Our Lady of Guadalupe, Mexico, 1531
https://virgendeguadalupe.org.mx/en/

Our Lady of Lourdes, France, 1858
https://www.lourdes-france.org/en/

Our Lady of Fatima, Portugal, 1917
https://www.fatima.pt/en

Our Lady of La Vang, Vietnam, 1798
http://denthanhlavang.org/

Our Lady of China, 1900, 1995
http://www.gcatholic.org/churches/asia/3644.htm

Our Lady of Good Health, India, 1500s, 1600s
http://www.vailankannishrine.net/

Our Lady of Walsingham, England, 1061
https://www.walsingham.org.uk/

Our Lady of Zeitoun, Egypt, 1968
https://www.stmaryztn.org/saintmary/en/

Our Lady of the Word, Rwanda, 1981-1983
http://kibeho-sanctuary.com/en/

Our Lady of Kazan, Russia, 1579
kazanskiy-tmb.pravorg.ru

Our Lady of Pilar, Spain, 40
http://www.basilicadelpilar.es/

Our Lady of Le Puy, France, ca. 250
https://www.cathedraledupuy.org/

Our Mother and Protectress, India, 335
http://kuravilangadpally.com/

Our Lady of the Snows, Italy, 352
http://www.vatican.va/various/basiliche/sm_maggiore/en/storia/
introduzione.htm

The Theotokos of Protection/ Pokrov, Turkey, 912
https://ec-patr.org/afieroma/churches/show.php?lang=gr&id=02

Our Lady of Mount Carmel, England, 1251
https://www.thefriars.org.uk/home

Our Lady of Good Counsel, Italy, 1467
http://www.turismoqr.it/genazzano/6.html

Our Lady of Consolation, Poland, 1578
http://kawnice.pl/kontakt

Our Lady of Good Event (*Buen Suceso)* of the Purification, Ecuador, 1594
https://www.nuestrasenoradelbuensucesodelapurificacion.com/

Our Lady of Akita, Japan, 1973
http://www.seitaihoshikai.com/us/

Our Lady of Soufanieh, Syria, 1982-1990
https://www.soufanieh.com/

Our Lady of Jerusalem, Israel 1954
www.copticj.com

Our Lady of Aparecida, Brazil, 1717
https://www.a12.com/

Our Lady of Ransom, India, 1752
https://www.vallarpadambasilica.com/

Our Lady of Ocotlan, Mexico, 1541
http://www.gcatholic.org/churches/northamerica/0806.htm

Our Lady of the Rosary of las Lajas, Colombia, 1754
http://santuariolavirgendelaslajas.com/index.html

Our Lady of Coromoto, Venezuela, 1651
http://www.santuariobasilicacoromoto.com/horario-misa-santuario-nacional-virgen-coromoto.html

Our Lady of Cuapa, Nicaragua, 1980
http://www.gcatholic.org/churches/centralamerica/6416.htm

Our Lady of Czestochowa, the Black Madonna, Poland, 1382, 1920
https://jasnagora.pl/en/about-sanctuary/miracolous-icon-of-our-lady/

Our Lady of Šiluva, Lithuania, 1608
https://siluva.lt/?id=66

Our Lady of the Miraculous Medal, France, 1830
https://www.chapellenotredamedelamedaillemiraculeuse.com/

Our Lady of Zion, Italy, 1842
https://www.madonnadelmiracolo.it/

Our Lady of La Salette, France, 1846
http://lasalette.cef.fr/

Our Lady of Hope, France, 1871
https://www.sanctuaire-pontmain.com/?lang=fr

Our Lady of Knock, Ireland, 1879
https://www.knockshrine.ie/

Our Lady of the Golden Heart, Belgium, 1932
https://www.sanctuairesdebeauraing.be/

The Virgin of the Poor, Belgium, 1933
https://web.archive.org/web/20120208132212/http://www.banneux-nd.be/gb/accueil.gb.htm

Our Lady of the Guard, Genoa, Italy 1490
http://www.santuarioguardia.it/

Our Lady of Lichen, Poland, 1815, 1830
http://www.lichen.pl/

Our Lady of Happy Meetings, France, 1664
http://www.sanctuaire-notredamedulaus.com/en/

Our Lady of Good Help, USA, 1859
https://championshrine.org/

One and Many – The Encounters Arranged as a Rosary

First decade —Top Ten Global Encounters

Our Lady of Guadalupe, Mexico, 1531

"Am I Not Here Who Am Your Mother?"

Witness: Juan Diego

Dates: December 9 to December 12, 1531

Enduring Evidence: Tilma with the Miraculous Image of Our Lady of Guadalupe that played an instrumental role in the conversion of the Aztecs. It might be said that this Image is a continuation of the original apparition of the Virgin making it the only apparition that is visible to all humanity. Conversion of eight million Aztecs in seven years.

Theme: Build a church to honor the Lord of Heaven and Earth and where the Virgin will offer consolation to all who come to her.

Image from –
https://en.wikipedia.org/wiki/Our_Lady_of_Guadalupe#/media/
File:Virgen_de_guadalupe1.jpg

Guadalupe remains the single most influential encounter with the Virgin Mary in history given its role in forming the very identity of a new nation. Fittingly, it comes with a startling seal of its own authenticity that has baffled scientists and skeptics for centuries and testifies to its own supernatural origin – the tilma.

The tilma is an all-but indestructible, self-mending burlap cloak with a super-power image of the Virgin. Every attempt to dispute the Guadalupe phenomenon has fallen apart in the face of this singular datapoint.

Three Hard Facts

The phenomenon itself is built on three hard facts that have stood the test of time

- the "founding event" of the appearance of the Virgin to an Aztec peasant that conforms to the pattern of such appearances from the first five centuries of Christianity to the present.
- The tilma, a cloth made of the agave popotule fiber with an indelible imprinted image of the Virgin as she appeared to her first witness.
- the inexplicable conversion of millions of indigenous people to an alien religion within a tiny window of time along with the historically continuous accounts of miracles associated with the phenomenon.

The face, hands, robe and mantle seen on the tilma were composed of pigments that cannot be identified by chemical analysis: it is known that the colors do not come from any known animal, vegetable or mineral dye. Despite having been exposed to smoke from thousands of candles through the centuries, infrared spectroscopy shows that there is none of the "wear and tear" which comes with age and pollution. The mysterious pigments refract light in such a way that the image continues to be singularly luminous. Also, unlike human paintings, there is no underdrawing below the mysterious image.

Even more extraordinary is the fact that an examination of the eyes of the Virgin shows reflections of actual persons in the pupils – a "technique" that ophthalmologists and others simply cannot comprehend. The reflections are apparently of the witness of the appearance, the church official to whom he reported it and an interpreter. Seeing is believing!

The image of the Virgin on the tilma is of the Woman Clothed with the Sun Standing on the Moon of *Revelation* 12 for she is surrounded by rays of the sun and her face is as bright as the sun (the strange luminosity mentioned above); her feet are on the moon. The turquoise, rose and gold colors on the tilma were the colors of royalty for the Aztecs. Though she was standing on the moon and had stars on her gown, she was no goddess because her hands were folded in prayer.

Here we will first consider the traditional Guadalupe origin story followed by a study of the tilma, a review of the historical core surrounding the phenomenon and, finally, an analysis of the claim that the Guadalupe appearance is simply a mixture of paganism and Christianity.

Critiques of Guadalupe span the spectrum from the silly to the solemn. These critiques include the allegations that the recipient of the encounter did not actually exist; that the image on the tilma is an ingenious albeit unique painting; that the devotion centered on it was simply a repurposing of Aztec religion; that the whole phenomenon was merely an ingeniously disguised Castilian import. For the most part, these critiques are built on fact-free speculation driven by a desperate need to deny the obvious.

None of the critiques address the three hard facts that undergird the phenomenon.

- How do you explain the unprecedented conversion of millions of Aztecs to a philosophically, culturally and morally foreign world-view in a seven year period – something never before or since witnessed in human history?
- How do you explain the tilma with its unnatural longevity and its "alternate reality" image – if the image was simply a human creation, how is it that no modern artists or scientists, with all the technologies at their disposal, have been able to create a replica with remotely similar properties?
- How is it that the account of the appearance and the messages transmitted at Guadalupe are almost identical to accounts of the Virgin's appearances in places and times across the world and

over 20 centuries – the request to build a church, the offer of maternal consolation? There is no parallel to this phenomenon in any non-Christian religion – but it is almost standard in Marian apparitions from the first to the twentieth centuries.

Guadalupe has drawn the ire and fire of assorted skeptics each with their own pet peeves because its three hard facts point to the immediate and undeniable reality of a supernatural order of reality. Interestingly, the critics who question the historicity of the event rarely study the scientific evidence in serious detail and the skeptics who deny the uniqueness of the tilma ignore the mystery of the sudden conversion of an entire nation. The Guadalupe phenomenon, in general, is especially lethal for skepticism because it is obvious and concrete. And the tilma, in particular, is deadly for self-styled rationalists because its ineffable attributes were "discovered" and then continually consolidated by modern science.

Only three systematic scientific hands-on studies have been done on the fibers making up the tilma and the image imprinted on it. These involved chemical and histological analysis and infra-red photography. All three studies confirmed the traditional affirmations that the preservation of the tilma and the infrastructure of the image are both scientifically inexplicable. None of the skeptics participated in these studies or addressed their results. As we will see, the skeptics have simply evaded the hard evidence while marketing irrelevant trivialities and wildly implausible speculation.

The renowned philosopher and historian of science, Stanley Jaki, winner of the Templeton Prize and the author of over 20 major scientific works, summarized the scientific verdict on the tilma: "While the stunning survival of the tilma should impress anyone who has watched a piece of burlap slowly disintegrate, it took a Nobel Prize winner chemist, Richard Kuhn, director of the Kaiser Wilhelm Institute in Heidelberg, to examine, in 1936, two fibers, one red, the other blue, from the tilma, *and reach the conclusion that neither contained any coloring*. Later, microscopic analysis of the tilma revealed that [it] showed no traces of brush strokes. Infrared investigation revealed no traces of pencil drawings. The eyes turned out to reflect the upper parts of the bodies of three men, in agreement with the Purkinje-Sanson effect, discovered in the 1830s. *Needless to say, no eyes in any painting show that effect. Its presence in the eyes of the Lady's image on the tilma forms a stunning scientific proof ... that the Lady was there in a mysterious though wholly real way* and that Bishop Zumarraga and two assistants *were seen by her "physically."* ... *A conclusion imposes itself, therefore, on any unbiased mind that in the image one is confronted with a miracle whose reality remains present as time goes on. There is no parallel to this in the annal of miracles....* [The image of] the Virgin of Guadalupe .. on Juan Diego's tilma *... has defied by its hues and texture the laws of decay now for almost half a millennium."*[1]

The Origin Story

The Guadalupe phenomenon begins with the appearance of the Virgin to Juan Diego, an Aztec peasant, in Mexico in 1531. Juan Diego was a convert to Christianity and his Aztec name was apparently Cuauhtlatoatzin (Talking Eagle). It is no exaggeration to say that this Marian apparition was primarily responsible for the Christianization of Latin America, home to nearly a fifth of the world's Christians.

The conquest of Mexico by Cortez had been accompanied and followed by atrocities by both Spaniards and Aztecs. Missionaries from Spain had little success in their attempts to convert the natives in view of the tensions between the Aztecs and their conquerors. Relations were also strained between the civil and the ecclesiastical authorities and the first bishop-elect in Mexico, Franciscan Prior Juan Zumarraga, had actually excommunicated the then civil administrator, Don Nuno de Guzman, for his continuing cruelty. (Bishop-elect Zumarraga served as administrator from 1528 and was formally consecrated as bishop in 1533).

Juan Diego, a fifty seven year old peasant, was an Aztec who had become a Christian. He was a widower who had been brought up by his uncle Juan Bernardino. The aged uncle was now under Juan Diego's care and they lived in the village of Tolpetlac.

According to the traditional narrative, on the morning of December 9, 1531, Juan Diego passed the hill of Tepeyac on his way to morning Mass in Tlaltelolco. He was startled by the ethereal quality of the birdsong he heard from the hill. Suddenly the singing of the birds ceased and he heard a young lady calling out to him, "Juan! Juan Diego! Juanito!"

On ascending the hill, he saw a fourteen year old girl, remarkable for her supernal splendor, beckoning to him. Speaking to him in his Aztec tongue, she said she was the ever-virgin Mary who was the Mother of God and explained that she wanted a church to be built on the hill. Juan Diego, she said, was to go to Tenochtitlan (Mexico City) and make this request to the bishop.

Juan Diego obediently went to the bishop's residence. After waiting for several hours, he was finally allowed to meet the bishop. Through an interpreter, Juan Gonzalez, he described his encounter and the Virgin's request to the bishop. The bishop was touched by the Aztec's sincerity and humility but found the story too extraordinary to believe. Although he could not agree to the request, he kindly told Juan Diego to visit him again later if he had anything more to say.

Juan Diego returned to the Virgin with the bishop's answer and suggested that she choose someone more important to deliver her message if she wanted the bishop to take it seriously. The Virgin insisted, however, that she had chosen him, Juan Diego, and prevailed on him to return to the bishop with the same request. When Juan Diego returned to the bishop he found that he had outworn his welcome; the bishop clearly had not expected him to return so soon. Juan Diego told him the Virgin asked that it be reiterated she was the Virgin Mary and that she desired a church built on the hill. The bishop answered that he wanted a sign from the lady to show that she was indeed the Virgin. When Juan Diego left, the bishop had him followed by two of his servants. But Juan Diego, who was unaware that he was being followed, disappeared from view when they reached the foot of Tepeyac and the servants returned to the bishop falsely accusing the Aztec of hiding from them. On Tepeyac, Juan Diego told the Virgin about the bishop's stance. She asked him to return at daybreak and she would give him the requested sign.

On returning to Tolpetlac, Juan Diego found that his uncle had been struck down with a deadly fever. He tended to Juan Bernardino's needs with herbs and medicines that night and all of the next day thus failing to keep his "appointment" with the Virgin. On the following day, December 12th, Juan Bernardino was convinced that he would die shortly and asked his nephew to bring a priest to administer the last rites. Tepeyac was on the way to Tlaltelolco, where the priest lived, but Juan Diego walked on the east side of the hill and not the west where the Virgin had appeared so as to avoid meeting her again and losing time. To his surprise, he saw the Virgin descending toward him from the hill. Juan Diego explained his uncle's condition to which she said "Am I not your mother?" and added that his uncle's health had been restored at that very moment. She asked Juan Diego to go to the top of the hill and bring her the flowers blooming there and these would be the sign requested by the bishop. Juan Diego was astounded to see that the top of the hill was covered with Castilian roses although it was the dead of winter.

He took off his cloak, called the tilma, and filled it with the roses; he used his tilma so as to protect them from the cold. When he brought them to the Virgin, she carefully arranged the roses on the tilma and asked him to present them to the bishop as the sign he required to build a church. No one else but the bishop was to be shown the contents of the tilma, she said.

When Juan Diego returned to the bishop, the servants tried to take the tilma with the roses away from him. But Juan Diego refused to give it up and insisted on seeing the bishop. When he was at last able to meet the bishop, Juan Diego unrolled the tilma and the roses fell to the ground. Juan Diego, who was holding the tilma away from himself was astonished to see the bishop suddenly kneel in front of it along with the others around him. On looking at the tilma, he saw why: for emblazoned on it was an image of the lady he had seen. The bishop now had no doubt about Juan Diego's story and took the tilma to his private chapel. Later, Juan Diego accompanied the bishop to the hill of Tepeyac and showed him where the church was to be built. The bishop's assistants then went with Juan Diego to his uncle. They found that Juan Bernardino had recovered completely. The Virgin had appeared to him as well saying he would be cured and asking that she and her image be called Santa Maria de Guadalupe.

The image on the tilma was of an Aztec girl but the name she had chosen was Spanish. As the Aztecs saw the image, hundreds and thousands of them converted to the Christian faith. Within seven years, eight million Aztecs had become Christians. By appearing as an Aztec and to an Aztec, the Virgin ensured that Christianity would not be perceived as an alien religion.

The Virgin's messages to Juan Diego have been recorded in the traditional accounts

"My dear little son, I love you. I desire you to know who I am. I am the evervirgin Mary, Mother of the true God who gives life and maintains its existence. He created all things. He is in all places. He is Lord of Heaven and Earth. I desire a church in this place where your people may experience my compassion. All those who sincerely ask my help in their work and in their sorrows will know my Mother's Heart in this place. I am your merciful Mother, the Mother of all who live united in this land, and of all mankind, and of all those who love me, of those who cry to me, of those who have confidence in me. Here I will see their tears; I will console them and they will be at peace. So run now to Tenochtitlan and tell the Bishop all that you have seen and heard."

"My little son, there are many I could send. But you are the one I have chosen."

"My little son, am I not your Mother? Do not fear. The Bishop shall have his sign. Come back to this place tomorrow. Only peace, my little son."

"Do not be distressed, my littlest son. Am I not here with you who am your Mother? Are you not under my shadow and protection? Am I not of your kind? Your uncle will not die at this time. There is no reason for you to engage a priest, for his health is restored at this moment. He is quite well. Go to the top of the hill and cut the flowers that are growing there. Bring them then to me."

"My little son, this is the sign I am sending to the Bishop. Tell him that with this sign I request his greatest efforts to complete the church I desire in this place. Show these flowers to no one else but the Bishop. You are my trusted ambassador. This time the Bishop will believe all you tell him."

[To Juan Diego's uncle]:
"Call me and call my image Santa Maria de Guadalupe."

The tilma, meanwhile, defied all natural explanation. It was made from cactus fibers and consequently should have turned into dust within twenty years – but it has remained on display to the faithful ever since the year of the apparition. Scientists have scrutinized the tilma on numerous occasions and have confirmed that it is made out of the low life-span cactus cloth.

Copies of the image were painted on two similar cloths made of cactus fibers in 1789 and left in the same environment as the tilma. Both disintegrated in a few decades. Similarly, when the tilma was embellished with additions such as a crown, these faded over time unlike the original image.

Two other events demonstrated the intrinsic power of the tilma.

In 1785, a worker cleaning the glass encasing the image accidentally spilled muriatic acid on the left side of the image. Remarkably, the acid caused no damage to the image or the fabric although a faint stain can still be seen in the area of the spill.

More seriously, on November 14, 1921, a saboteur hid several sticks of dynamite in a bouquet of flowers that he placed at the foot of the image. The resulting explosion was so powerful that it was heard for a radius of one kilometer and destroyed nearby windows. Although it bent back the stout bronze crucifix and the candlesticks on the altar, it caused no damage to the tilma or its glass frame.

Human Creation or Celestial Imprint?

In studying the foundations of the Guadalupe phenomenon, we start with the ultimate "smoking gun" pointing to its celestial provenance – the tilma. By "smoking gun" we mean "incontrovertible evidence."

Two dimensions of the tilma are central to its unique stature: the material of which the tilma was made and the nature of the image imprinted on it.

As highlighted in the original narrative, the tilma was made of cactus fibers. Cloths produced with 16th century looms were narrow and the tilma is, in fact, made up of two cloths tacked together with a vertical seam in the middle. It was mounted on a wooden stretcher frame.

Agave fiber cloths are notoriously non-durable as can be demonstrated even today. At best they last twenty to thirty years. But the tilma has continued to subsist over a period now approaching five centuries.

Secondly, the original image on the tilma was not made out of any known natural pigment and it continues to manifest properties that have yet to be replicated. The image, it is claimed, was miraculously imprinted on the tilma – not painted but imprinted.

It was taken for granted that some of the non-essential parts of the image on the tilma could have been later additions and these parts were sometimes "touched up" over the centuries – but these had no relevance for the origin and nature of the original image.

These two dimensions of the tilma (its longevity and the mystery of its image) were repeatedly confirmed in the only major scientific studies done on the tilma as we shall see below. But given the overpowering evidence for the tilma, we might wonder how anyone could remain a skeptic. Here we are dealing with a mystery of human psychology not facts and figures. As it turns out, the best-known critics of the tilma were not scientists who had done studies on its material and image. And, of these, the two most relevant were the art restorers Jorge Sol Rosales and José Antonio Flores Gómez. They performed no chemical or infrared analysis but were concerned by issues that actually did not pertain to the traditional claims about the tilma.

Rosales acknowledged the good state of preservation of the image and admitted that there was no varnish on the image or any visible brush strokes. He was concerned by the paint loss and abrasion and apparent primer in certain points of the image – but these were precisely the points which are thought to be later additions and which are therefore likely to manifest such lacunae. José Antonio Flores Gómez was perturbed by certain cracks but these were the cracks caused by the stress of the wooden stretcher frame used to support the image and were only to be expected; they were not cracks in the original image. Neither Rosales nor Gómez did any chemical analysis of the image and so were not in a position to make scientific judgments on the tilma or its image.

Another critic, Leoncio Garza-Valdés, was a pediatrician with no specialized knowledge relevant to a scientific analysis of the tilma. But this did not stop him from making outlandish claims. Garza-Valdés claimed to see images in the tilma that no one else could see but brought no evidence to bear in supporting this claim. Daniel Castellano points out that Garza-Valdés "is not a professional scientist, nor is he an expert in painting or in infrared photographic analysis. His lack of expertise is shown by his employment of ultraviolet photography on the Image while it was still in its glass case, which makes UV imaging practically useless."[2] Garza-Valdés' co-investigator and physician colleague, Gilberto Aguirre, had an entirely different appraisal of his work. The photos taken by Garza-Valdés, says Aguirre, "don't show any underpaintings at all and… the photos can't be relied upon because the Plexiglas blocked some of the light and created reflections. Besides, he says, ultraviolet photographs detect only the surface of paintings, not the subsurface painting. Scientists, as it turns out, have to have faith too—in their experiments. Aguirre has none. "This is a totally flawed scientific study," he says. "It proves nothing."[3]

Then we have Joe Nickell, an amateur magician and blackjack dealer, who is a regular columnist for *Skeptical Inquirer*, an American publication serving skeptics of the supernatural. As with most of his critiques of claims of the supernatural, Nickell simply cites third party critics to make his case. He brings nothing new to the table, simply reciting issues that have already been addressed: additions and touchups which everyone already accepts; cracks in some parts of the tilma – again something that is accepted by Guadalupe devotees. Other than citing fellow skeptics, Nickell has nothing of his own to say.

Much like Nickell, Jeanette Favrot Peterson, an art history professor with her self-created history of Guadalupe, says that the image is not supernatural because of its evident additions and touchups (none of which is denied by anybody). But she herself has not reviewed the scientists' analyses of the tilma and consequently cannot make any relevant comments on its scientific status. Her self-created history is not supported by any evidence other than her arbitrary subjective speculation and, of course, does not explain the phenomenon as a whole in any sense.

The issues brought up by the critics are unsurprising given some of the later additions and touch ups. They have no bearing on the enduring mystery of the original image or the longevity of the cloth. We will now turn to the actual evidence provided by the only scientific studies done on the tilma.

Accordingly, we provide below excerpts and summaries of the major scientific studies done on the tilma, all of which highlight its uniqueness.

The most important of these was the study carried out by Dr. Philip Callahan, a University of Florida biophysicist and authority on infrared photography. Callahan was given unique extended access to the image with the latest equipment for infra-red photography. The glass was removed from the image and, after an initial investigation with the naked eye, his crew took seventy five photographs, forty of which were on special infra-red film.

Dr. Jody Smith, who was with Callahan, noted that their "close examination with the naked eye confirmed the remarkable state of preservation of the original image." Smith remarked too that "There is no evidence whatsoever of cracking. Yet paintings less than half the age of the Guadalupe image commonly show a web of hairline cracks across the entire surface, caused by the drying of the paint."[4]

In his own report, Callahan notes,

> The mantle is a dark turquoise blue … This presents an inexplicable phenomenon because all such pigments are semi-permanent and known to be subject to considerable fading with time, especially in hot climates. The Indian Maya blue wall paintings are already badly faded. The blue mantle, however, is bright enough to have been laid last week.

> The most notable feature of the robe is its remarkable luminosity. It is highly reflective of visible radiation yet transparent to the infrared rays…. As in the case of the blue mantle, the shadowing of the pink robe is blended into the paint layer and no drawing or sketch is evident under the pink pigment….

The pink pigment appears to be inexplicable.… One of the really strange aspects of this painting is that not only is the tilma not sized, but there is absolutely no protective coating of varnish. Despite this unusual lack of any protective overcoating, the robe and mantle are as bright and colored as if the paint was newly laid.

The head of the Virgin of Guadalupe is one of the great masterpieces of artistic facial expression. In subtleness of form, simplicity of execution, hue and coloring, it has few equals among the masterpieces of the world. Furthermore, there are no portraits that I have ever observed which are executed in a similar manner.…

One of the truly marvelous and inexplicable techniques utilized to give realism to the painting is the way it takes advantage of the unsized tilma to give it depth and render it lifelike. This is particularly evident in the mouth, where the coarse fiber of the fabric is raised above the level of the rest of the weave and follows perfectly the ridge at the top of the lip. The same rough imperfections occur below the highlighted area on the left cheek and to the right and below the right eye. I would consider it impossible that any human painter could select a tilma with imperfections of weave positioned so as to accentuate the shadows and impart realism. The possibility of coincidence is even more unlikely.…

The black of the eyes and hair cannot be iron oxide or any pigment that turns brown with age for the paint is neither cracked nor faded with age. The truly phenomenal thing about the face and hands is the tonal quality which is as much a physical effect from the light reflecting off the coarse tilma as the paint itself.[5]

He adds:

The original figure including the rose robe, blue mantle, hands and face… is inexplicable. In terms of this infra-red study, there is no way to explain either the kind of color pigments utilized, nor the maintenance of color luminosity and brightness of pigments over the centuries. Furthermore, when consideration is given to the fact that there is no under-drawing, sizing, or over-varnish, and that the weave of the fabric is itself utilized to give the portrait depth, no explanation of the portrait is possible by infra-red techniques. It is remarkable that in over four centuries there is no fading or cracking of the original figure on any portion of the ayate tilma, which being unsized, should have deteriorated centuries ago.[6]

Callahan's colleague Smith observes, "To account for the brightness of the colors in mantle and robe, many people have suspected that artists employed by the church have, from time to time, in the last four hundred and fifty years been called to retouch the portrait. But in the original portions of the portrait there is absolutely no sign of retouching – no brushstrokes, no cracked or chipped pigment, no layering of paint. In short, the unfading brightness of the turquoise and rose colors remains inexplicable."[7]

With regard to the later additions to the tilma, Callahan believes that the gold trim and fleur-de-lis on the robe and the bottom part of the image were added later. Others have argued that these elements were part of the original image because they are found in the first replica of the image made in 1570. Charles Wahlig believes that they are painted overlays intended to embellish the appearance of the images underneath.

The two other scientific studies done on the tilma were histological and chemical analyses and these are usefully summarized by physicist Daniel J. Castellano in his encyclopedic work *Historiography of the Apparition of Guadalupe*:

> Although many experts have given educated opinions about the composition of the cloth and its paints, none of these carry much evidentiary value without histological and chemical analysis. At most two such studies have been conducted, in 1936 and 1946.
>
> Our only definite source for the 1936 study is the testimony of the well-known Mexican forensic scientist Ernesto Sodi Pallares (1919-1977), who devoted much of his time to Guadalupan investigations. One version of his account is mentioned in a February 1976 report that he and fellow criminologist Roberto Palacios Bermúdez gave to the Guadalupan researcher Manuel de la Mora Ojeda.

According to the lab results, the chemical composition of the fiber coloring did not match any natural mineral, vegetable, or animal pigment. The results were consistent with a variety of synthetic pigments, yet these were all invented in the late nineteenth century or later.

It was Pallares who sent fibers from the tilma to the Nobel Prize winning chemist Richard Kuhn for his analysis.

Castellano then describes the second study which was

> a 1946 chemical and microscopic analysis, done at the National University of Mexico (UNAM). A signed letter from the biologist Isaac Ochoterena (1885-1950), then honorary director of the Institute of Biology, is still available in the library of the Basilica of Guadalupe

> The purpose of this study was to determine the composition of the tilma itself, rather than its pigments....

> Ochoterena reports that the cloth appeared coarse like a sack, and the removed fibers had a dressing (aderezo), part of which must have been flaxseed (linaza). We note that flaxseed or linseed oil is an ordinary component of oil paint, but is not used as sizing, since it causes fabric to rot. Since Ochoterena perceives the cloth to be quite old, this evidence of paint without sizing is remarkable.

Ochoterena's histochemical studies excluded "most non-lignin fibers" and eliminated "most synthetic fibers. The fibers did not dissolve in any of the reagents, which eliminates cotton, silk and linen." His microscopic examination eliminated "cotton, which has unicellular fibers, as well as flax and hemp, which have much longer cells."

> Judging from the size, rectilinear configuration, and structure of the cells, Ochoterena concluded that the plant was an agave of indeterminate species.

> To this day, this has been the only technical analysis competent for determining the composition of the cloth. All other expert opinions, given before or since, have been based on ocular or low-

power microscopic examination, without any chemical analysis or precise measurement. In a word, they are educated guesses, based on the weave and texture of the cloth. Only Ochoterena has made proper cellular and histochemical analysis, a task for which he was eminently qualified, and his verdict was that the cloth is made of a species of agave.

The abbot of the basilica Feliciano Cortés Mora said in 1949 that a separate study done on a thread from the tilma showed it to be agave.[8]

More recently, in 2009, Dr. Aldofo Orozco, a physicist from the National University of Mexico pointed out that the conservation of the tilma over five centuries "is completely beyond any scientific explanation."

A news story elaborates further on his conclusions

> "All the cloths similar to the Tilma that have been placed in the salty and humid environment around the Basilica have lasted no more than ten years," he explained. One painting of the miraculous image, created in 1789, was on display in a church near the basilica where the Tilma was placed. "This painting was made with the best techniques of its time, the copy was beautiful and made with a fabric very similar to that of the Tilma. Also, the image was protected with a glass since it was first placed there."
>
> However, eight years later, the copy of the image of Our Lady of Guadalupe was thrown away because the colors were fading and threads were breaking. In contrast, Orozco said, "the original Tilma was exposed for approximately 116 years without any kind of protection, receiving all the infrared and ultraviolet radiation from the tens of thousands of candles near it and exposed to the humid and salty air around the temple."
>
> Dr. Orozco then discussed the Tilma's fabric. He noted that "one of the most bizarre characteristics of the cloth is that the back side is rough and coarse, but the front side is 'as soft as the most pure silk, as noted by painters and scientists in 1666, and confirmed one century later in 1751 by the Mexican painter, Miguel Cabrera."

Following an analysis of some of the fibers in 1946, it was concluded that the fibers came from the Agave plant.[9]

Another unique dimension of the image on the tilma are the images reflected in the eyes of the Virgin. Says Castellano,

> From the 1950s through the 1970s, various experts in photography and ophthalmology have attested that the image of one or more human figures can be found in the Virgin's eyes. Ordinarily, we might dismiss such claims as mere coincidence. After all, the human brain is highly proficient at facial recognition, accounting for our propensity to recognize faces in clouds and other amorphous objects.

> Yet there are two considerations that might make us take the claims more seriously. First, the same figure seems to be in both eyes. Second, in the right eye, which is more clearly rendered, there are two or possibly three instances of the human figure, in the locations, sizes and orientations one finds in the reflections on a human eye, known as Purkinje-Sanson images. Both of these considerations greatly reduce the likelihood that we are dealing with mere coincidence.[10]

Other remarkable features of the image have been highlighted in recent years. For instance, the 46 stars on the Virgin's mantle reflect the position of the constellations in the night sky in Mexico on December 12, 1531.

Most important in hastening the conversion of the Aztecs was the fact that the tilma contained codes that they could decipher instantly. These are enumerated in *The Guadalupe Mysteries*[11]

An Image as an Aztec Codex

Mary's maskless face signifies that she is human and not a goddess; her loose hair signifies she is a virgin.
The blue mantle signifies heaven, the abode of the supreme gods.

> The mantle's covering the sky signifies that the Lady rules the stars, not vice versa.
>
> Mary's obscuring the sun signifies that she is more powerful than the sun itself, the greatest life-giving force on earth.
>
> The arrangements of stars on Mary's mantle, clear to the Aztec priests, corresponds with their location on December 12, 1531, not as seen from earth but from outer space.
>
> The pink tunic, the color of the rising sun, is a sign of the renewal of life.
>
> The moon, a footstool for Mary, signifies the dethronement of the moon gods.
>
> Hands folded in prayer honor someone more powerful than oneself.
>
> The blue mantle's covering the flora on the dress shows heavenly care of the earth.

The mantle held a different set of codes for the Spanish Christians ranging from the cross to the hands folded in prayer.

As revealed by both historical reports and archaeological evidence, human sacrifice was a regular feature of Aztec life throughout the year. With the coming of the Mother, such sacrifice came to an end. Msgr. Eduardo Chavez, cofounder and dean of the Higher Institute for Guadalupan studies and today's pre-eminent Guadalupan researcher, notes that "The plain cross at her neckline signifies the end of Aztec human sacrifice, as her son was a sacrifice for all on the cross."[12]

Did Juan Diego Exist?

Does the Guadalupe phenomenon exist? Yes. But what is it? It is the conviction of millions through the centuries that the Mother of God appeared to an Aztec peasant named Juan Diego, exhorted him to come to her for help and consolation along with all who live in his land and finally left behind a tangible token of her appearance. No such claim is made in any religion other than Christianity and so it is simply inconceivable that it would spontaneously arise in an Aztec milieu. Appearances of a human messenger from Heaven are peculiar to Christianity.

Since we know the phenomenon exists, we have to ask how it arose. If we say, Juan Diego never existed, as some writers have uncritically said, we are still left with the problem of accounting for the phenomenon. Was it a Spanish import? This is hard to believe since some of the Spanish religious leaders were initially opposed to Guadalupe for theological reasons. And the Spanish civil authorities had no particular interest in religion. Was it an Aztec creation? That is even harder to believe given that the Aztecs did not have a theological framework of such appearances. Nor would they be trying to promote a Christian cause.

So we are still left with the problem. But it is a problem we have created for ourselves because we have failed to take the phenomenon seriously or grasp the big picture.

Our task is to explain the phenomenon in a way that remains faithful to the available data. Given the diversity of the data, the only viable route is the holistic one. We have to look at the big picture and consider the cumulative case. To "explain" the phenomenon, we have to study it as a whole on its own terms instead of brandishing some arbitrary 21st century methodology. We have to study all of the data and not just a sub-set.

Sixteenth century Mexico did not have social media platforms or television networks. There was no possibility of headlines like "Virgin Mary appears to Juan Diego." But the communities of that time had scribes and archivists who recorded events and life-stories. There were also buildings, artworks and customs related to events. This is how we recreate what took place in the past. Recreating the past, then, involves taking evidence that is available to us today.

And it also means an openness to all data. We should not shut our minds to claims that undermine our preconceptions and biases. We are not dealing with a mere academic discussion or a chemical lab analysis. Rather this is an existentially urgent question that has created communities and changed lives. It should not be reduced to polemics or pointless wordplay.

Concrete written testimonies to the historicity of Juan Diego and his encounter with the Virgin date from the time of the apparition itself. Certainly there is more contemporary documentary evidence of this kind for Juan Diego's existence than for Alexander the Great, Socrates and many ancient historical figures whose existence we accept. The three most significant documents testifying to Juan Diego's historicity are the *The Cuautitlán testament* of 1559, the *Nican mopohua* which describes the apparition and has been dated to the mid-sixteenth century (its author is believed to have lived from 1520 to 1606) and the *Codex Escalada* of 1548 (some find the *Codex* controversial because it was discovered relatively recently).

One of the earliest written references to Juan Diego and the apparition is found in the will of an Aztec convert, variously known as Gregoria Maria and Juana Martin (being the daughter of Juan Martin), who was from Cuautitlán the same town as Juan Diego. The document dates back to March 11, 1559, and is written in Nahuatl, the Aztec tongue. She writes, "here [Cuautitlán] grew up the young man Juan Diegotzin; …after he left, through her revered mediation her miracle was worked, there on Tepeyac … where the precious lady holy Mary appeared, whose image we see there in Guadalupe, which is our venerable possession in our town of Cuauhtitlán."

Shockingly, dogmatic deniers of the historicity of Juan Diego and his encounter like Stafford Poole are reduced to calling the Aztec witnesses liars while admitting that they do not know how to explain the positive testimony of the leaders. Poole writes:

> "This would not bother me if it involved only the Indian witnesses, because they have always been inclined toward marvelous narratives and not well known for telling the truth; but when I see that serious priests and illustrious gentlemen affirm the same falsehood, I cannot but be confused."

About Poole, Castellano writes, "Remarkably, some of the more strident anti-apparitionist authors have found themselves forced to accuse the most upstanding citizens of Mexico of false testimony, in order to sustain their improbable thesis that no one knew of the apparition story before 1648. While it was relatively easy to dismiss the Indian witnesses as ignorant, credulous or mendacious, it is much more problematic to do the same for the witnesses in Mexico City."[13]

Castellano argues that "The Cuautitlán testament of 1559 and the testimonies of 1666 amply establish that Juan Diego was a real person, personally known by many in Cuautitlán, and that he was a man of exceptional character and a devout Christian. The Indians asked for his intercession in life and in death, and verified miracles have resulted from his intercession."[14]

L'Osservatore Romano has provided a helpful overview of the currently available historical data on Juan Diego and Guadalupe

> In analyzing the event of Guadalupe, an effort has been made to refer to the various kinds of written historical sources (accounts, letters, legal and administrative documents), archaeological, figurative and "industrial". These sources basically derive from three distinct cultural patterns: the "strictly Indian and indigenous", the "Spanish" and the "mestizo". The treatment of each source is determined by the nature of the source: to attribute the correct value to the sources, the cultural language of the two worlds must be taken into account as well as the way in which they were transmitted. At times, the written sources are in the form of annals, chronicles, "songs", etc., that determine an oral tradition. The epistolary sources are almost entirely Spanish, while the juridical sources vary considerably and have to do with Church government or worship … The administrative sources reflect the organization of the new Hispanic territory in censuses and maps (some very early ones even show the first shrine at Tepeyac). Among the indigenous sources, the oral ones deserve mention. These are important in popular cultural traditions, such as the Mexican, that were mainly oral….
>
> The historical period in which the events of Guadalupe occurred explains the scarcity of direct Guadalupan documentation from the earliest times. However, there are accounts that date back to the first 20 years after the events and others that treat the topic from the middle of the 16th century with recourse to ancient documents or testimonies, as in the case of Fernando de Alva Ixtlilxóchitl, and above all the *Informaciones Jurídicas* of 1666 that collected many of these testimonies, including those of people who were acquainted with contemporary witnesses of the events and their protagonists….

Many indigenous codices were destroyed, as the friars Fr
Bernardino de Sahagún and Fr Gerónimo de Mendieta affirm
… Theft, fire [especially the fire in the Municipal Archives of
Mexico City in 1692], the recycling for commercial use of written
legislation, etc., further explain the scarcity of archival sources. In
1578, the Dominican Friar Diego Durán realized that he had
erred in the destruction of the indigenous codices. In spite of all,
a few indigenous codes with references to Guadalupe have been
preserved, for example the "Crónica de Juan Bautista" (1563-
1574), kept in the Archives of the Basilica of Guadalupe.…

We should remember the document known as the *'informaciones de
los viejos de Cuauhtitlán'*, said to be the native village of Juan Diego.
These testimonies, gleaned from the lips of various indigenous
men and women, advanced in years … certainly shed light on
the figure of Juan Diego. The abundant, coinciding information
they provide on him deserves to be taken into consideration".…

Many "Guadalupan" documents of the 16th century "of Spanish
provenance, refer mainly to the devotion to the Mexican Virgin
of Guadalupe. The subject of numerous other documents is
donations or acts of Guadalupan devotion; yet others refer
to juridical questions concerning the Shrine of Guadalupe or
to controversies connected with the devotion.… In the work
cited, "El encuentro de la Virgen de Guadalupe y JuanDiego",
documents concerning "Guadalupe" were presented which date
from the mid-16th century (from about 1555) to 1630: in all,
there are 9 testaments, 2 documents concerning donations, 2
of a juridical kind (controversies); there are 11 references to
Guadalupe in contemporary chronicles.…

Recent research and discoveries have confirmed the ancient data
of a constant "traditio" of Guadalupe from the 16th century,
and even lead to the confirmation of the actual existence of
Juan Diego. Among them, we recall the study on the Escalada
Codex … that includes the death certificate of Juan Diego
Cuauhtlatoatzin, with the signatures of Antonio Valeriano and
of the friar, Fr Bernardino de Sahagún.…

Investigations made by researchers in other archives, until very recently unknown, at the ancient Dominican Friary of San Vicente Ferrer Chimalhuacan (founded in 1529), has resulted in the discovery of important material concerning the early years of the conquest and some of its protagonists, both Indian and Spanish. This material shows Juan Diego's cultural and family background that is closely linked to the site of the friary and its foundation....

The results of the examination of the sources show convergence on the essentials. At the beginning of the Spanish presence in Mexico and precisely in the Anahuac Valley, after a dramatic conquest and divisions in the "Nahuatl" political world, a church was built in a place of religious significance to the indigenous community: the hills of Tepeyac. This church was dedicated to the Blessed Virgin Mary with the title of "Guadalupe", and coincides only in name with the one in Spain ... The Shrine of Guadalupe became an incredibly powerful symbol of a new history of Christianity and of the convergence between two worlds, which until then had been tragically opposed.... In the places linked to Juan Diego's life, a living memory of him has been preserved among the indigenous since the 16th century.... Moreover this was often the case with distinguished figures, both indigenous and Spanish. In Guadalupe, according to one tradition, a "chapel" was built on the site of Juan Diego's hut, not far from Our Lady's shrine. Tradition claims that Juan Diego withdrew to the "shrine". This is normal in the Christian tradition, as it also was in the indigenous Mexican tradition.[15]

About the *Nican mopohua*, Castellano writes,

"The New York [Nican mopohua] manuscripts do nothing but confirm what we already could gather from a careful examination of the seventeenth-century Guadalupan authors, namely that a written Nahuatl tradition of the apparition narrative existed long before 1648, and this tradition already included fixed wording for the dialogue between Our Lady and Juan Diego. The discovery of the oldest manuscript confirms that Lasso preserved a sixteenth century version verbatim, though we cannot say for certain that it is the oldest version of the tradition....

Nonetheless, the manuscripts are prima facie evidence against the claim that there is no written testimony of the traditional apparition narrative prior to 1648. Their antiquity does not compel us to believe that they are accurate in every detail, but they do constitute evidence that the basic apparition story as we know it was already known to the Indians of the sixteenth century.

It is not reasonable to demand an absolutely original manuscript as a guarantee of authenticity, for much of our historical and literary knowledge is well established without autograph originals. As Burrus noted, we possess no manuscript originals for any of the Greek or Latin classics, nor of Dante and Shakespeare, yet we can establish that the extant content of these works has been preserved with substantial accuracy.[16]

The *Codex Escalada*, discovered in 1995, and dating back to 1548

"depicts the Virgin of Guadalupe and Juan Diego on Tepeyac, and accompanying text mentions the apparition in 1531, the death of Juan Diego, and the year 1548. The codex bears the glyph of Antonio Valeriano, reputed author of the Nican mopohua or one of its variants, and is signed by Bernardino de Sahagún....The codex is the earliest witness to the 1531 date of the apparition. We know from other sources that the apparition was known as "Guadalupe" as early as 1555, and the indigenous writer renders this as "Gadalope." We also find an early mention of Juan Diego by his indigenous name, Cuauhtlactoatzin. The testament of 1559 shows that Juan Diego was already well known as the seer of Guadalupe, at least in the vicinity of Cuautitlán. When Fray Bernardino de Sahagún put his signature on this codex, there was nothing in its content that he would find objectionable.... [The Codex] does provide important evidence of mid-sixteenth century belief in a Guadalupan apparition to an Indian named Cuauhtlactoatzin. It is the oldest extant document attesting to the traditional 1531 date of the apparition, not counting annals whose entries cannot be definitively dated.[17]

In each decade from the Thirties through the Sixties, Mexican historians produced classic research studies on the historicity of Juan Diego and the Guadalupe apparition:

> Mariano Cuevas, *Album Historico Guadalupano del IV centenario*, 1930
> Jose Bravo Ugarte, *Cuestiones Historicas Guadalupanas*, 1946
> Alberto Junco, *Un Radical Problema Guadalupano*, 1953
> Laura Lopez Beltran, *La Protohistoria Guadalupana*, 1961

The big picture before us is this:

- A set of historical documents from the sixteenth century that narrate the Juan Diego story.
- A community of millions of believers in Mexico that not only claims that its ancestors received the faith from the appearance to Juan Diego but whose very religious identity is inseparable from its origin in Guadalupe and Juan Diego. In this particular case, *the community IS its history*.
- This community preserves a living tradition of specific places, persons, events and dates associated with the Guadalupe phenomenon – principally Tepeyac itself.
- The religious life of the community has been governed for centuries by devotional traditions specific to Guadalupe that withstood the onslaught of time and co-exist with traditional Christian practices.
- Certain miraculous phenomena have been traditionally associated with the phenomenon: protection from natural disasters, healing from diseases, help for countless needs.
- Starting in the sixteenth century, Church authorities have consistently held to the tradition that the Virgin appeared to Juan Diego and eventually secured papal approval and praise. The historian David Blackbourn notes that in the case of Marian apparitions, "For all historians of the subject, clerical approval has created superior documentation."
- The continuing miracle that is the tilma.

When the mists of history clear away, we are left with an extraordinary immovable fact: the inexplicable instantaneous genesis and enduring subsistence of a new Christian community made up of an indigenous people that once followed a religion as different from Christianity as can be imagined.

So the question arises: how did this community spring up? Was the Juan Diego story simply an embellishment designed to inflate their self-importance? Was it all a conspiracy cooked up in later centuries? On the face of it, the conspiracy suggestion seems far-fetched. Did someone a few centuries ago simply come up with the idea of the Virgin appearing to an Aztec peasant – something without precedent in that community.

Or is it possible that they were affirming what they knew to be true? After all, if the Virgin did appear to an Aztec peasant as described, then everything makes sense. All the dots can be connected to give us a coherent and comprehensive picture.

In actual fact, we should say that the burden of proof should rest with those who wish to deny either the existence of Juan Diego or his encounter with the Virgin. If they deny either, then they should provide an explanation of all the disparate facts to which we have drawn attention. But all alternate explanations fail and none of the critics have even tried to provide any with some degree of plausibility. Moreover, this pattern of the Virgin Mary appearing to humble natives of different lands is found all over the world in every century. And the kind of messages she transmitted in various cultures and communities separated by space and time are identical to those she delivered in Guadalupe. The messages of a mother assisting her children.

The Guadalupe community literally kept the Faith – a faith whose zeal and depth, given the constraints of isolation in space and time, could only have been birthed by an actual encounter with the Virgin mediated through a chosen messenger. How else could so novel and life-changing a vision as the Christian idea have so rapidly taken root in a people who were as sociologically, culturally and theologically distant from the Spaniards as the Aztecs were? The community itself, we might say, embodies the truth of its birth at the hands of the Virgin and her witness Juan Diego.

Marian Apparition or Pagan Cult?

We have seen good reason to affirm the uniqueness of the tilma and the historicity of Juan Diego. But whom did Juan Diego encounter? Was it the Virgin Mary or Tonantzin, the Aztec goddess of fertility, as loosely asserted by some writers? Or was this just part of a cycle of peasants discovering images of the Virgin much like in Europe as airily claimed by a professor of art (this is a demonstrably erroneous claim given that very few of the prominent European encounters with the Virgin involve the finding of an image)?

As already pointed out, the idea of appearances of the Virgin Mary is unique to Christianity. The gods and goddesses of the Aztec religion and of every pre-Christian religion were not human and there was no tradition of them "appearing" to their devotees. The attitude toward these deities was one of appeasing them. None of them were benevolent. "Tonantzin was the source of both life and death, a terrifying goddess who eventually consumed everything she created."[19] Tonantzin was also known as Cihuacotl, the serpent woman. This goddess could not be more different from the tender, loving mother who says. "Am I not here with you who am your Mother? Are you not under my shadow and protection? Am I not of your kind?" The coming of the Virgin ended the practice of human sacrifice common in Aztec religion.

In any case, why would a goddess fold her hands in prayer as we see in the case of the Virgin?

These confused notions of associating the Virgin with local goddesses or speaking of Guadalupe as a Spanish import is based on sheer ignorance of the global phenomenon of Marian apparitions. Mythologies do not produce mass conversions or create powerhouses like the tilma. Marian apparitions, on the other hand, have a track record of changing hearts and minds and leaving behind lasting "signs". We can make sense of the Guadalupe phenomenon only within the framework of apparitions of the Virgin Mary. Much as we can make sense of the falling of an apple only within the framework of gravity.

For the appearance of the Virgin to Juan Diego does fit within a pattern, a universal paradigm. But it is not the pattern promoted by certain scholars of syncretic synthesis with local deities or importation of alien religious cults. Such scholars are guided not by the available evidence but their own fanciful ideas. Rather, what we have here is the Contact of *Revelation* 12, the Woman Clothed with the Sun.

This is what the Guadalupe phenomenon is all about.

But Guadalupe is different from all the other encounters with the Virgin in one unique respect. In her appearance, she had assured Juan Diego, "Am I not here who am your mother?"

Amazingly, the Virgin Mother is present with her children through her tilma inviting them to come to her with all their needs. All who seek and all who doubt can "see" her today as did Juan Diego in 1531.

The Virgin continues to be with us to this very day. Guadalupe is an apparition that never ended.

NOTES

[1]Stanley L. Jaki, *The Drama of Guadalupe* (New Hope, KY: Real View Books, 2009), 24-5, 35.

[2] https://www.arcaneknowledge.org/catholic/guadalupe13.htm

[3]https://www.texasmonthly.com/articles/quite-contrary/

[4]Jody Brant Smith, *The Image of Guadalupe* (Macon, Georgia: Meridian University Press, 1994), 63.

[5]Philip S. Callahan, "The Tilma Under Infra-Red Radiation," *CARA Studies on Popular Devotion*, Volume II: *Guadalupan Studies*, No 3 (Washington, 1981), pp. 9-15.

[6]Cited in Christopher Rengers, *Mary of the Americas*, (New York: Alba House, 1989), 92.

[7]Jody Brant Smith, op cit., 72.

[8]https://www.arcaneknowledge.org/catholic/guadalupe13.htm

9http://www.mariancongress.org/mcongress/en/presentations/orozco-cna.html

10https://www.arcaneknowledge.org/catholic/guadalupe13.htm. Carlos Salinas and Manuel de la Mora, *Descubrimento de un Busto Humano en los Ojos de la Virgen de Guadalupe* (Mexico: Editorial Tradición, 1980).

11Grzegorz Gorny and Janusz Rosikon, *The Guadalupe Mysteries* (San Francisco, CA: Ignatius Press, 2016), 64.

12https://catholickey.org/2016/04/15/who-is-our-lady-of-guadalupe/

13https://www.arcaneknowledge.org/catholic/guadalupe7.htm

14https://www.arcaneknowledge.org/catholic/guadalupe11.htm

15*L'Osservatore Romano*, 23 January 2002, page 8

16https://www.arcaneknowledge.org/catholic/guadalupe5.htm#ch9

17https://www.arcaneknowledge.org/catholic/guadalupe11.htm#ch17

18https://fullerstudio.fuller.edu/the-virgin-of-guadalupe/.

Our Lady of Lourdes, France, 1858

"I Do Not Promise to Make You Happy in This World,
But in the Next"

Witness: Bernadette Soubirous, 12
Dates: February 11 to July 16, 1858
Enduring Evidence: Healing spring, incorrupt body of St. Bernadette
Messages: Healing, Call to Penance, Secret
Description of the Virgin: "She has the appearance of a young girl of sixteen or seventeen. She is dressed in a white robe, girdled at the waist with a blue ribbon which flows down all along Her robe. She wears upon Her head a veil which is also white; this veil gives just a glimpse of Her hair and then falls down at the back below Her waist. Her feet are bare but covered by the last folds of Her robe except at the point where a yellow rose shines upon each of them. She holds on Her right arm a Rosary of white beads with a chain of gold shining like the two roses on Her feet."

Image source –
https://en.wikipedia.org/wiki/Our_Lady_of_Lourdes#/media/
File:France-002009_-_Our_Lady_of_Lourdes_(15774765182).jpg

The Apparitions

Bernadette Soubirous, the oldest of four children, lived in Lourdes, a town in the foothills of the Pyrenees mountains in France. Her father had been financially ruined and the family lived in a small room in a building that was once the town jail. Here, in Bernadette's own words, is an account of her first encounter with the Virgin:

> The Thursday before Ash Wednesday (February 11, 1858) it was cold and the weather was threatening. After our dinner, our mother told us there was no more wood in the house and she was vexed. My sister Toinette and I, to please her, offered to go and pick up dry branches at the riverside. My mother said no, because the weather was bad and we might be in danger of falling into the Gave. Jeanne Abadie, our neighbour and friend, who was looking after her little brother in our house and who wanted to come with us, took her brother back to his house and returned the next moment telling us that she had leave to come with us. My mother still hesitated, but seeing that there were three of us, she let us go. We took first of all the road which leads to the cemetery, by the side of which wood shavings can sometimes be found. That day we found nothing there. We came down by the side which leads near the Gave and having arrived at the Pont Vieux we wondered if it would be best to go up or down the river. We decided to go down and taking the forest road we arrived at Merlasse. Then we went into Monsieur de la Fittes field, by the mill of Savy.
>
> As soon as we had reached the end of this field, nearly opposite the grotto of Massabieille, we were stopped by the canal of the mill we had just passed. The current of this canal was not strong for the mill was not working, but the water was cold and I for my part was afraid to go in. Jeanne Abadie and my sister, less timid than I, took their sabots in their hands and crossed the stream. However, when they were on the other side they called out that it was cold and bent down to rub their feet and warm them. All this increased my fear and I thought that if I went into the water I should get an attack of asthma. So I asked Jeanne, who was bigger

and stronger than I, to take me on her shoulders. 'I should think not!' she answered 'If you won't come, stay where you are!'.

After the others had picked up some pieces of wood under the grotto, they disappeared along the Gave. When I was alone, I threw some stones into the water to give me a foothold, but it was no use. So I had to make up my mind to take off my sabots and cross the canal as Jeanne and my sister had done.

I had just begun to take off my first stocking when suddenly I heard a great noise like the sound of a storm. I looked to the right and to the left, under the trees of the river, but nothing moved; I thought I was mistaken. I went on taking off my shoes and stockings, when I heard a fresh noise like the first. Then I was frightened and stood straight up. I lost all power of speech and thought when, turning my head toward the grotto, I saw at one of the openings of the rock a bush only one moving as if it were very windy. Almost at the same time, there came out of the interior of the grotto a golden coloured cloud, and soon after a Lady, young and beautiful, exceedingly beautiful, the like of whom I had never seen before, came and placed herself at the entrance of the opening, above the rose bush. She looked at me immediately, smiled at me and signed to me to advance, as if she had been my Mother. All fear had left me, but I seemed to know no longer where I was. I rubbed my eyes, I shut them, I opened them; but the Lady was still there continuing to smile at me and making me understand that I was not mistaken. Without thinking of what I was doing I took my Rosary in my hands and went on my knees. The Lady made with her head a sign of approval and herself took into her hands a Rosary which hung on her right arm. When I attempted to begin the Rosary and tried to lift my hand to my forehead, my arm remained paralysed, and it was only after the Lady had signed herself that I could do the same. The Lady left me to pray all alone; she passed the beads of her Rosary between her fingers but she said nothing; only at the end of each decade did she say the Gloria with me.

> When the recitation of the Rosary was finished, the Lady returned to the interior of the rock and the golden colored cloud disappeared with her.

Bernadette described her experience to her sister Marie (Toinette) asking her to keep it to herself. But when Bernadette began to cry during evening prayers, Marie went ahead and told their mother all about the incident. Her mother said it was just an illusion and forbade Bernadette to go back to Massabieille. For the next few days she was firm in her refusal but finally the two sisters and Jeanne persuaded her to let them return. On February 14, along with some friends they started off carrying with them a bottle of holy water. When they reached the grotto, Bernadette saw the Lady again and knelt down. She poured the holy water on the ground and this seemed to please the Lady. By now Bernadette had entered the state of ecstasy characteristic of most apparitions: her eyes were focused on a particular location (which seemed to be just empty space to the other observers) and she was entirely oblivious to the presence of her friends. At this time, Jeanne hurled a rock down the incline near the grotto into the river. This startled the children who scattered in different directions and their cries attracted the attention of a nearby miller and his family. The miller took Bernadette into his house. On being informed of the incident, Bernadette's mother arrived to pick her up and would have punished her severely but for the miller's intervention.

It seemed unlikely that Bernadette would ever again be allowed to go back to the grotto but then a prominent local lady, Madame Milhet, and her seamstress, Antoinette Peyret, came to Bernadette and her mother and asked them if they might be able to go together to the grotto. The mother found it impossible to say "no" to two such influential ladies and on the morning of February 18 the two of them went with Bernadette to the grotto. The ladies brought a blessed candle and a pen and paper with which they hoped to record the Lady's name during the apparition. When the Lady appeared to Bernadette, she appeared to have no objection to the presence of the two women but said it was not necessary when Bernadette gave her the pen and paper. The Lady told Bernadette she was to come another fifteen times and promised her happiness not in this world but the next. At the request of the two ladies, Bernadette's mother and aunt accompanied her on the next two visits on February 19th and 20th. On the 20th, the Lady taught Bernadette a secret prayer which she recited for the rest of her life.

On February 21st, her sixth visit, Bernadette was accompanied by Dr. Dozous, the town's most eminent doctor, who evaluated her physiological condition during the ecstasy and announced that there was nothing abnormal about it, no indication of "nervous excitement." Bernadette was asked to pray for sinners. By this time, large crowds were following Bernadette to the grotto and the local authorities were becoming concerned about safety hazards. Bernadette was separately interrogated by the Imperial Procurator, who said she was imagining things, and the Chief of Police, who said she was lying. The Chief warned her that she would be imprisoned if she made any further visits to the grotto. Despite this threat she returned there the next day followed by two policemen. On this occasion, the Lady did not appear to her and she was taunted and mocked by many of the locals. As if to reward her for her perseverance, on the next day, the 23rd, the Lady again came to her and gave her "three wonderful secrets" that have never been revealed. On February 24th, she was given repeated injunctions of "Penitence" and on February 25th she was commanded to drink and bathe in the fountain. Since there was no fountain there, Bernadette started to dig up the gravel with her hands and soon a small pool had formed from which she drank and washed her face. The pool became a stream and its ability to heal and cure became evident almost instantly when, shortly after this apparition, a man who was going blind recovered his sight after bathing his eyes in its waters and a lady's paralyzed hand was restored to normal use. On February 26th Bernadette was told to "kiss the ground in behalf of sinners," on February 27th she was asked to tell the clergy that they should build a chapel at the grotto and on March 1st that the people should come in a procession to this chapel.

Bernadette was more afraid of the parish priest, Abbe Peyramale, than of the civil authorities. When she fearfully told him of the Lady's requests he was quite severe with her and said that he did not deal with strangers and that she, Bernadette, must first find out from the Lady who she was. On March 4th, over twenty thousand people had gathered to watch Bernadette at the apparition site. Although Bernadette saw the Lady again, this was the fifteenth apparition, the crowds were clearly disappointed that they did not witness any kind of "sign and wonder." The Abbe Peyramale had specified the sign he wanted: the blooming of a rose bush in winter. The Lady declined to comply with the Abbe's demand.

The next apparition was on March 25th, the Feast of the Annunciation, and it was then that the Lady finally responded to Bernadette's request to reveal her identity. Her answer, which Bernadette did not quite comprehend, was "Que soy era Immaculado Conceptiou": "I am the Immaculate Conception." The crowds grew larger after this announcement and the authorities became even more concerned. Lourdes fell under the jurisdiction of the Baron Massy, the Prefect of Tarbes, and the Baron who was quite annoyed by the entire phenomenon asked three prominent physicians to examine Bernadette. Their diagnosis, like that of Dr. Dozous, was that she was physically and mentally sound.

On April 7th, when Bernadette was in the state of ecstasy, she accidentally moved her right hand into the flame of the candle that she always held at the apparitions (before the ecstasy began she had been holding the hand near the flame to ward off the wind). Although the hand remained in the flame, she continued in her ecstasy for another fifteen minutes without showing any sign of pain and with no damage to her skin. When the apparition was over, however, and Dr. Dozous touched her hand with a lighted candle, she reacted with pain and surprise.

After this apparition, the civil authorities blocked public access to the grotto. Bernadette felt that since the Lady had both revealed her identity and appeared to her as many times as she promised there was no urgency about returning to the grotto. On July 16th, the Feast of Our Lady of Mount Carmel, she received one more "invitation" to come to the grotto - and there saw the Lady for the last time in this world (the eighteenth apparition). With the end of the apparitions, Bernadette went to study at a hospice run by the Sisters of Nevers. Eventually, she resolved to join the Sisters of Nevers and left Lourdes for the last time on July 4, 1866. Always sickly, Bernadette died at the age of 35 on April 16, 1879. Miraculously, to this day, like that of Sister Catherine Laboure of the Miraculous Medal, Bernadette's body remains incorrupt and lies in the convent chapel in Nevers. She was canonized on December 8, 1933.

As for the spring which Bernadette uncovered under the direction of the Lady, it is now the source of nearly fifteen thousand gallons of water a day. Over five thousand cures have been attributed to the waters of Lourdes – of which the Church has rigorously investigated and validated just sixty five. Nearly five million pilgrims visit Lourdes every year.

A little-known and yet significant event, in this context, was the effect of the water on the son of the then-emperor of France, Napoleon III. In August 1858, the two-year old prince imperial "contracted dangerous sunstroke and the threat of meningitis from it." The royal governess was instructed to bring water from Lourdes which was then sprinkled on the child. The child was subsequently cured and in October the Emperor ordered the local officials to remove the barricades set up around the grotto.

After an investigation of nearly four years, the bishop of the Diocese of Tarbes (to which Lourdes belongs) declared on January 18, 1862: "We judge that Mary Immaculate, Mother of God, really appeared to Bernadette Soubirous on 11 February 1858, and on subsequent days, eighteen times in all. The faithful are justified in believing this to be certain." There are now four churches in Lourdes and the processions of the pilgrims (requested by the Lady) are a regular part of the ceremonies at this great shrine of healing.

The Song of Bernadette

The story of Lourdes was memorably captured in a best-selling 1941 novel, *The Song of Bernadette*, by the Austrian Jewish writer Franz Werfel. Werfel was a novelist who left Austria for France with his wife when the Nazis came to power. When the Nazis invaded France, Werfel, who had angered the Gestapo with his writings, had to flee yet again. On this perilous journey the Werfels spent five weeks in Lourdes where they were hospitably received by the townspeople and the staff of the shrine. During this time, their hosts, some of whom knew the visionary of Lourdes, told Werfel about Bernadette and her visions.

Moved by the hosts' outpouring of love, Werfel vowed to set aside all projects to write a book about Lourdes if he and his wife were able to escape safely. Eventually the Werfels made their way to the US via Spain and Portugal. Once in the US, Werfel wrote *The Song of Bernadette*. The book was an instant bestseller and stayed on the *New York Times bestseller* list for a year: it was #1 for thirteen weeks. The book was the basis of the movie of the same name which was similarly successful and received four Oscars.

Paradoxically, it was Werfel, a Jew, who played a pivotal role in making Lourdes widely known in the English-speaking world and in intellectual circles. Werfel's preface to *The Song of Bernadette* is a poignant testimony to the role he himself felt was assigned to him by Providence:

> In the last days of June 1940, in flight from our mortal enemies after the collapse of France, we reached the city of Lourdes.... It was in this manner that Providence brought me to Lourdes, of the miraculous history of which I had hitherto had but the most superficial knowledge....
>
> It was, I repeat, a time of great dread. But it was also a time of great significance for me, for I became acquainted with the wondrous history of the girl Bernadette Soubirous and also with the wondrous facts concerning the healings of Lourdes. One day in my great distress I made a vow. I vowed that if I escaped from this desperate situation and reached the saving shores of America, I would put off all other tasks and sing, as best I could, the song of Bernadette.
>
> This book is the fulfilment of my vow. In our epoch an epic poem can take no form but that of a novel. *The Song of Bernadette* is a novel but not a fictive work. In face of the events here delineated, the sceptical reader will ask with better right than in the case of most historical epic narratives: "What is true? What is invented?" My answer is: All the memorable happenings that constitute the substance of this book took place in the world of reality. Since their beginning dates back no longer than eighty years, there beats upon them the bright light of modern history and their truth has been confirmed by friend and foe and by cool observers through faithful testimonies. My story makes no changes in this body of truth.

I exercised my right of creative freedom only where the work, as a work of art, demanded certain chronological condensations or where there was need of striking the spark of life from the hardened substance.

I have dared to sing the song of Bernadette, although I am not a Catholic but a Jew; and I drew courage for this undertaking from a far older and far more unconscious vow of mine. Even in the days when I wrote my first verses I vowed that I would evermore and everywhere in all I wrote magnify the divine mystery and the holiness of man--careless of a period that has turned away with scorn and rage and indifference from these ultimate values of our mortal lot.[1]

Lourdes and Science

As with the site of many Marian apparitions, Lourdes is renowned for its healing miracles. But Lourdes is different from other such sites in that from the beginning it has subjected claims of its alleged cures to scientific scrutiny. The Medical Bureau of Lourdes was set up precisely to analyze such claims. After starting with primitive resources, the Bureau is now known for its rigor and the stature of its scientific and medical team.

We will consider the scientific status of the healings attributed to Lourdes by reference to three sources: the Nobel Prize winner Alexis Carrel who won his Nobel for his work on wound healing and the surgical techniques later used for organ transplants and open heart surgery, who made several trips to Lourdes and who witnessed at least two scientifically remarkable cures; the paleontologist Teilhard de Chardin who authored internationally known popularizations of science; and a 2014 evaluation of the Lourdes cures published by the Oxford University Press in its *Journal of the History of Medicine and Allied Sciences*.

Right at the start, as Ruth Cranston points out in her classic work *The Miracle of Lourdes*, a scientific study showed that "chemically the water of the spring at Lourdes contains no curative or medicinal properties whatsoever."

A laboratory analysis of the water showed "that the water from the Grotto of Lourdes has a composition that may be considered as a drinking water similar to most of those found in the mountains where the soil is rich in calcium. The water contains no active substance giving it marked therapeutic properties. It can be drunk without inconvenience. ... The extraordinary effects which are claimed to have been obtained following the use of this water cannot, in the present state of science, be explained by the nature of the salts of which the analysis shows the science."

Remarkably, a study of the water used by infected patients at Lourdes showed that it did not have any negative effect despite an abundance of toxins:

> A bacteriological study of the water from the baths of the sick did, however, bring a remarkable discovery. As we have said, while only a small percentage of the sick who go to the baths are cured, the uncured suffer no harm or any further infection after their immersion....

> Two samples of water were taken from the last bath where men's wounds are bathed, and these were sent with all proper precautions [to two laboratories to be tested on guinea pigs]. ... The resulting reports ... stated: 'The water contains microbes of the most varied order - colon bacillus, staphylococcus, pyocyaneus, etc. But none of these microbes, after culture, showed itself pathogenic to the guinea pig.' Experiments made the same year at Tarbes produced a similar report: colon bacillus, streptococcus, staphylococcus, diplococcus, cocobacillus. That is to say, water polluted in the extreme. Six months after being inoculated with this water, all guinea pigs were living and normal and in healthy condition. In short, Lourdes water, even when polluted, remained perfectly harmless. Billions of bacilli were found, but they were inert. At the same time, guinea pigs inoculated with water from another source containing much the same bacilli, died.[2]

We turn now to the three scientific sources cited earlier.

Alexis Carrel

Nobel Prize winner Alexis Carrel had not only witnessed cures relating to Lourdes but wrote a book titled *The Voyage to Lourdes*. Philosopher-historian of science Stanley Jaki wrote the preface to the 1994 edition of the book and his summary of Carrel's experiences with one of these cures is of particular interest:

> Marie Bailly was born in 1878. Both her father, an optician, and her mother died of tuberculosis. Of her five siblings only one was free of that disease. She was twenty when she first showed symptoms of pulmonary tuberculosis. A year later she was diagnosed with tuberculous meningitis, from which she suddenly recovered when she used Lourdes water. In two more years, in 1901, she came down with tubercular peritonitis. Soon she could not retain food. In March 1902 doctors in Lyons refused to operate on her for fear that she would die on the operating table.
>
> On May 25, 1902, she begged her friends to smuggle her onto a train that carried sick people to Lourdes. She had to be smuggled because, as a rule, such trains were forbidden to carry dying people. The train left Lyons at noon. At two o'clock next morning she was found dying. [Alexis] Carrel was called. He gave her morphine by the light of a kerosene lamp and stayed with her. Three hours later he diagnosed her case as tuberculous peritonitis and said half aloud that she would not arrive in Lourdes alive. The immediate diagnosis at that time largely depended on the procedure known as palpation.
>
> In Lourdes Marie Bailly was examined by several doctors. On May 27 she insisted on being carried to the Grotto, although the doctors were afraid that she would die on the way there. Carrel himself took such a grim view of her condition that he vowed to become a monk if she reached the Grotto alive, a mere quarter of a mile from the hospital.
>
> The rest is medical history. It is found in Dossier 54 of the Archives of the Medical Bureau of Lourdes. The Dossier contains the immediate depositions by three doctors, including Carrel, and

Marie Bailly's own account, which she wrote in November and gave to Carrel, who then duly forwarded it to the Medical Bureau in Lourdes.

The highlights of Marie Bailly's own account are as follows: On arriving at the baths adjoining the Grotto, she was not allowed to be immersed. She asked that some water from the baths be poured on her abdomen. It caused her searing pain all over her body. Still she asked for the same again. This time she felt much less pain. When the water was poured on her abdomen the third time, it gave her a very pleasant sensation.

Meanwhile Carrel stood behind her, with a notepad in his hands. He marked the time, the pulse, the facial expression and other clinical details as he witnessed under his very eyes the following: The enormously distended and very hard abdomen began to flatten and within 30 minutes it had completely disappeared. No discharge whatsoever was observed from the body.

She was first carried to the Basilica, then to the Medical Bureau, where she was again examined by several doctors, among them Carrel. In the evening she sat up in her bed and had a dinner without vomiting. Early next morning she got up on her own and was already dressed when Carrel saw her again.

Carrel could not help registering that she was cured. What will you do with your life now? Carrel asked her. I will join the Sisters of Charity to spend my life caring for the sick, was the answer. The next day she boarded the train on her own, and after a 24-hour trip on hard benches, she arrived refreshed in Lyons. There she took the streetcar and went to the family home, where she had to prove that she was Marie Bailly indeed, who only five days earlier had left Lyons in a critical condition.

Carrel continued to take a great interest in her. He asked a psychiatrist to test her every two weeks, which was done for four months. She was regularly tested for traces of tuberculosis. In late November she was declared to be in good health both physically and mentally. In December she entered the novitiate in Paris.

Without ever having a relapse she lived the arduous life of a Sister of Charity until 1937, when she died at the age of 58.[3]

Teilhard de Chardin

The Jesuit priest Pierre Teilhard de Chardin was both a paleontologist and the author of works of popular science. His assessment of Lourdes is of interest given his scientific background:

> If a common antecedent for the cures could only be discovered; if we could extract from all these authentic facts something which marks them off or conditions them! But we find only this: *Lourdes*; and it is not the Lourdes imagined or hoped for in the excitement of the pilgrimages ... but it is Lourdes alone – Lourdes, a naked and objective reality, to which is attached a mysterious virtue, independent of anything the sick and the praying crowds can take there.

> If the cures of Lourdes were characterized by any family likeness, attached to one category of diseases or appeared under determinate circumstances of time or place, I might invoke with show of reason, some magnetism, some appropriate vibration with which the human body would enter into a vivifying resonance. The precise cause would escape me, but a certain regularity in the phenomena would assure me of the existence of this cause and entitle me to imagine it. But there is nothing of the kind ... effects follow each other without apparent rule. These cures are distributed as if by chance.[4]

"The Lourdes Medical Cures Revisited," Journal of the History of Medicine and Allied Sciences, 2014

Oxford University's *Journal of the History of Medicine and Allied Sciences* is "internationally recognized as one of the top publications in its field." Its paper "The Lourdes Medical Cures Revisited" has been widely reprinted in various scientific settings. Below are relevant excerpts:

> The Lourdes phenomenon, extraordinary in many respects, still awaits scientific explanation. Lourdes concerns science as well as religion....

Any assessment of the Lourdes cures must take into account a hidden face of Lourdes. As previously mentioned by Harris, our inquiry has led us to conclude that, in addition to "regular" pilgrims, many others, who were convinced they were cured in Lourdes, were not known to the Medical Bureau. To the routine question now asked by the nuns of the Department of Archives "Why don't you report to the Bureau?," the usual answer is "There's no point going there," and to the next question "For what reason have you been here?," the answer is "The Virgin knows why." Many of these people elect to have commemorative plaques put in the Lourdes basilicas or in the crypt. The annual number of new plaques has increased from fifty-seven in 2004 to ninety-four in 2008. Other pilgrims, about four hundred a year, who do not report to the Bureau, bring personal items or gifts to the Lourdes Department of Archives as tokens of their gratitude for the grace they have been granted and as evidence of their willingness to share their good fortune. Leaving gifts in Lourdes has been "integral to the spiritual journey," as mentioned by Harris. Today, votive offerings range from gold, rings, jewels, wedding gowns, and children's clothes to frames, textiles, crutches and canes, and prostheses of all kinds. These anonymous believers have been estimated to be five to ten times more numerous than the patients known to the Medical Bureau and this introduces another strong bias in the study of Lourdes. Moreover, a number of people whose pathological disorders were not influenced by the Lourdes pilgrimage maintain that they have experienced inward changes that help them cope with their pains and handicap. The Lourdes appeal, it appears, is more vibrant and enduring than suggested by statistics. A shrine devoted to prayers and penance, Lourdes remains a spiritual and charismatic healing space....

The least that can be stated is that exposures to Lourdes and its representations (Lourdes water, mental images, replicas of the grotto, etc.), in a context of prayer, have induced exceptional, usually instantaneous, symptomatic, and at best physical, cures of widely different diseases....

Years have passed and the sanctuary's followers are not quite the same, but the Lourdes appeal endures. Numerous astounding cures have been attended by hundreds of honorable physicians and thousands of witnesses. These are facts that cannot be ignored. Prayer is the fulcrum of the Lourdes cure, the essential condition for a miracle to occur....

Uncanny and weird, the cures are currently beyond our ken but still impressive, incredibly effective, and awaiting a scientific explanation.[5]

How Can the Cures be Explained?

That there are cures at Lourdes cannot be reasonably denied at least at a medical level. How can these be explained?

The favorite escape route of skeptics at this juncture is to attribute these cures to "unknown natural forces" that may be discovered in the future. But whatever else it might be, this explanation is not scientific since science can only operate within a framework of universal, predictable laws of nature.

As Cranston points out,

the action of the forces of nature is always general, universal, permanent and unchanging. ... So would it have to be with the "unknown natural forces" alleged to be responsible for the Lourdes cures. They would have to act the same for all persons under similar conditions. Though their formulas are still unknown, their operation would have to show the same characteristics of *generality*, *universality*, *permanence* and *changelessness*: the undeviating marks of the forces of nature.

But with Lourdes cures we see the exact opposite. Here these 'unknown forces' act neither constantly nor uniformly. They act today, but not tomorrow; for some people, but not for others. They have their privileged persons.[6]

Or, as Teilhard de Chardin put it,

> In all truth, what renders Lourdes altogether extra-medical is less what occurs there than the manner in which the prodigies take place. If what happens there astonishes the scientists, the way it happens is absolutely beyond him.[7]

So what seems like a reasonable explanation for these cures? Cranston notes,

> A Lourdes cure, as we repeatedly see, involves a profound spiritual as well as physical experience, and a profound and permanent spiritual transformation. These being the effects, we logically infer that the producing cause behind them must partake of the same qualities – in even larger measure: that the force which produces such profound spiritual transformation must be a force of tremendous spiritual power.
>
> To bring about both physical and spiritual transformation, revolutionizing the whole being in an instant, it must be a magnificent force indeed.[8]

This same point was made with pellucid clarity in 1971 by a group of Lutheran theologians from the then-Communist country of East Germany:

> At Lourdes, Fatima and other Marian sanctuaries, impartial criticism is faced with supernatural facts, which have a close relation to the Virgin Mary, either because of the apparitions, or because of the miraculous graces obtained by her intercession. These facts defy any natural explanation. Until now, 1,200 of the cures that have taken place at Lourdes were recognized as scientifically inexplicable by medical doctors. Yet the Catholic Church has only declared miraculous 44 of them. For thirty years, 11,000 doctors, without distinction of religion or scientific opinions, had free access to the Office of Medical Observations. Therefore, a cure declared miraculous has the greatest possible guarantee.[9]

Messages

Thursday 18 February 1858
Bernadette:
"She said to me, 'I do not promise to make you happy in this world, but in the next'."

Sunday 21 February 1858
Bernadette:
"The Lady, looking away from me for a moment, directed Her glance afar, above my head. Then, looking down upon me again, for I had asked her what had saddened her, she replied 'Pray for the sinners'. I was very quickly reassured by the expression of goodness and sweetness which I saw return to her face, and immediately she disappeared."

Wednesday 24 February 1858
Bernadette:
"Penitence...penitence...penitence!"

Thursday 25 February 1858
Bernadette:
"Whilst I was in prayer, the Lady said to me in a serious but friendly voice 'Go, drink and wash in the fountain'. As I did not know where this fountain was, and as I did not think the matter important, I went towards the Gave. The Lady called me back and signed to me with her finger to go under the Grotto to the left; I obeyed but I did not see any water. Not knowing where to get it from, I scratched the earth and the water came. I let it get a little clear of the mud then I drank and washed."

Saturday 27 February 1858
The Virgin:
"Go, and kiss the ground in penance for sinners."
"Go and tell the Priests to have a Chapel built here."

Tuesday 2 March 1858
Bernadette (to Abbe Peyramale):
"The Lady has ordered me to tell you that she wishes to have a chapel at Massabieille and now she adds 'I wish people to come here in procession'."

Wednesday 3 March 1858
Bernadette (to Abbe Peyramale):
"She smiled when I told her that you were asking her to work a miracle. I told her to make the rose bush, which she was standing near, bloom; she smiled once more. But she wants the Chapel."

Thursday 25 March 1858
Bernadette:
"Whilst I was praying, the thought of asking her name came to my mind with such persistence that I could think of nothing else. I feared to be presumptuous in repeating a question she had always refused to answer and yet something compelled me to speak. At last, under an irresistible impulsion, the words fell from my mouth and I begged the Lady to tell me who she was.

"The Lady did as she had always done before; she bowed Her head and smiled but she did not reply.

"I cannot say why, but I felt myself bolder and asked her again to graciously tell me her name; however, she only smiled and bowed as before, still remaining silent.

"Then once more, for the third time, clasping my hands and confessing myself to be unworthy of the great favour I was asking of her, I again made my request.

"The Lady was standing above the rose bush, in a position very similar to that shown on the Miraculous Medal. At my third request, her face became very serious and she seemed to bow down in an attitude of humility. Then she joined her hands and raised them to her breast. She looked up to Heaven.

"Then slowly opening her hands and leaning towards me, she said to me in a voice vibrating with emotion:

"'I AM THE IMMACULATE CONCEPTION'
(Que Soy Era Immaculada Conceptiou)

"She smiled again, spoke no more, and disappeared smiling."

NOTES

[1]Franz Werfel, *The Song of Bernadette* (San Francisco, CA: Ignatius Press, 2006), xiv-xv.

[2]Ruth Cranston, *The Miracle of Lourdes* (New York: Doubleday, 1988), 58-9

[3]https://www.catholicculture.org/culture/library/view.cfm?id=2866

[4]Teilhard de Chardin, "Les Miracles de Lourdes et les enquetes canoniques," *Etudes* 118 (1909), 161-183.

[5]https://www.ncbi.nlm.nih.gov/pmc/articles/PMC3854941/

[6]Cranston, op cit., 264.

[7]Teilhard de Chardin, op cit.

[8]Cranston, op cit., 265.

[9]Excerpt from the "Travel and Mission Notebook #113" by FJE and included in Brother Albert Pfleger's *Marian Collection* (1991).

Our Lady of Fatima, Portugal, 1917

"Various Nations Will be Annihilated"

Witnesses: Lucia dos Santos, 9, Francisco Marto, 8, Jacinta Marto, 6.
Dates: May 13, 1917 to October 13, 1917.
Enduring evidence: Sun miracle and other luminous phenomena visible by those present, fulfilled prophecies
Theme: Reparation, Salvation, Prophecy
Description of the Virgin:
"It was a Lady dressed all in white, more brilliant than the sun, shedding rays of light clearer and stronger than a crystal glass filled with the most sparkling water and pierced by the burning rays of the sun."

https://en.wikipedia.org/wiki/Our_Lady_of_F%C3%A1tima#/media/
File:Pf%C3%A4rrich_Pfarrkirche_Marienstatue_aus_Fatima.jpg

Fatima is without question the greatest of the twentieth century encounters with the Virgin, one which has had a profound impact both on the faith of millions and on central events of that century. A September 27, 1991, *Wall Street Journal* story subtitled "Believers say Blessed Virgin beat CNN to the news by more than 74 years," considered the impact of Fatima on current events in Russia: "Says William Fairman, a 62-year-old chemist recently retired from Argonne National Laboratory in Lemont, Ill.: 'Our Lady is simply fulfilling her promise back in 1917 to convert Russia.' Francis Irons, 62, a former Defense Department analyst agrees: Recent events in the Soviet Union are 'only explainable in supernatural terms,' he says."

It is now hardly remembered that no serious analyst, even as recently as in 1988, would dare to have suggested that the Soviet Union could give up Communism or that the Communist regimes of eastern Europe might relinquish power. But these implausible events were predicted by the Virgin at Fatima in 1917 – and those who believed in her promises from the very start continued to pray for this turn of events despite its utter unlikelihood. The Virgin had predicted first that Russia would spread its errors around the world – this was before the Communists came to power and hence did not sound realistic – and then that Russia would be "converted" upon the fulfillment of certain conditions, a turnaround that could not have been contemplated during the nightmare of the Cold War and the Iron Curtain.

As in many of her other apparitions, these and similar predictions were fulfilled in future events.

The improbability of the fulfillment of the Fatima prophecy concerning Russia was highlighted in a 2021 story, again in the *Wall Street Journal* (February 8 2021), on the end of Communism in Europe: "The Soviet Union [in 1982], possessing a huge arsenal of nuclear weapons, was led by Yuri Andropov, a determined communist opponent of the West. Hard to believe now, but Europe then was still divided by what Winston Churchill called an 'iron curtain,' which separated the free democratic nations of Western Europe from the closed, Soviet-dominated nations to the east. Millions were imprisoned in these countries, unable to emigrate. Those who tried to flee could be imprisoned or shot. The competition between the U.S. and the Soviet Union was global.... Some 30 years after the Cold War ended with the West's victory, we tend to forget how contingent and difficult the struggle was."

As we have seen, on March 25, 1984, Pope John Paul II had made the consecration required by the Virgin at Fatima, in union with bishops around the world. In July 1989, Sister Lucia confirmed that the fruits of that consecration would be visible. The 2021 *Journal* story continues, "By 1989, communist regimes were collapsing across eastern Europe. The symbolic end of the Cold War came with the fall of the Berlin Wall."

Beginnings

The apparitions of the Virgin at Fatima in 1917 were in some respects a direct response to a plea from Pope Benedict XV who implored the intercession of the Blessed Mother in bringing the Great War to a halt. On May 5, 1917, the Pope sent out a pastoral letter to the world in which he asked the faithful to petition Mary the Mother of Mercy in "this awful hour" "that her most tender and benign solicitude may be moved and the peace we ask for be obtained for our agitated world." Within eight days, on the 13th of May, the Mother of Mercy appeared at Fatima with her own "peace plan" for the world. In the third of the Fatima apparitions, the Virgin said that the present war would come to an end (something that most people found unbelievable at the time) but a new and greater war would begin during the papacy of Piux XI.

After the overthrow of the monarchy in 1908, Portugal was ruled by anti-Christian groups who killed thousands of priests, nuns and monks between 1911 and 1916 (source: Ingo Swann). Public religious ceremonies were forbidden in Portugal just as they were in Mexico. It was into this unpromising environment that the Lady of the Rosary made her world-changing entrance.

The Fatima apparitions were preceded by three appearances of the Guardian Angel of Portugal in which he prepared the three tiny sheep-herder visionaries for the coming of the Mother of God. Lucia, Francisco and Jacinto had taken their sheep to a hilly area called the Chousa Velha. At this time, wrote Lucia, "a strong wind shook the trees and above them a light appeared, whiter than the driven snow. As it approached, it took the form of a young man, transparent and resplendent with light. He began to speak. 'Fear not. I am the Angel of Peace. Pray with me.' He knelt on the ground, bowed low, and three times recited a prayer: 'My God, I believe, I adore, I hope and I love You. I ask pardon of You for those who do not believe, do not adore, do not hope and do not love you.' Then he arose and said: 'Pray this way. The Hearts of Jesus and Mary are attentive to the voice of your supplications.'" On another occasion, the angel told them, "The Hearts of Jesus and Mary have designs of mercy for you. Offer unceasingly to the Most High prayer and sacrifices. Offer up everything within your power as a sacrifice to the Lord in reparation for the sins by which he is so much offended and of supplication for the conversion of sinners. Thus bring down peace upon your country. I am the Guardian Angel of Portugal. More than all else, accept and bear with resignation the sufferings that God may send you."

The angel also brought them holy communion and prostrating himself in front of the Eucharist repeated a prayer that is now synonymous with Fatima: "Most Holy Trinity, Father, Son and Holy Ghost, I adore You profoundly and I offer You the most precious Body, Blood, Soul and Divinity of Jesus Christ, present in all the tabernacles of the world, in reparation for the outrages, sacrileges and indifference by which He Himself is offended. And by the infinite merits of His Most Sacred Heart and the Immaculate Heart of Mary, I beg of You the conversion of poor sinners." Offering them communion, he said, "Take and drink the Body and Blood of Jesus Christ, horribly outraged by ungrateful men. Make reparation for their crimes and console your God."

The apparitions of the angel were followed by six apparitions of the Virgin to the three children from May 13 to October 13, 1917 and numerous subsequent appearances and messages to Lucia. In some respects Lucia was a living testament to the Fatima event, called to carry out a mission that began in 1917 and that continued until her death in 2005, over 80 years later. The apparitions themselves were public events so that even onlookers were aware of something extraordinary taking place most especially on October 13, 1917.

On May 13, the three children had taken their sheep to a part of the Chousa Velha called the Cova da Iria when they were alarmed by a sudden flash of light from the clear blue sky (literally a bolt from the blue). As they ran toward their sheep, they saw another flash of light and then a ball of light alighting on a holm oak tree (called *carrasqueira*). In the luminous ball was a beautiful lady. Although they were terrified, the woman calmed their fears telling them softly that she would not hurt them. She told them she was from Heaven and that she wanted them to come to the Cova on the thirteenth of each month for six months and that she would tell them who she was in her last appearance and explain what she wanted of them. The Lady told them that all three of them would go to Heaven although Francisco would have to say many rosaries. She asked them if they wanted to offer themselves to God and suffer for the reparation of sin and the conversion of sinners. When they said yes, she told them they would suffer a lot but be strengthened by God's grace; they were to say the rosary for peace and the end of the war. With this, the Lady glided toward the east until she was out of sight.

Although the father of Francisco and Jacinto accepted their accounts of the event, Lucia's mother was convinced she was lying, gave her a painful beating and tried to make her retract her story but in vain. On June 13th, the children went back to the Cova despite their parents' attempts to get them to come to the festival for St. Antony of Padua. The Lady appeared again at noon - onlookers saw the sun dim at this precise time - and asked that they pray five rosaries a day and continue to come back on the 13th of each month. The children were to learn to read. The Lady told Lucia that Francisco and Jacinta would be taken to Heaven soon and she alone would be left in the world - and her mission would be to spread devotion to the Lady's Immaculate Heart for this devotion was of great assistance on the journey of salvation. She left as before in the direction of the east.

After this apparition, both Lucia's mother and the parish priest were adamant that the Lady of the apparitions was of diabolic origin. Lucia was confused and fearful and decided not to go again. But just as the time of the apparition drew near on July 13th, her mind found serenity and she left for the Cova with Francisco and Jacinta (who would not have gone without her). Two to three thousand people awaited them there.

This apparition was especially important for those who wonder whether Marian apparitions are diabolic in nature. As if to show the difference between her and the diabolic world, the Lady spread out her hands and the light that poured out from them went into the depths of the earth to show the terrified visionaries a sea of fire filled with demons and the damned. "Even the earth itself seemed to vanish," wrote Lucia, "and we saw huge numbers of devils and lost souls in a vast and fiery ocean. The devils resembled black animals, hideous and unknown, each filling the air with despairing shrieks. The lost souls were in their human bodies and seemed brown in color, tumbling about constantly in the flames and screaming with terror. All were on fire, within and without their bodies, and neither devils nor damned souls seemed able to control their movements. They were tossing about like coals in a fiery furnace, with never an instant's peace or freedom from pain."

The Lady told them that God wanted to establish devotion to her Immaculate Heart precisely to bring more souls to salvation. She warned that a greater war than the last one would break out under the next pontificate if people did not stop offending God. When an unknown light illumined the night, it would be a sign that a divine chastisement would soon begin. She also asked for a consecration of Russia to her Immaculate Heart by the Pope and communion of reparation on First Saturdays. If this were not done, Russia would spread its errors and entire nations would be annihilated – but in the end her Immaculate Heart would triumph because the Pope would consecrate Russia to her and the country would be converted followed by a short time of peace. The First Secret of Fatima was the vision of Hell and the Second Secret was the revelation of the importance of devotion to the Immaculate Heart. The children were also given the Third Secret that was revealed to the world in 2000. Here the apparition ended.

The fourth apparition, scheduled for August 13, did not take place as planned. The children were kidnapped by one of the anti-clericalists committed to wiping out the Church, the civil Administrator, who threatened the children, in individual sessions, with death in a red-hot frying pan unless they admitted that the alleged experience was a mere deception or told him the secrets they had been told. Heroically, the children held out and after three days the Administrator was finally forced to return them to their village. Meanwhile, on the 13th, at the apparition site, the 18,000 people who were present witnessed a sign of Heaven's displeasure at this arrogant action. There was lightning and thunder, the sun turned pale and there was a yellowish haze in the atmosphere. A white cloud settled on the oak tree and rapidly changed colors taking on all the colors of the rainbow. The children saw the Lady again on August 19th and at this time she spoke of the need for penance for one's sins and those of the world; many souls were damned because there was no one to pray for them.

On September 13th, the assembled multitudes, now some 30,000 strong, again saw the sun dim at noon and then a globe of light descending on the oak tree. They also saw white roses falling from the sky. The visionaries were once again reminded of the importance of saying the rosary to end the war. She told them that in October she would be accompanied by St. Joseph and the Child Jesus.

The Miracle of the Sun

By October 13, the whole country had heard of Fatima. 70,000 people had arrived at the Cova. The night before, a terrible (some said diabolic) storm swept through Europe and it was still raining hard by the noon of the 13th. When the Lady appeared to the visionaries, she said she was the Lady of the Rosary, that she wanted a chapel built at the Cova and that people must amend their lives and not offend the Lord since He was already greatly offended. Then she stretched out her hands again and rays of light went toward the sun. Thus began the famous miracle of the sun.

The sun now seemed to be a silver disk and the multitudes could look straight into it without shading their eyes. Suddenly it started shooting off different colored rays in all directions and then spinning on its axis. And then just as suddenly it seemed to be hurtling towards the earth. The terrified onlookers dropped to their knees convinced that the end had come and many sought forgiveness for their sins. Just when it seemed that there would be a cataclysmic collision, the sun returned to its normal position and everything was as before. Miraculously, drenched clothes had dried up and there was neither water nor mud to be seen anywhere. The miracle of the sun was witnessed not just by those in the Cova but by people thirty miles away (thus ruling out the possibility of mass hysteria). While the crowds were gazing at the solar phenomena, the visionaries were witnessing various scenes in the heavens: Jesus in red blessing the crowds, then Jesus as an infant with Mary and Joseph, and finally Mary in the brown robes of Our Lady of Mount Carmel. With this magnificent display, the apparitions of Fatima came to an end – but its impact on the century had only just begun.

The miracle of the sun was reported in the non-religious media. A story in the *Washington Post*, on the 100th anniversary of Fatima, cites these reports:

> "Before the astonished eyes of the crowd, whose aspect was biblical as they stood bareheaded, eagerly searching the sky, the sun trembled, made sudden incredible movements outside all cosmic laws — the sun 'danced' according to the typical expression of the people," reported O Seculo, a Lisbon newspaper.

> The strange phenomena included odd colors.

> "Looking at the sun, I noticed that everything was becoming darkened. I looked first at the nearest objects and then extended my glance further afield as far as the horizon. I saw everything had assumed an amethyst color. Objects around me, the sky and the atmosphere, were of the same color. Everything both near and far had changed, taking on the color of old yellow damask," said José Maria de Almeida Garrett, a science professor from Coimbra, Portugal, who was at the scene.

> Onlookers from as far as 25 miles away noted the strange phenomena in the sky.[1]

What caused the phenomenon called the "miracle of the sun"? Philosopher and historian of science Stanley Jaki has suggested that everything witnessed by the thousands present could have been caused by an "air lens". Predicting the appearance of the air lens months before would have been humanly impossible given that this kind of an event has never been observed before although it was scientifically possible.

This is Jaki's description of the admittedly speculative air lens scenario which would be compatible with both astronomical observations of the sun at the time as well as the phenomenon witnessed by the 70,000:

> An air lens formed in the cloudy sky at about 500 meters above the ground. That air lens contained ice crystals that can refract the rays of the sun into the main colors of the rainbow. Then two streams of air, blowing from two different angles at the air lens, could have put it in a circular motion, exactly as happens when a tornado is formed....

> All the morning of October 13, 1917 the wind was blowing hard over the Covia. It was noted that even during the phenomenon clouds moved at a fast clip in front of the sun. Many observed that the unusually cold air suddenly warmed up on the ground, a clear case of rapid temperature inversion. Its dynamics could then push downward the air lens, which, since it already had a lateral push, had to move not in a vertical direction but along an ellipse, with small spirals imposed on it. In other words, the air lens flew as does a boomerang. Owing to the presence of ice crystal in the air lens, it dispersed the rays of the sun. This was observed by the crowd who found themselves covered in yellow, violet, and reddish hues, the main components of the rainbow....

> No such phenomenon had been previously observed, or at least there was no record of such observations.... *To predict the occurrence of such a phenomenon three months in advance should seem to be a genuine prophecy, especially since the prophets were three illiterate children of the land....*

> Even more importantly, *the size of the air lens had to be such as to resemble the apparent size of the sun* whose brightness had been dimmed by a veil of clouds in front of it. The air lens also had to form at a given moment, when the sun was more or less at its zenith. The phenomenon occurred shortly after noon, real time, as predicted.[2]

Francisco died in April 1919 and Jacinta in February 1920. Both were victims of the great global influenza epidemic. Jacinta heroically endured excruciating pain in the last months of her life and her body was found to be incorrupt when it was exhumed in 1935 and 1950. As she lay dying, she once asked Lucia, "Why doesn't the Lady show Hell to everybody? Then nobody would ever again commit a mortal sin."

At the local bishop's recommendation, Lucia was sent to a girls school run by the Sisters of St. Dorothy in 1921. In 1926 she entered the novitiate of this order and in 1934 made her final vows. In 1925 both the Virgin and the Christ Child appeared to Lucia. At this time, Jesus asked the whole world to institute the practice of Reparation to the Immaculate Heart on the first Saturdays of every month: those who, for five consecutive first Saturdays, received communion, went for reconciliation, recited five decades of the rosary and meditated for fifteen minutes on mysteries of the rosary, all of this done in reparation to the Immaculate Heart, would receive the graces required for salvation. In 1929, the Virgin told Sister Lucia that this was the time for the consecration of Russia to the Immaculate Heart.

In October 1930 the Bishop of Leiria declared the apparitions of Fatima worthy of belief. Ever since millions of pilgrims have journeyed to Fatima every year.

At the request of Sister Lucia, the bishops of Portugal consecrated their country to the Immaculate Heart in 1938 – and with good reason it is believed that, as a result of this act, Portugal was not drawn into the Second World War.

Prophecy and Fulfillment

Lucia entered the Carmelite order in 1948. In 1989, Sister Lucia sent a communication to the world announcing that the consecration of Russia and the world to the Immaculate Heart, made by Pope John Paul II on March 25, 1984, had been accepted by God and that its results would become apparent later that year. As noted, in late 1989 the Berlin Wall had fallen. By August of 1991 Russia was no longer Communist. The Communist coup against Gorbachev was launched on August 19, 1991, the same day as the delayed fourth apparition of Fatima. The coup failed and Gorbachev was set free on August 22, the Feast of the Queenship of

Mary. Gorbachev was held as a prisoner for three days as were the Fatima visionaries.

The Third Secret of Fatima which concerned the future assassination of a Pope and the persecution of the Church was officially released by the Vatican in the year 2000 (see below).

Over the years there has been controversy as to whether the 1984 papal consecration met the conditions laid down by the Virgin. As shown in the report below (one of many), Sister Lucia herself affirmed to several interviewees that the consecration met these conditions and that the promised "period of peace" was the era following the fall of communism in Europe. She went on to say that the consecration averted a nuclear war that would have taken place in 1985.

> On October 11, 1992, during [a] meeting, at the Carmel of St. Teresa Convent in Coimbra, Portugal, when asked by Cardinal Padiyara of Ernakulam, India, the loaded question of whether, on March 25, 1984, Pope Saint John Paul II had finally accomplished a key request of Our Lady — consecration of Russia to her Immaculate Heart, which she told the seers would bring about the conversion of that threatening, atheist empire — the seer replied (as if expecting the question): "Yes. Yes. Yes. The consecration was already partially done. Pope Pius XII made it in 1942, on October 31, but it lacked union with all the bishops of the world, which Pope John Paul II finally managed to unite in 1984."

> This was a bombshell. For decades, aficionados of Marian apparitions have debated whether indeed the requested consecration was properly carried out when, in 1984, John Paul II consecrated the "world," but in the prayer did not specifically name "Russia." Few controversies in the field have been quite as red-hot. It remains a controversy to this day. Apparently, the Vatican long had been wary of overt mention, which would be seen as stepping on Soviet toes during this tense period of Cold War.

> Yet there on October 11, 1992, was the only living Fátima seer answering the question in a way that was as unequivocal as it has been ignored.

Sister Lucia went on to explain that Paul VI had also made an attempt at consecration at the close of Vatican II, but that when she asked the Blessed Mother — who continued to appear or at least speak to her after the 1917 apparitions — Our Lady had said, "no," that she had wanted the bishops to be in their own dioceses for the consecration (not all gathered at an event far from their flocks).

There was also an attempt at fulfilling the consecration, as spelled out at Fátima, by John Paul II in 1982 (at which Lucia was present), but this consecration lacked union with all the bishops, the seer told the cardinal. The 1984 consecration, on the other hand, had that union with bishops, said the seer.

Even though Russia was not mentioned by name, said the cloistered nun, "God knew that the Pope's intention was Russia," as did the bishops. She told the cardinal, bishop, and priest that Our Lady never required that Russia be mentioned by name (the key sticking point in lingering controversies.)

Remarkably, just weeks after that consecration — on May 13, 1984, the Fátima anniversary — an explosion at the Soviets' Severomorsk Naval Base destroyed two-thirds of all the missiles stockpiled for the Soviets' Northern Fleet. It also destroyed workshops needed to maintain the missiles and killed hundreds of technicians. Western military experts called it the worst naval disaster the Soviet Navy had suffered since WWII.

The consecration was also followed, in an even more astonishing way, with the collapse in 1988 of Communism in Poland, followed in 1989 by the fall of atheistic Communism in East Germany, Czechoslovakia, Hungary, Romania, and Bulgaria. (Remember the "Berlin Wall" and the "Iron Curtain"?).

No state department specialist, no Ivy League academic, no political leader, and no television analyst would have dared to have predicted this.

Within two years, Communism was falling in the Soviet Union itself: Latvia, Lithuania, Estonia, Ukraine, Armenia, Azerbaijan, Belarus, Georgia, Kazakhstan, Kyrgyzstan, Moldova, Tajikistan, Turkmenistan, and Uzbekistan, followed by the fall of the Communist dictatorship in Russia.

No one expected such a thing in his or her lifetime — never mind a few short years. Albania and Yugoslavia soon joined the others.

Sister Lucia noted, during the 1992 meeting, that "the news speaks for itself."

She further stated that the collapse of Communion in Soviet-held territories constituted a "period of peace" predicted during the apparitions if the consecration was accomplished. She said this peace pertained to the greatly lessened tensions between the Soviet Union (or now just "Russia") and the rest of the world. It was a "period" of time that had been foreseen, she said — not an "era" (as many have interpreted the message).

Most remarkably, in a second meeting exactly a year later — on October 11, 1993 — she reportedly told Cardinal Ricardo Vidal of the Philippines and eight others (including two priests) that "the consecration of 1984 prevented an atomic [nuclear] war that would have occurred in 1985." She said the Triumph of Our Lady's Immaculate Heart had begun but was (in the words of the interpreter, Carlos Evaristo) an "ongoing process."

As the Irish Democrat noted in a 1993 review of the translator's work, "This 32-page pamphlet detailing a precise and accurate two-hour interview with Sister Lucia in 1992 [along with the 1991 conversation] is a must for all devotees and others interested in the apparitions of Fátima. Clearly from this meticulously recorded interview, many of the abounding theories surrounding these protracted controversies can now be discarded."[3]

Did the consecration prevent a possible nuclear war? Consider this:

The March 25, 1984, prayer by Pope John Paul II and the bishops was followed *on the Fátima anniversary day of May 13, 1984* (less than two months later), by a devastating explosion at the key Soviet ammunition depot at Severomorsk, crippling the fighting capacity of the Northern Fleet, the strongest of the Soviet Navy's four high-sea fleets; the mysterious death that same year of the Soviet Minister of Defense (who had designed plans for invasion of Europe); the rise of Mikhail Gorbachev the following year; and then an incredible meeting between Gorbachev and President Ronald Reagan; followed by the phenomenal, unforeseen collapse in 1988 of Communism in Poland which in its turn was followed in 1989 by the fall of atheistic Communism in East Germany, Czechoslovakia, Hungary, Romania, and Bulgaria. Within two years, Communism was collapsing in the Soviet Union itself ...

The year before the consecration, in 1983, nuclear negotiations had collapsed. Back then, there were 50,000 nuclear devices in the world's arsenals![4]

N.B. In the early Nineties, the present author personally met with Cardinal Antony Padiyara at his office in Ernakulam, India, and he confirmed that Sister Lucia had indeed told him that the consecration performed by Pope John Paul II met the conditions stipulated by the Virgin.

Backstory

The cause-and-effect laws at work in the spiritual world are evident in the effects of the consecration requested at Fatima. What is less well-known is the rationale behind the selection of Fatima and Portugal as the site of one of the Virgin's pivotal appearances.

In 1646, after winning victories against vastly superior armies, King John IV of Portugal offered his crown to Our Lady of the Immaculate Conception and then declared her the Patroness of Portugal. No king of Portugal since then wore a crown. Fatima, a town in Portugal, was named after a Moslem princess who had become a Catholic. General Nuno Alvares Pereira, an ancestor of John IV, led the Portuguese to victory against the Castilian army at the Battle of Aljubarotta in 1385. On the eve of the battle, Nuno "asked for a sign from God that his greatly outnumbered army would be victorious through the intercession of 'Our

Lady Queen of Portugal.' When the advancing troops arrived at the Cova da Iria of Fatima, the horses began to kneel and Nuno was led to a place upon the Mount of Saint Michael where the apparitions of Fatima occurred in 1917."[25]

Here, Nuno "was reportedly told the ground he knelt on was holy and that one day God would bring victory over evil on this very spot and an era of peace would be granted to the world."[6] Nuno's victory – aided it is said, by apparitions to the soldiers of St. Michael and the Blessed Virgin – had significant consequences: "Nuno achieved his victory the next day, opening the way, even historians concur, for the great evangelization and exploration of the new world that would arise from Portugal because of this significant event."[7] After the victory, at the request of the King of Portugal, Pope Boniface IX, on May 13, decreed that all the Cathedrals in Portugal should be dedicated to the Virgin Mary: not by coincidence, the first apparition of Fatima took place on May 13 several centuries later.

Messages

May 13, 1917
"Do not be afraid. I will do you no harm."

"I am from heaven."

"I have come to ask you to come here for six months in succession, on the 13th day, at this same hour. Later on, I will tell you who I am and what I want. Afterwards, I will return here yet a seventh time."

"Are you willing to offer yourselves to God and bear all the sufferings He wills to send you, as an act of reparation for the sins by which He is offended, and of supplication for the conversion of sinners? . . . Then you are going to have much to suffer, but the grace of God will be your comfort."

"Pray the Rosary every day, in order to obtain peace for the world, and the end of war."

(Excerpted from *Fatima, in Lucia's Own Words* by Sister Lucia)

June 13, 1917:

"I wish you to come here on the 13th of the next month, to pray the Rosary every day and to learn to read. Later, I will tell you what I want."

The Virgin's response to Lucia's request for the cure of a sick person:

"If he is converted, he will be cured during the year."

Response to Lucia's request that she take them to heaven:

"Yes, I will take Jacinta and Francisco soon. But you are to stay here some time longer. Jesus wishes to make use of you to make me known and loved. He wants to establish in the world devotion to my Immaculate Heart."

Response to Lucia's concern that she would be alone:

"No, my daughter. Are you suffering a great deal? Don't lose heart. I will never forsake you. My Immaculate Heart will be your refuge and the way that will lead you to God."

July 13, 1917

"I want you to come here on the 13th of next month, to continue to pray the Rosary every day in honour of our Lady of the Rosary, in order to obtain peace for the world and the end of the war, because only she can help you."

"Continue to come here every month. In October, I will tell you who I am and what I want, and I will perform a miracle for all to see and believe."

"Sacrifice yourselves for sinners, and say many times, especially whenever you make some sacrifice: O Jesus, it is for love of You, for the conversion of sinners, and in reparation for the sins committed against the Immaculate Heart of Mary."

After the vision of Hell:

"You have seen hell where the souls of poor sinners go. To save them, God wishes to establish in the world devotion to my Immaculate Heart. If what I say to you is done, many souls will be saved and there will be peace. The war is going to end: but if people do not cease offending God, a worse one will break out during the pontificate of Pius XI. When you see a night illumined by an unknown light, know that this is the great sign given you by God that He is about to punish the world for its crimes, by means of war, famine, and persecutions of the Church and of the Holy Father.

"To prevent this, I shall come to ask for the consecration of Russia to my Immaculate Heart, and the communion of Reparation on the First Saturdays. If my requests are heeded, Russia will be converted and there will be peace; if not, she will spread her errors throughout the world, causing wars and persecutions of the Church. The good will be martyred, the Holy Father will have much to suffer, various nations will be annihilated ... [At this point, our Lady revealed what has become known as the third part of the Fatima secret.] In the end, my Immaculate Heart will triumph. The Holy Father will consecrate Russia to me, and she will be converted, and a period of peace will be granted to the world. In Portugal, the dogma of the Faith will always be preserved. Do not tell this to anybody. Francisco, yes, you may tell him."

"When you pray the Rosary, say after each mystery: O my Jesus, forgive us, save us from the fire of hell. Lead all souls to heaven, especially those who are most in need."

August 19, 1917
"I want you to continue going to the Cova da Iria on the 13th, and to continue praying the Rosary every day. In the last month, I will perform a miracle so that all may believe."

Response to Lucia's question on the money left by visitors:

"Have two litters made. One is to be carried by you and Jacinta and two other girls dressed in white: the other one is to be carried by Francisco and three other boys. The money from the litters is for the "festa" of Our Lady of the Rosary, and what is left over will help towards the construction of a chapel that is to be built here."

Response to Lucia's request for cures: "Yes, I will cure some of them during the year."

"Pray, pray very much, and make sacrifices for sinners: for many souls go to hell because there are none to sacrifice themselves and to pray for them."

September 13, 1917
"Continue to pray the Rosary in order to obtain the end of the war. In October Our Lord will come, as well as Our Lady of Dolors and Our Lady of Carmel. Saint Joseph will appear with the Child Jesus to bless the world. God is pleased with your sacrifices. He does not want you to sleep with the rope on, but only to wear it during the daytime."

Response to Lucia's request for cures:

"Yes, I will cure some, but not others. In October I will perform a miracle so that all may believe."

October 13, 1917
"I want to tell you that a chapel is to be built here in my honor.

I am the Lady of the Rosary. Continue always to pray the Rosary every day.

The war is going to end, and the soldiers will soon return to their homes."

Response to Lucia's request for cures and conversions:

"Some yes, but not others. They must amend their lives and ask forgiveness for their sins."

"Do not offend the Lord our God any more, because He is already so much offended." After this statement, the Miracle of the Sun took place.

Messages to Jacinta

"The sins of the world are very great ... If men only knew what eternity is, they would do everything in their power to change their lives."

"Fly from riches and luxury; love poverty and silence; have charity, even for bad people."

"More souls go to Hell because of sins of the flesh than for any other reason."

"Certain fashions will be introduced that will offend Our Lord very much."

Jacinta also said –

"Our Lady can no longer uphold the arm of Her Divine Son which will strike the world. If people amend their lives, Our Lord will even now save the world, but if they do not, punishment will come. "

"People must renounce sin and not persist in it, as has been done until now. It is essential to repent greatly."

Later Apparitions

"On December 10, 1925, the Most Holy Virgin Mary appeared to her [Lucia is writing in the third person]. By her side, elevated on a luminous cloud was a Child. The most holy Virgin rested Her hand on her shoulder. As She did so, she showed her a Heart encircled by thorns which She was holding in Her other hand. At the same time, the Child said, 'Have compassion on the Heart of your most holy Mother, covered with thorns, with which ungrateful men pierce it at every moment, and there is no one to make an act of reparation to remove them.'

"Then the Most Holy Virgin said, 'Look my daughter, at my Heart, surrounded with thorns with which ungrateful men pierce it at every moment by their blasphemies and ingratitude. You at least try to console me and say that I promise to assist at the hour of death, with the graces necessary for salvation, all those who, on the first Saturday of five consecutive months, shall confess, receive Holy Communion, recite five decades of the Rosary, and keep me company for fifteen minutes while meditating on the mysteries of the Rosary, with the intention of making reparation to me.'"

On February 26, 1926, Jesus asked her, "What is being done to promote the devotion to the Immaculate Heart of Mary?"

Then, finally, in 1929, He said, "I want My entire Church to know that this favor [the conversion of Russia] was obtained through the Immaculate Heart of My Mother so that it may extend this devotion later on and put the devotion to this Immaculate Heart beside the devotion to My Sacred Heart."

The Secrets

In the year 2000, the Vatican released the Third Secret of Fatima. The first two Secrets, already described, "refer especially to the frightening vision of hell, devotion to the Immaculate Heart of Mary, the Second World War, and finally the prediction of the immense damage that Russia would do to humanity by abandoning the Christian faith and embracing Communist totalitarianism."[2] The Third Secret concerned the future assassination of a Pope and the persecution of the Church.

Below is the text of the Secret:

> After the two parts which I have already explained, at the left of Our Lady and a little above, we saw an Angel with a flaming sword in his left hand; flashing, it gave out flames that looked as though they would set the world on fire; but they died out in contact with the splendour that Our Lady radiated towards him from her right hand: pointing to the earth with his right hand, the Angel cried out in a loud voice: 'Penance, Penance, Penance!'. And we saw in an immense light that is God: 'something similar to how people appear in a mirror when they pass in front of it' a Bishop dressed in White 'we had the impression that it was the Holy Father'. Other Bishops, Priests, men and women Religious going up a steep mountain, at the top of which there was a big Cross of rough-hewn trunks as of a cork-tree with the bark; before reaching there the Holy Father passed through a big city half in ruins and half trembling with halting step, afflicted with pain and sorrow, he prayed for the souls of the corpses he met on his way; having reached the top of the mountain, on his knees at the foot of the big Cross he was killed by a group of soldiers who fired bullets and arrows at him, and in the same way there died one after another the other Bishops, Priests, men and women Religious, and

various lay people of different ranks and positions. Beneath the two arms of the Cross there were two Angels each with a crystal aspersorium in his hand, in which they gathered up the blood of the Martyrs and with it sprinkled the souls that were making their way to God.[8]

NOTES

[1]https://www.washingtonpost.com/news/retropolis/wp/2017/10/13/our-lady-of-fatima-the-virgin-mary-promised-three-kids-a-miracle-that-70000-gathered-to-see/

[2]Stanley Jaki, *The Sun's Miracle* (New Hope, KY: Real View Books, 2000), 25-6.

[3]https://spiritdailyblog.com/apparitions/the-fatima-what-sister-lucia-reportedly-said

[4]https://spiritdailyblog.com/apparitions/eyewitness-mailbag-sister-lucia-said-consecration-was-done

[5]http://bit.ly/2pjvaoU

[6]Petrisko, *The Fatima Prophecies* (McKees Rock, PA: St. Andrews, 1998), 4.

[7]Ibid., 5.

[8]http://www.vatican.va/roman_curia/congregations/cfaith/documents/rc_con_cfaith_doc_20000626_message-fatima_en.html

Our Lady of La Vang, Vietnam, 1798

Date: 1798
Enduring Evidence: Image of Our Lady of LaVang, Church on the site of the apparitions, pilgrimages

Christianity was first brought to Vietnam by French missionaries in 1533. Vietnamese Christians were persecuted by their rulers almost from the beginning. The Christians, who numbered over one hundred thousand in less than a hundred years after the introduction of the new Faith, were severely persecuted in 1698 and the three following centuries with thousands being martyred. It was during this persecution, in 1798, that the Virgin appeared to the Christians.

This is the traditional account of what happened:

> In the late eighteenth century, the Vietnamese emperor was afraid the fast increasing number of Catholics in the kingdom would threaten his throne. He then started persecuting Catholic Vietnamese and the Catholic priests who were mainly foreigners. All 37 parishes in Dinh Cat were destroyed – the churches were burnt down and [thousands of] Vietnamese Catholics died as martyrs.
>
> A good number of Catholic Vietnamese hid in the rainforest in La Vang. Many died from bitter cold, being attacked by wild animals, starvation and sickness but every night they all gathered around a tree, saying their rosary.
>
> One night up in the branches of the tree, they saw a lady wearing the traditional Vietnamese ao dai dress with a child in her arms and two angels beside her. They believed it was the Virgin Mary and the infant Jesus. They said she comforted them and told them to boil the yellow striped leaves called *la vang* from the trees and drink it to cure them of their illness. Which they did and they were.
>
> A few years later, a new emperor ascended the throne and he allowed Christianity to flourish. So the Catholics returned to their villages and the story of the apparition spread. Many came to pray at the site and years later a chapel was built. A new wave of persecution followed and the chapel was destroyed but a new one was later built and this chapel was consecrated in honour of Our Lady.
>
> In 1954, the Vietnamese Bishops Conference made the church of Our Lady of La Vang a national shrine in honour of the

Immaculate Conception. In 1961, La Vang became the National Marian Center of Vietnam and later that year the Pope John XXIII elevated the Church of Our Lady of La Vang to the rank of a minor basilica.… In 1998, Pope John Paul II publicly recognised the importance of Our Lady of La Vang and expressed [the] desire to rebuild the La Vang Basilica in commemoration of the 200th anniversary of the first vision.[1]

The Virgin had promised the persecuted Christians that anyone who sought her assistance at the site of her appearance would be protected by her. Many miracles and cures have been reported at La Vang.

The initial church built at La Vang had been burned down during the different persecutions but the altar, which marked the spot of the apparition, survived. A new brick church was built in 1900. This church was again damaged during the Vietnam War but the outside altar again was untouched by the bombs and bullets.

In April 2020, the President of the Vietnamese Bishops Conference, celebrated a special Mass at the shrine of Our Lady of La Vang asking for her intercession. He said, "We are here like our ancestors in the past to commend our life and all things to Mother, Queen of Peace."

NOTES

[1] https://www.journeywithus.asia/our-lady-of-la-vang/

R.A. Varghese

Our Lady of China, 1900, 1995

Dates – 1900, May 23-24, 1995
Witnesses – Christians of Dong Lu and their enemies
Enduring Evidence – Christian community in Dong Lu, Image of Our Lady of China

In 1900, and then again in 1995, the Blessed Virgin appeared to Christians and their enemies in Dong Lu, a village in Baoding in the Hebei Province in north China. Missionaries had established a Christian community in the impoverished Dong Lu village. When the Boxer rebellion broke out in 1900, nearly ten thousand hostile soldiers attacked the Dong Lu Christians who numbered less than a thousand.

What happened next was unexpected:

> "The soldiers, in senseless rage, started to shoot into the sky. Then suddenly they fled, frightened, and never came back again.... A woman in white appeared above the settlement, and the rioters' bullets were aimed at her. When the apparition did not fade, attackers had not even time to reorganize because a strange horseman [believed to have been St. Michael the Archangel] put them to flight.

> "Soon after they had disappeared beyond the horizon. Father Wu, a Chinese priest, confessed to his flock that he invoked the help of Mary. A new church was built on the site and Father Wu placed a picture of Our Lady on the main altar."[1]

The Virgin is shown in this image as a Chinese empress with the infant Jesus in her hands. In 1924, the Bishops Synod of China chose this image to be honored as "Our Lady of China"/"Our Lady Queen of China". In 1932, Pope Pius XI approved the church with the image as an official Marian shrine. Although the church was destroyed in 1951, the image is still extant.

In the early 2000s. Donglu had a population of 8,000 of whom 80% are Christian. The Virgin was again witnessed on May 23 and 24, 1995, the vigil and feast days of Our Lady of China. One hundred and fifty priests and five bishops celebrated Mass for thousands of Chinese Christians on these special days. During the Mass, a colorful cloud covered the altar and during the consecration the cloud surrounded the sun which started spinning in different directions. The cloud lifted the sun higher and the awe-struck participants saw Our Lady of China and the child Jesus in the sky and also the Holy Family, the Heavenly Father, the Holy Spirit in the form of a dove and angels. This apparition was reported in American and other international publications.

There is a sad footnote to these accounts of the apparitions of Our Lady of China at Dong Lu. Catholic News Service had this report on February 7, 1999: "Underground Catholic peasants in Baoding Diocese were attacked at Christmas time, according to reports received in Hong Kong. Father Peter Hu Duo of the Diocese of Baoding had been arrested and seriously beaten by officials December 20 in his sister's home in Xushui County, near Baoding City. ... Chinese sources say the whereabouts of two underground prelates, Bishop Su Zhimin of Baoding and his auxiliary, Bishop An Shuxin, remained unknown. Both were arrested in 1996. Father Cui Xingang, pastor of Donglu Church, also arrested in 1996, was still detained in Qingyuan County, southeast of Baoding, they added. Government forces demolished the popular Donglu Marian shrine near Baoding in 1996 and have forbidden the large annual May pilgrimage to the site since."[2]

A later news story, "Chinese Police continue to Bar Pilgrims from Honoring Our Lady in Dong Lu" by Margaret Galitzin, reported that, "Every year, throughout the month of May, the Chinese government sends extra police forces to lock down the village of Dong Lu in Hebei, a few hours drive from Beijing. Officers sitting in blue tents erected as checkpoints on access roads stop every car and force most travelers, including reporters, to turn back."[3]

NOTES

[1]https://indefenseofthecross.com/marian-apparitions/our-lady-of-china/

[2]Catholic News Service, February 7, 1999

[3]"Police surround China village for Catholic celebration," May 26, 2012, Times of Oman online.

Our Lady of Good Health, India, 1500s, 1600s

Date –1500s, 1600s
Place –Vailankanni, India
Witnesses –Village boys, Portuguese sailors
Enduring Evidence – Image of Our Lady of Vailankanni, Healing Spring and Basilica on the site of the apparitions.

It was in Vailankanni in the state of Tamil Nadu, India, in the 16th century, that Our Lady first healed a young lame boy and then appeared several years later to yet another boy. In the 17th century, on the feast of her Nativity, she miraculously saved a band of Portuguese sailors from a storm in response to their prayers. As this Marian shrine with its miraculous pond became a source of healing and other miracles for millions of pilgrims through the centuries, Pope John XXIII elevated the local church to a basilica thus publicly recognizing the ministry of Marian intercession taking place there.

Below is an excerpt from the official history of the shrine of Vailankanni authored by Fr. S.R. Santos:

> As in Fatima the Blessed Mother appeared only to shepherds of a tender age, likewise in Vailankanni she appeared to a shepherd boy and a lame boy with miracles. The apparition in Vailankanni is one of the earliest Marian apparitions. She appeared here in the 16th century and has been continuously present until now with miracles and wonders. She has attracted and gathered pilgrims of all religious communities whether Catholic, Protestant, Hindu, Muslim or Parsee. Pilgrims from far and wide pour in and this alone is the sign that her name and fame are being echoed throughout India and even in distant places of the world. Many visit this shrine to invoke her blessings and many are here to offer thanks to her for the gifts that they have received.
>
> Here is a description of the apparitions:
>
> **1. Our Lady's apparition to a shepherd boy**
>
> In the 16th century, by the side of a street named "Anna Pillai" in Vailankanni, there was a small pond and on its bank was a huge banyan tree. The passersby used to drink water in that pond. A shepherd boy as usual was carrying milk to his master's house which was in Nagapattinam a town near Vailankanni. The day was extremely hot. He felt tired and thirsty. After having quenched his thirst at the pond, he sat down to rest a while under the cool shade of the tree.

At that time, he was startled by a bright vision of a beautiful Lady standing before him, holding a lovely child in her arms. He was spell-bound by her celestial beauty. Her serene face with its glorious appearance astonished him immensely. The child's face was bright and glorious as the sun. Both wore celestial haloes around their heads. Fascinated by this rare phenomenon, the simple shepherd boy was deeply moved and was at a loss for words. His heart was filled with a sense of awe mingled with reverent fear. With childlike innocence, he clasped his hands together and gently bowed his head in utter humility to give her a deep reverence.

The Lady, however greeted him with a motherly smile and asked him to give some milk for her child. The boy joyfully gave her the milk and then noticed the smile of satisfaction springing from the baby's face. The shepherd boy rushed to Nagapattinam carrying the remaining milk in his pot. There he reported the whole strange happening to his master and thus the reasons for his unusual delay. He also begged him to excuse him for the shortage of milk in the pot. Great was their astonishment when upon lifting the lid of the milk pot, it was full to the brim with milk and overflowing from the pot. The master was astonished for a moment over this strange and extraordinary event. He hastened with the boy to Vailankanni and came precisely to the pond, where the boy had seen the lady with a child. The gentleman prostrated himself on the ground with awe and reverence, with his forehead pressed close to the holy spot indicated by the shepherd boy.

The story of this miraculous happening soon spread throughout Vailankanni, Nagapattinam and the neighbourhood. The Christians in Nagapattinam who heard about it, were certain that the vision was of the Blessed Virgin Mary with the Child Jesus. They were filled with joy and reverence and felt proud that their gracious Mother should have thus deigned to honour their neighbourhood. From that day the pond near Anna Pillai street in Vailankanni came to be known as 'Matha Kulam' (Our Lady's Pond). To this day it is known by that glorious name. Millions of pilgrims visit the pond with faith and reverence. She has blessed them all with plentiful graces; worries and diseases disappear as the mist at the sight of the morning sun.

2. Apparition to the lame boy, a buttermilk vendor

Some years after the first miraculous vision, our gracious Mother deigned to appear again with her Son in her arms to a poor lame boy of the village.

During the 16th century, there lived a poor widow in the village of Vailankanni. She had a son who was lame from birth. In order to eke out a living the widow used to carry a butter milk pot to the place called 'Nadu Thittu'. It was a little elevated place then where there was a huge banyan tree with outstretched branches. The boy used to sit there and sell buttermilk to the weary wayfarers who would come to take shelter from the burning sun. The cool shade of the tree attracted the passersby and the lameboy's stall gradually became known to many people. As he was on the look out for customers, he suddenly found standing before him a lady of peerless beauty, holding in her arms a still more beautiful child, both attired in spotless garments. Sweetly smiling, the lady approached the poor cripple boy and asked him for a cup of buttermilk for the baby. The boy felt immensely happy and proud to be privileged to oblige such a distinguished customer. Without a moment's hesitation he gave her a cup to drink. She started feeding the child with the butter milk. The boy observed all this, and was rooted to the spot where he sat. The lady then cast a look of benevolent pity on the poor boy and turned to the child in her arms. She pleaded to the child to cure the lame boy who had quenched His thirst. The Mother's request was granted within a second. The boy did not realize the miracle that had been worked on him, but he was intently gazing at the Mother and the Child. She gratefully smiled at the boy for his drink and requested him to do her an additional favour.

The lady asked the lad to go to Nagapattinam and apprise a certain rich Catholic gentleman of this incident and inform him that she desired to have a chapel built in her name at Vailankanni. With a look of veneration and selfpity the lad pleaded that it was physically impossible for him even to walk. He was lame! The Lady graciously smiled and bade him stand up and walk because he was no longer lame! On this the lad jumped up with joy, and leaped from place to place realizing the pleasant sensation of the earth for the first time. The boy finally reached the town. There he met the Catholic gentleman and revealed the message of the Lady. The gentleman had no difficulty in believing him, for he had himself a similar vision of Our Lady in his sleep on the previous night. The good man had already made up his mind to build a small chapel in Vailankanni in honour of the Blessed Virgin as directed by her in the vision. He went with the boy to the place where Our Lady had appeared in the vision to the boy. With the willing cooperation of the people of the locality whose imagination was stirred by the miraculous cure of the widow's cripple son, the wealthy man from Nagapattinam soon set up a small thatched chapel in Vailankanni. It was fitted with an altar and a beautiful statue of Our Lady with the Infant Jesus in her left arm was placed on the altar.

Soon the news spread everywhere. Christians and nonChristians flocked to the spot. Many were the favours granted to the people who came to pray so that the fame of the little thatched Shrine and the statue of the miraculous Mother with the divine Child in her arms spread far and wide. As a result of the striking cure of the lame boy and other subsequent cures that took place there, the Mother of God came to be known and incessantly invoked as "Our Lady of Health Vailankanni" (Vailankanni Arokia Matha).

3. The stormtossed Portuguese ship

The 16th century was particularly memorable for the attempts of European merchants to establish trading centres in India. In those days there were no steam ships but only sailing vessels. They had to sail all round Africa to reach the Indian Ocean, because the Suez Canal had not yet been dug. The first European country to accomplish the arduous task of reaching India by sea round the Cape of Good Hope, was Portugal. For about one hundred years, the Portuguese had a monopoly on trade between Europe and the Far East. They were good seamen and at the same time ardent Catholics with a tender devotion to Our Blessed Mother Mary the 'Star of the Sea'. In all their perils at sea they naturally invoked her protection. In the 17th century a Portuguese merchant vessel was sailing from Macao in China to Colombo in Sri Lanka. They started their voyage and the ship was sailing towards the west to reach the Bay of Bengal. During the crossing the ship was caught in a terrible storm. The gale grew furious, the waves lashed high and the fate of the vessel with all on board seemed sealed. The helpless sailors instinctively threw themselves on their knees and with all the fervor of sinking souls, besought Mary, to succor them. They vowed to build a church in her name wherever they could land safely on shore. Their earnest prayer was instantly granted; for there was a sudden and miraculous lull in the winds; the waves fell and the sea became calm. Very soon the tattered ship was safely pushed to the shore of Vailankanni.

On landing, the first thing the sailors did was to fall on their knees and express their grateful thanks to God and to Mary the Virgin Mother of God. They were soon surrounded by a large group of fishermen who lived nearby and who were sure that the strangers were Christians because they prayed to God on their knees. They guided the stranded seamen to the thatched chapel erected by the Catholic gentleman of Nagapattinam. On entering the chapel the grateful sailors once more reverently fell on their knees before the image of Our Lady with the Child Jesus in Her arms, but for whose miraculous help they might all have met a watery grave. They soon learnt from the local fishermen that the village was called Vailankanni and that the chapel was dedicated to Our Lady of Health. All these strange things happened on the 8th of September, the feast of the Nativity of our Lady, the Mother of Jesus.

The zealous and devoted clients of Mary soon set about to find out the best way to fulfill their vow and built a permanent chapel at the place. A modest brick and mortar chapel 24 feet by 12 feet with a dome overhead and with windows in the usual western style, was soon constructed. The statue of Our Lady of the old thatched chapel graced the altar in the masonry structure. The day of the completion of the chapel was celebrated with touching veneration and great rejoicing which demonstrated their heartfelt gratitude for the signal graces which the Blessed Virgin and her divine Son had showered on them. They dedicated the new church to the Nativity of Our Lady in order to perpetuate the day of their landing at Vailankanni.

The Portuguese sailors were not satisfied with all that they had done for the chapel on the spur of the moment. On their subsequent voyages they visited Vailankanni and made many improvements to the chapel. Among them may be mentioned the rich and rare porcelain plates illustrating scenes from the Bible. These plates from China may still be seen fixed round the high altar of the Shrine Basilica of Vailankanni.

Thus, with the landing of the stormtossed Portuguese ship on the coast of Vailankanni, a new chapter emerged in the history of the shrine. The Vailankanni Shrine was initially a part of the Nagapattinam parish. In those days Nagapattinam was under the control of the Portuguese. But in 1660 the Dutch captured Nagapattinam and its flourishing trade from the Portuguese. The Dutch new-comers were hostile to the Catholic Church since they were Reformed Protestants. So the one hundred years of Dutch rule in Nagapattinam limited the progress made on Our Lady's Shrine at Vailankanni.

In 1962, the Bishop of the Diocese, Dr.R.A.Sundaram, went to Rome to attend the second session of the Second Vatican Council. At this time, he requested the Holy Father to raise the ancient Shrine of Our Lady's at Vailankanni to the high rank and dignity of a 'Minor Basilica'. The request was carefully looked into and magnanimously granted. His Holiness Pope John XXIII graciously issued orders raising the shrine to the exalted state of a 'Minor Basilica' Thus the shrine Basilica of Vailankanni became linked to the St.Mary Major Basilica of Rome. In his Apostolic Brief, the Pope noted:

"TO PERPETUATE THE MEMORY OF THE EVENT: We learn that at the illustrious church of Vailankanni within the limits of the Diocese of Tanjaore (India) the august Virgin Mary through her powerful intercession imparts to her clients health and is venerated with deep devotion. For, pilgrims in large numbers approach the spot even from distant parts and participate in the sacred services especially during the Novena preceding the Nativity of the Mother of God, so much so that this Shrine is not undeservedly hailed as the 'Lourdes of the East'. This singular zeal for the Marian Veneration has been practiced from fairly ancient times."

Today, throughout India there are shrines of our Lady of Good Health of Vailankanni. In fact the old chapel built in 1551 upon the cave where the apostle St. Thomas lived in Madras is the chapel of the Mother of Good Health of Vailankanni.

At Vailankanni, Mary evangelizes in a special manner through her miracles and wonders. Through her motherly affection she touches the hearts of the millions of devotees who come to Vailankanni every year to meet their heavenly Mother. The power of the Mother acts within them even without their knowledge and they receive the power to relinquish evil from their life and to begin changing to goodness by accepting the ways of Jesus, her Son. The Holy Spirit descends upon them and changes them through her intercession. These experiences are reserved not only for Catholics but for all those who come to her whoever they may be, whether Hindu, Muslim or Protestant. Adjoining the Basilica is a 'Museum of Offerings' with gold and silver and other gifts from the thousand of grateful pilgrims who have experienced miraculous healings and wonders through the intercession of their Mother Mary. The two central pilgrimage spots in Vailankanni are the healing Pond where the Virgin first appeared and the Basilica with the miraculous image which is the site of the second apparition.

During the Asian tsunami of 2004, Vailankanni was in the news because of the miraculous preservation of the shrine basilica. This was highlighted in the media:

Like many Southeast Asian coastal areas, the Diocese of Thanjavur was hit hard by tsunamis resulting from the magnitude-9 earthquake beneath the Indian Ocean Dec. 26. As of Jan. 3, the death toll was more than 155,000 in 12 countries.

But diocesan officials say they saw a miracle at the Basilica of Our Lady of Good Health amid the tragedy that took more than 1,000 lives locally, including those of hundreds of pilgrims.

"The killer waves surged and came up to the entrance of the main basilica where the statue of Our Lady of Vailankanni is present and receded after touching the first steps of the basilica's outer door," church officials said in a Dec. 30 statement.

"Faith always rewards," they added.

Quoting eyewitnesses, diocesan officials said the waves stopped at the entrance of India's most popular Marian shrine, which draws 20 million pilgrims a year. Water inundated a bus stand a quarter mile behind the shrine, but on [the] same elevation.

"Who can deny and say this is not a miracle? The powerful blessing of Our Lady of Vailankanni has saved thousands of lives, as people who were inside the basilica were untouched by the monstrous killer waves," the statement said.

More than 2,000 pilgrims — including hundreds attending Mass — were at the basilica and its sprawling compound when the waves struck.

The shrine, facing the Bay of Bengal, has a history as a miraculous safe haven. Portuguese sailors escaped a devastating cyclone in the bay in the 17th century and built the shrine in thanksgiving (see sidebar). Today, the shrine is a replica of Our Lady of Lourdes in France.

"The shrine is just 325 feet from the beach. Yet, the water did not enter the basilica compound," said Bishop Devadass Ambrose of Thanjavur who has been camping at the basilica to oversee relief work despite lack of water and electricity for the first four days after the tragedy."[1]

NOTES

[1] "Miracles and Horrors," *National Catholic Register*, January 8, 2005.

Our Lady of Mount Carmel, England, 1251

Date – July 16, 1251
Place – Ayleshire, England
Witness – St. Simon Stock
Enduring Evidence – The Brown Scapular

Image source –
https://en.wikipedia.org/wiki/Simon_Stock#/media/File:Pietro_Novelli_Our_Lady_of_Carmel_and_Saints.JPG

The Brown Scapular is one of the three Marian devotions closely associated with apparitions of the Virgin. The other two are the Rosary and the Miraculous Medal. The origin of the Rosary predates St. Dominic but it is the subject of many messages of the Virgin in various apparitions. The Miraculous Medal originated with the apparition to St. Catherine Laboure.

The Rosary - centered as it was (before the addition of the Luminous Mysteries) on the 150 psalms and the Gospel narratives of the life and death of Christ - went through many stages of development over the centuries but all the traditions concerning the brown scapular focus on its origin in an appearance of the Virgin to a great Carmelite monk, St. Simon Stock, in the thirteenth century. Accounts of this apparition were recorded regularly from the time that the Order started putting its traditions in writing and the promises of the Scapular had become an established tradition in the Order within a hundred years of the death of St. Simon Stock.

Simon Stock, an Englishman, decided to join the Order of Our Lady of Mount Carmel while visiting the Holy Land. This Order claimed to have as its founder the Prophet Elijah and its hermits lived on the Mount Carmel made famous by the Prophet. As the Saracens intensified the persecution of the Christian religious orders in the Holy Land, the Carmelites migrated to Europe. In 1241, the Earl of Kent gave the Carmelites a house on his property of Ayleshire.

In England the Carmelites were not popular with the other clergy who even conspired against them in Rome; their brown cloaks were also viewed with great suspicion. Simon Stock, who had been elected the head of the Order in England, was deeply discouraged by the climate of antagonism and spent the night of July 15, 1251, in prayer to the Virgin seeking her assistance. In the early morning of July 16, the Virgin appeared to him along with the infant Jesus and a host of angels and handed him the scapular along with the following promise:

"My beloved son receive this scapular for your Order. It is the special sign of a privilege which I have obtained for you and for all God's children who honor me as Our Lady of Mount Carmel. Those who die devotedly clothed with this scapular shall be preserved from eternal fire. The brown scapular is a badge of salvation. The brown scapular is a shield in time of danger. The brown scapular is a pledge of peace and special protection, until the end of time."

This promise was eventually given a seal of approval - as a private revelation worthy of belief - by the undivided Western Church and became established throughout Christendom. Many miracles were reported by those who wore the scapular - signaling Heaven's approval - ranging from the sudden conversion of unbelievers to protection from fires, floods, diseases, bullets, swords and other physical dangers. On the day that he received the scapular, Lord Peter of Linton called Simon Stock to his brother's deathbed saying that he was dying in despair. St. Simon placed his own scapular on the dying man who repented shortly after and then died. The scapulars with which many saints were buried were found to be perfectly preserved when the bodies were exhumed centuries later.

The Carmelite Order flourished after the apparition to St. Simon Stock. During the Black Death in the fourteenth century, when many Carmelites sacrificed their lives to help the dying, it was feared that the Order would die out. Again the Virgin appeared to St. Peter Thomas to reassure him that the Order would last until the end of history because its patron, the Prophet Elijah, had specially requested this of the Lord and his petition had been granted.

It has been pointed out that the scapular message is specially related to the parable of the one lost sheep. Just as the divine Shepherd goes to great lengths to save the one lost sheep, the scapular seeks the salvation of every lost sheep. The scapular is made of wool - just as sheep have woolen fleece. And it is worn as a "shoulder garment" (the meaning of scapular), just as the Shepherd wraps the lost sheep around his neck and over his shoulders.

The scapular has deep roots in the grace of final perseverance. It is not magical. It signals the wearer's commitment to seek to continue in final perseverance aided by the grace of God. It requires an act of free will on the part of the wearer - and the rest is left to God. It is offered as a gift by the Mother who wishes to make every means of grace available to her children - so that none may be lost.

The importance of the scapular devotion and Our Lady of Mount Carmel is evident from its role in two of the greatest modern apparitions: the last apparition of Our Lady of Lourdes was on July 16, the Mount Carmel feast day, and in her last apparition, on October 13, Our Lady of Fatima appeared in the livery of Our Lady of Mount Carmel.

Our Lady of Zeitoun, Egypt, 1968

Dates – April 2, 1968 to May 2, 1971
Place – Zeitoun, Egypt
Witnesses – Thousands of people of every religion
Enduring Evidence: Photographs of the Virgin as she appeared above the church in Zeitoun. Miraculous cures.

Image source –
https://en.wikipedia.org/wiki/Our_Lady_of_Zeitoun#/media/File:Zeitun.gif

Many of the appearances of Mary occur in places that have some special significance in their own right. Fatima of Portugal, for instance, had been the venue of supernatural events in the past and it had been prophesied that even greater events would take place there in the future. Knock of Ireland had been specially blessed by St. Patrick who apparently prophesied that it would be a center of pilgrimage for multitudes in the future.

Zeitoun in Egypt belongs to this category of a place with a particular supernatural significance. In ancient times, Zeitoun was known as Mataria and it was to this city that Joseph, Mary and the infant Jesus came when they escaped from Herod. St. Mary's Church, an ancient shrine, had been built on the precise spot where the Holy Family had been living in exile. The shrine had disappeared and was then rebuilt - and this went on several times with the shrine finally disappearing by the turn of the century. In 1918, the property was owned by the wealthy Coptic Christian Khalil family. The Virgin revealed to a member of the family that this location was important for her and that fifty years from that date she would bring a special blessing to the church to be built there. The Khalils gave the property to the Coptic Orthodox Church and the Church authorities constructed a Coptic St. Mary's Church on it.

On April 2, 1968, at 8:30 p.m., a lady dressed in a robe of light was observed walking back and forth on the dome of the church by Moslem workmen. She was seen kneeling beside a cross on top of the dome. The mechanics who saw her thought she was a nun about to jump off the building and one of them pointed his finger at her imploring her to stop. The finger he had pointed was gangrenous and was to be amputated. The next day the finger was found to have been completely healed. A crowd gathered but gradually the luminous lady disappeared before their eyes. Seven days later she was again seen over the church and was identified as the Virgin. This time she went on appearing at different periods up to May 2, 1971. The crowds that came to see her were sometimes as large as 250,000 and included Jews and Moslems and Protestant, Orthodox and Catholic Christians. The Virgin would often bow to the crowd (a typical gesture in the Middle East) or bless them. Sometimes she held out an olive branch to them (Zeitoun means "olive" in Arabic). Her apparitions on the dome were sometimes accompanied by other miraculous phenomena such as the sudden emission of incense from the dome of the church into the crowd or the flight of dovelike creatures around her. Many miracles and cures were reported by people who came to see her.

The Coptic Patriarch Anba Kyrillos VII appointed a Commission to investigate the phenomenon on April 23, 1968. Among the miracles attributed to the Virgin of Zeitoun and reported to the Commission were various cancer cures, recovery of sight for those totally blind and the like. The Commission accepted the authenticity of the apparitions and declared on May 5 that "These appearances have been accompanied by two great blessings: the first being that of engendering and strengthening faith, and the second is the miraculous cures of desperate cases." Cardinal Stephanos I, the Patriarch of the Catholic Copts, issued a statement declaring that "It is undoubtedly a real apparition, confirmed by many Coptic Catholic members of the highest integrity and reliability."

The General Information and Complaints Department of Zeitoun, Egypt, released its own report in 1968 and declared, "Official investigations have been carried out with the result that it has been considered an undeniable fact that the Blessed Virgin Mary has been appearing on Zeitoun Church in a clear and bright luminous body seen by all present in front of the church, whether Christian or Moslem."

An envoy sent by Pope Paul VI witnessed the apparition and wrote this report:

> The apparitions occurred on many different nights and are continuing in different forms. The Holy Virgin Saint Mary appeared sometimes in full form and sometimes in a bust, surrounded with a halo of shining light. She was seen at times on the openings of the domes on the roof of the church, and at other times outside the domes, moving and walking on the roof of the church and over the domes. When She knelt in reverence in front of the cross, the cross shone with bright light. Waving Her blessed hands and nodding Her holy head, She blessed the people who gathered to observe the miracle. She appeared sometimes in the form of a body like a very bright cloud, and sometimes as a figure of light preceded with heavenly bodies shaped like doves moving at high speeds. The apparitions continued for long periods, up to 2 hours and 15 minutes as in the dawn of Tuesday

April 30, 1968 (the 22nd of Barmouda, 1684 A.M.), when She appeared continuously from 2:45 am till 5:00 am. Thousands of people from different denominations and religions, Egyptians and foreign visitors, clergy and scientists, from different classes and professions, all observed the apparitions. The description of each apparition as of the time, location and configuration was identically witnessed by all people, which makes this apparition unique and sublime.[1]

Among those who witnessed the apparitions was the then President of Egypt:

Even the Egyptian government investigated the apparition. President Gamal Abdel Nasser witnessed the apparition and the Egyptian police could not find any natural way to explain the phenomenon. Everyone was universally stunned by what they saw and no one could offer a scientific explanation.[2]

NOTES

[1] https://aleteia.org/2019/05/05/this-marian-apparition-in-egypt-was-witnessed-by-at-least-250000-people/

[2] Ibid.

Our Lady of the Word, Rwanda, 1981-1983

"The World is on the Edge of Catastrophe"

Dates – November 1981 to 1983
Place – Kibeho, Rwanda
Witnesses – Alphonsine, Nathalie, Marie-Clare
Enduring Evidence – Solar phenomena visible to all present, fulfilled prophecies
Theme – Reparation, Conversion, Prophecy
Feast Day – November 28

Image source –
http://www.kibeho-sanctuary.com/en/about/places-of-worship.html

The Marian apparitions of Kibeho in Rwanda, perhaps the poorest country in Africa at the time (one known also as the "Switzerland of Africa" for its many mountains), were witnessed by seven principal visionaries. The apparitions share many common features with the great apocalyptic visions of the past. As in the nineteenth century French apparitions and at Fatima and Akita, the Virgin announced impending bloodshed on a horrific scale. Moreover, as in some other instances, the apparitions themselves took place in the very region that would shortly become synonymous around the world with genocide and systematic butchery. The warnings issued at Rwanda were not only prophetic but unmistakably accurate and, because they were not heeded, the fate of the nation seemed sealed; the Virgin finally even urged the visionaries to flee their homeland before the onset of the wars ahead.

The apparitions began on November 28, 1981, when Alphonsine Mumureke, a 16 year old student in a Catholic convent, heard a voice calling out "my daughter" to her as she was helping in the dining room. She left the room and saw a beautiful lady in white in the corridor. When Alphonsine asked her who she was, the lady replied, "I am the Mother of the Word," speaking in Kinyarwanda, the language of the Rwandans. The Virgin asked her which of the religions she liked to which Alphonsine replied, "I love God and His Mother who have given us Their Son who has saved us." The Virgin commended her and said that she wished that some of her friends would have more faith since some did not believe enough. She then asked Alphonsine to join a lay evangelization group called the Legion of Mary and said that she wanted to be loved and trusted as a Mother so that she could lead people to her Son Jesus. (The Legion of Mary is one of the largest lay Christian organizations in the world and one of the pioneers of the Legion from Ireland, Edel Quinn, had devoted her life to the work of the Legion in the neighboring country of Kenya.) The Virgin then gracefully arose until she was out of sight. As she departed, Alphonsine dropped to the ground and was unconscious for about fifteen minutes.

The other children had heard Alphonsine engaged in conversation and were curious to find out what had happened. When Alphonsine narrated her experience, both her friends and the nuns were skeptical and scornful. Alphonsine witnessed another apparition of the Virgin on the next day in which she was told that the Virgin liked her children to see her as a mother. Again she lost consciousness at the end of the apparition and again she told the others what had happened but was met with the same ridicule. The apparitions continued through December. Most of the girls continued to mock Alphonsine, even throwing rosaries at her during the apparitions, but some prayed that others could also share the experience so that they could find out if Alphonsine was being truthful.

On January 12, 1982, these prayers were answered and Nathalie Mukamazimpaka, a 16 year old girl who was already a member of the Legion of Mary, witnessed an apparition of the Virgin. The messages she received focused on prayer, humility and self-sacrifice. Once Nathalie started witnessing the apparitions, most of the community accepted Alphonsine's veracity. The continuing apparitions were now beginning to transform the spiritual life of the students. On March 22, yet another student, 22 year old Marie-Claire Mukanganga, reported seeing the Virgin as well. She had been one of the most ardent scoffers and now begged forgiveness for her disbelief. She said that the Virgin wanted everyone to meditate on the Passion of Jesus and the sorrow of His mother and asked them to pray the rosary and the beads of the Seven Sorrows to receive the grace of repentance.

By now news of the apparitions had spread around Rwanda and visitors were coming to Kibeho from all over the country. To accommodate the hundreds of onlookers, special platforms were constructed for the visionaries in the convent yard and the crowds could now see them as they entered the state of ecstasy which often lasted three to four hours. The girls would sing songs or pray the rosary until the coming of the Virgin at a pre-set time.

Huge crowds watched the visionaries as they went into ecstasies that lasted several hours. During the ecstasies, the visionaries were not affected when observers pricked them with knives or burnt them with candles or shone bright lights into their eyes; they were also "frozen" so that their arms and legs could hardly be moved. Sometimes, during the apparitions, the assembled multitudes also witnessed various supernatural phenomena such as miracles of the sun (including the dancing of the sun and multi-colored displays as at Fatima), stars turning into crosses at night and heavy rains that came when the visionaries asked the Virgin to bless the crowds (cures were reported from the water collected from the rain). After warning observers that this would happen, the visionaries went into comatose states for extended periods in which they were taken to Heaven, Purgatory and Hell. They were also shown a vision of the savage future awaiting Rwanda: rivers of blood, burning trees and countless rows of corpses, many of them headless. They were shown "a river of blood, people who were killing each other, abandoned corpses with no one to bury them, a tree all in flames, bodies without their heads." This glimpse of the future, given in an eight-hour-long apparition on August 15, 1982, had such a terrifying effect on the visionaries that it shook even the onlookers. The visionaries were told that there would be a "river of blood" if Rwanda did not come back to God.

The apparitions went on for various spans of time for each visionary: Marie-Clare up to September 15, 1982, Nathalie to December 3, 1983 and Alphonsine all the way through November 28, 1989. Bishop Jean Baptiste Gahamanyi, bishop of the diocese of Butare to which Kibeho belonged, had appointed investigative commissions of doctors, psychiatrists and theologians in March 1982. Public devotions at the site of the apparitions were permitted by the bishop on August 15, 1988. Although some other young people claimed to have seen the Virgin and her Son, only the first three witnesses were considered credible by the investigative commission.

The Rwandan civil war began in 1991 and took a toll of over five million lives by the time the conflict ended. The visionary Marie-Clare was one of the slain. Alphonsine's entire family was killed although she herself escaped. She became a member of the monastery of the Poor Clares in Abidjan, Ivory Coast. Nathalie was determined to remain in Kibeho but eventually had to flee as well. She later returned to serve pilgrims coming to Kibeho. Bishop Gahamanyi is one of the hundreds of clergy who were killed in the civil war. Thousands of dead bodies were thrown into rivers that turned putrid. Thousands of other corpses, many of them decapitated, were left unburied on shore.

A new diocese of Gikongoro was created in 1992 and Kibeho came under its jurisdiction. The investigation continued under the new bishop of Gikongoro, Augustin Misago. On June 29, 2001, Bishop Misago, after approval from both the Vatican and the bishops of Rwanda, announced the Church's final judgement on the apparitions of Kibeho:

1. Yes, the Virgin Mary appeared at Kibeho on November 28th, 1981 and in the months that followed. There are more reasons to believe in the apparitions than to deny them. Only the three initial testimonies merit being considered authentic; they were given by Alphonsine Mumureke, Nathalie Mukamazimpaka, and by Marie Claire Mukangango. The Virgin appeared to them with the name "Nyina wa Jambo", that is "Mother of the Word", which is synonymous to "Umubyeyl W'iamna" that is, "Mother of God", as she herself explained. The visionaries said to have seen her sometimes with joined hands, sometimes with outstretched arms.

2. Various reasons justify the choice by Our Lady of these three visionaries already approved as visionaries. These witnesses, historically linked, were the only ones on the scene for some months, at least up to June 1982. They are the ones who made Kibeho known as a place of apparitions and pilgrimage causing crowds of people to flock there.

What is more important is that Alphonsine, Nathalie and Marie Claire corresponded satisfactorily to all the criteria established by the Church in the matter of private apparitions and revelations....

3. In the evaluation of the facts and the messages, only the public apparitions are taken into consideration. Public are those apparitions that take place in the presence of various testimonies, which does not necessarily mean a crowd....

5. In the case of the three visionaries named above, who are at the origin of the fame of Kibeho, nothing that they said or did during the apparitions is contrary to Christian faith and morals. Their message is in conformity with the Sacred Scripture and the living Tradition of the Church.

Description of the Virgin:

Alphonsine: She "was not really white like we see her in pictures. I could not determine the color of her skin, but she was of an incomparable beauty."

Messages

To Marie-Clare:

"I am concerned not only for Rwanda or for the whole of Africa. I am concerned with, and turning to, the whole world. The world is on the edge of catastrophe."

"I have come to prepare the way for my Son for your good and you do not want to understand. The time remaining is short and you are absentminded. You are distracted by the goods of this world which are passing. I have seen many of my children getting lost and I have come to show them the true way."

To Alphonsine:

"I love a child who plays with me because this is a beautiful manifestation of trust and love. Feel like children with me because I, too, love to pet you. No one should be afraid of their Mother. I am your Mother. You should not be afraid of me but you should love me."

[At the last apparition]: "I love you, I love you, I love you very much. Never forget the love I have for you in coming among you. These messages will do good not only now but also in the future."

To Nathalie:

"Wake up, stand up. Wash yourself and look up attentively. We must dedicate ourselves to prayer. We must develop in us the virtues of charity, availability and humility."

Our Lady of Kazan, Russia, 1579

Date – July 8, 1579
Place – Kazan, Russia
Witness – Matrona
Enduring Evidence: Copies of the icon of Our Lady of Kazan and associated miracles.

Russia is among those nations like Poland and Mexico that has built its national identity around a treasured icon of the Virgin. The great national icon of Russia is Our Lady of Kazan – an image of the Virgin with the infant Jesus. Russia has, in fact, been called the "house of Mary" because of the numerous icons of the Virgin and shrines and churches dedicated to her all across the country. The icon of Kazan has been called "the protection of Russia" because of its role in protecting Russia from invaders.

The origin of the icon of Our Lady of Kazan is unknown. But it is known to have been housed in Kazan possibly from the eleventh century. In the thirteenth century Kazan was conquered by the Moslem Tartars and the icon disappeared. In 1552, the troops of Ivan the Terrible liberated Kazan from the Khanate. And the lost icon was miraculously discovered in 1579 on July 8.

According to the traditional account, "the Mother of God appeared to Matrona, a nine-year-old daughter of … [a member of the Russian infantry regiment] …and told her to find her icon amid the ashes of a burned house. After the first vision nobody believed the girl. But the apparitions of the Queen of Heaven continued and the girl kept asking the adults to find the icon. Soon Matrona's mother turned to Orthodox priests, asking them to help her. However, the clerics didn't believe her story and were reluctant to search for the icon. It was not until numerous appeals to the bishop of Kazan that it was decided to try and find the holy object. At last the icon (wrapped in an old cloth) was found. According to tradition, as soon as Matrona started digging she discovered it. By orders of Tsar Ivan IV a convent in honor of the Mother of God and a church were built on this site, and the first copy of the icon was sent to Moscow."

The icon became known for its healings and miracles. "The Kazan icon was particularly venerated in Russia, and the Mother of God healed the sick and saved that country through the petitions of the faithful who prayed before it…. Prayer before the wonderworking Kazan icon saved Russia from the Polish invasion in 1613. In 1812, the Army of Napoleon, one of the most famous military commanders in the world, attacked Russia, and the prayer to the Queen of Heaven again helped the nation defeat the aggressors."[1]

In 1904, the icon was stolen. "From the moment of its appearance, the original icon was kept at the Convent of the Holy Theotokos in Kazan until the early twentieth century. But in those troubled years of the revolution the Lord took this wonderworking icon away from His people, perhaps for their edification or humility. Over that period many Russian people apostatized and drifted away from their faith, the faith of their forefathers. This was most likely one of the reasons for that tragedy."[2]

The thieves claimed to have burned the icon. An old copy of the icon was received by Pope John Paul II who then gifted it to the Russian Patriarchate in 2004. "Initially it was believed to be the original icon that had been found in 1579. However, the joint Russian-Vatican commission determined that it was a later seventeenth-century copy."[3]

In 2019, a copy of the icon in Moscow exuded a miraculous ointment on four occasions.

"In a church in the center of Moscow... the icon of Our Lady of Kazan, has for the fourth time released rivets of miraculous ointment (miron, a term also used for the Sacred Chrism).

The news was confirmed and made public in an authoritative way by Metropolitan Ilarion (Alfeev), head of the Foreign Affairs Department of the Moscow Patriarchate."[4]

For centuries, a copy of the icon had been kept in a great basilica in Moscow. At the time of the Communist revolution, the Bolsheviks destroyed this basilica. The date on which the destruction of the basilica took place is significant: October 13, 1917 – the same day on which the Miracle of the Sun took place in Fatima and the Virgin warned the visionaries of the errors that would come out of Russia while also prophesying the future conversion of Russia.

NOTES

[1] https://orthochristian.com/114554.html

[2] Ibid.

[3] Ibid.

[4] http://www.asianews.it/news-en/Moscow,-miraculous-ointment-from-an-icon-of-Our-Lady-of-Kazan-48207.html

Second decade – First Century through the 1500s

Our Lady of Pilar, Spain, 40

Date – 40 A.D.
Place – Zaragoza, Spain
Witness – St. James the Greater
Enduring Evidence – Ancient column of jasper and image of Our Lady of the Pillar
Feast Day – October 12

The first ever appearance of the Virgin outside Scripture was witnessed by the Apostle James the Greater, the brother of St. John the Evangelist. St. James was reputedly the Virgin's favorite Apostle and she had promised to assist him in his effort to evangelize Spain. The apparition took place in Zaragoza, Spain, in 40 A.D. when St. James was preaching on the banks of the Ebro River. Since the Virgin was still alive at the time, this apparition was actually an instance of bilocation. A number of saintly people have shown this capability for bilocation (St. Antony of Padua, St. Padre Pio) whereby they would be at prayer in one place and simultaneously be physically present at another location.

St. James, who is said to have come to Spain in 35 A.D., was discouraged by his lack of progress. Here is the traditional story of the appearance of the Virgin:

> When St. James traveled through Spain in the first century preaching the Gospel, he encountered much difficulty. One night, as he and his disciples were walking along the River Ebro, in Caesar Augustus (present day Zaragoza, Spain), he prayed for help. Suddenly, a flash of light lit up the night sky and heavenly music was heard. Our Lady appeared to St. James seated on a throne surrounded by angels, and she told him she had come to help. Our Lady asked that a church be built on the spot in her honor, where the faithful would receive all the graces they asked of her Son through the invocation of her name. She then gave St. James a small wooden statue of herself with the child Jesus in her arms, on a column of Jasper. Our Lady then said,

> "This pillar will remain here, and on it my own image, which in this place where you will build my temple, will last and endure with the Holy Faith until the end of time."

> While many chapels were built on the site of the apparition over the years, the statue of Our Lady has always remained in the same place. The column can be seen today on display in the Basilica of Our Lady of the Pillar, in Zaragoza, Spain. The construction of the Basilica began on the feast of St. James (July 25) in 1686.

The statue, affectionately known by the Spanish people as La Pilarica (the little pillar), has survived wars with the Romans, Goths, and Moors. Miraculously, although it is over 1,900 years old, it shows no sign of decay. During the Spanish Civil War (1936-1939) three bombs were dropped on the Basilica, but none of them exploded. These bombs are on display in the Basilica, and they are a vivid testament to the power of Our Lady's promise.[1]

In her appearance to him, the Virgin is supposed to have told St. James that the Lord wanted him to return to Jerusalem to become the first of the martyrs. St. James was martyred in Jerusalem in 44 A.D. – a fulfillment of the prophecy of Matthew 20:20-23 where Jesus says that James would drink of His cup.

The people of Spain and, in particular, of Zaragoza remain deeply devoted to the Virgin of Pilar – "The sentiment of the Saragossans toward their beloved *Virgen del Pilar* is far different from the ordinary devotion paid to a favorite saint. It is an inheritance from their forefathers, a love that is born with them, and ends only with their lives. It is interwoven with their patriotism, with their nationality, with their home life, and with their daily tasks and amusements… In their talks, she is the ever-recurrent theme, and in their patriotic songs, they acclaim her as the leader of their nation. Saragossans say that the church of the *Virgen del Pilar* was the first raised in her honor and will last as long as the faith."[2]

The Spanish Feast of El Pilar is on October 12. It was on October 12, 1492, that Christopher Columbus, sailing on the Santa Maria and funded by the Spanish monarchy, arrived in the New World. Consequently, Nuestra Señora del Pilar is not only the patroness of Spain but of all Hispanics.

NOTES

[1] https://www.catholicnewsagency.com/cw/post.php?id=673

[2] https://www.catholicculture.org/culture/library/view.cfm?recnum=2983

Our Lady of the Holy Trinity, Asia Minor (Turkey), 238

> *Date* – 238 A.D.
> *Place* – Neocaesarea/Niksar
> *Witness* – St. Gregory Thaumaturgus ("the Wonderworker")
> *Enduring Evidence* – The book *The Exposition of Faith*

The second major encounter with the Virgin is distinctive in three respects: Marian doctrine is as old as the doctrine of the Trinity and here we have a Marian apparition that is mainly concerned with the doctrine of the Trinity; the witness of the first apparition was an Apostle in the Apostolic age and the witness of this second apparition is a Church Father in the succeeding Patristic era; the Woman Clothed with the Sun of *Revelation* 12 was witnessed by St. John the Evangelist and here the Virgin appears with St. John.

The Protestant Christian magazine *Christianity Today* has called this "the first recorded Marian apparition" (technically, Pilar preceded it): "Gregory's writings are strong defenses of Trinitarian doctrine. According to Eastern tradition, his principal work, *The Exposition of Faith*, was given to him in a vision of John the Evangelist with the intercession of the Virgin Mary—the first recorded Marian apparition."[1]

Gregory (213-268) was a pagan student of the Church Father Origen who subsequently converted to Christianity. He later became the Bishop of Neocaesarea, his region of Asia Minor, and was so renowned for his miracles that he was called Thaumaturgus – "the Wonderworker".

Gregory had been confused by the debates on the Holy Trinity, the revelation that there are Three Persons in One God, and sought divine assistance. His prayers were answered when the Virgin appeared to him as a beautiful woman along with St. John the Evangelist, who came as an old man. The Virgin asked St. John to explain the mystery of the Trinity to Gregory. St. John told him, "I will gladly comply with the wishes of the Mother of God" and after giving a summary, concluded with these words, "There is therefore nothing created, nothing greater or less in the Trinity, nothing superadded ... The Father has never been without the Son, nor the Son without the Spirit; and this same Trinity is immutable and forever unalterable."

Below is Gregory of Nyssa's account of the apparition to St. Gregory Thaumaturgus cited in Bernard Buby's *The Marian Heritage of the Early Church* (Buby notes that, "The value of Gregory's testimony is that even in patristic times apparitions were recorded"). This account is notable for its restraint and is considered quite reliable:

> "Now, as he was one whole night long pondering on the words of faith, and bringing up all sorts of reasonings - for there were at that time, too, some who sought to adulterate the orthodox teaching, and often made the truth ambiguous even to the learned and prudent through plausible arguments - while, I say, he was thus lying awake thinking anxiously about the truth, there appeared to him one in human shape, of aged mien, and of sacred character, by the form and arrangement of his garb, showing marks of great virtue by the grace of his countenance and his whole bearing. Gregory, amazed at the vision, was about to rise from his bed, and to ask him who he was, and wherefore he had come. But the other calmed the troubles of his mind, speaking with gentle voice, and telling him that it was by divine command he appeared - on account of the questions that were exercising him - for the revealing to him of the truth of the orthodox faith. At these words Gregory began to take courage, and to regard him with mingled feelings of joy and awe. The latter then stretched forth his hand, and with fingers extended, pointed to Gregory at what was appearing on the other side. Gregory turning his eyes in the direction of the hand, beheld facing him another vision in woman's form more excellent than human. Struck again with awe he let fall his gaze, lost in bewilderment at the apparition, and unable to bear the sight of the vision - for what was most astonishing in the vision was that, though it was deep night, a light shone forth on him from those who appeared, as though some bright blazing torch were kindled. While then his eyes could not bear the apparition,

he heard them conversing together on the subject of his doubts, and thereby not only gained a true knowledge of the faith, but also learned their names, as they addressed each other by their respective titles. And thus he is said to have heard the person in woman's shape bid 'John the Evangelist' disclose to the young man the mystery of godliness, while he replied that he was ready to comply in this matter with the wish of 'the Mother of the Lord.' He then pronounced a formulary well-turned and complete." (*De Vita, S. Greg. Thaum.*).[2]

This appearance of the Virgin is depicted in a fresco in the Borghese Chapel in Rome's St. Mary Major Basilica. The inscription on the fresco reads: "On the left, the painting represents the apparition of the Madonna and St. John the Evangelist to St. Gregory the Wonderworker; on the right it shows people bitten by the serpent of heresy before the Temple of God among a crowd of true believers."

NOTES

[1]https://www.christianitytoday.com/history/people/evangelistsandapologists/gregory-thaumaturgus.html)

[2]Bernard Buby, *The Marian Heritage of the Early Church*

R.A. Varghese

Our Lady of Le Puy, France, circa 250

Date – Between the third and fourth centuries
Place – Le Puy
Witness – Villa, a noblewoman who converted to Christianity
Enduring Evidence – The "stone of the apparitions" and the ancient cathedral at the site of the apparition

Image source –
https://www.roman-catholic-saints.com/our-lady-of-puy.html

The Virgin of Le Puy has traditionally been called the Queen of France.

The Cathedral of Le Puy in the mountains of south-central France stands on a site that has been an epicenter of Christian worship from ancient times. Pilgrims, including Gregory of Tours in the 500s and the Emperor Charlemagne in the 700s, have been visiting it for centuries. It has been called the Lourdes of the Middle Ages. Its fame derives from its being the locus of an apparition of the Virgin and of associated healing miracles.

The medieval French historian Bernard Gui, among others, documented the traditions associated with the origin of the shrine. An aristocratic lady named Villa living between the third and fourth centuries A.D. was a convert to Christianity. She happened to fall very sick but was shown in a dream that she should go to the top of Mount Anis (also known as Corneille Rock). Here the Virgin Mary appeared to her and told her to rest on a volcanic stone there. On doing so, she was healed of her ailment and the stone came to be called the "fever stone." She was asked to help build a church at the location. An angel is reported to have said, "The Queen of Heaven has chosen this place as her domain, to receive and answer prayers here." Eventually the local bishop gave his approval for the construction of a church. It became one of the earliest churches honoring the Virgin. The present twelfth century cathedral was built on the site of the original church.

Both the apparition of the Virgin and the healing stone attracted pilgrims to Le Puy from all over Europe. Writing in the sixteenth century, Mathurin des Roys pointed out that pilgrims came there because "they receive health, and healing, which has been experienced and approved by all, and which is very corroborative of faith."

Our Mother of Protection, India, 335

Date – 335 A.D.
Place – Kuravilangad, Kerala, India
Witnesses – Three young boys
Enduring Evidence – The spring said to have been unveiled by the Virgin continues to flow to the present day. It has been the site of many reported healing miracles over the centuries. And it has traditionally been a pilgrimage destination for people of all religions who come to partake of its healing waters.

ST. MARY'S FORANE CHURCH,
KURUVILANGAD

St. John Offset Printers. Si...

From the earliest days of Christianity, the leaders of the Church of East and West have testified that the Apostle Thomas came to India in the first century. He began a Christian community in the South Indian region now known as Kerala and perhaps one in northwestern India. Many of the Christians in Kerala today trace their ancestry to the first converts of St. Thomas. In its first days, the Kerala Christians were primarily based in a place today known as Kuravilangad which was known for its spices and also for transactions with the Jewish community. A church is believed to have been built there in 105 A.D. The head of the Christian community in India was always based here from the fourth through the seventeenth centuries.

This is because it was at the site of this church that the Virgin Mary is reported to have appeared to three young boys in 335 A.D as the Protectress of the community.

According to the traditional story, the boys were thirsty. It is then that the Virgin appeared and herself cleared the soil in the area and revealed a fountain from which they drank. This spring is connected to a stream. The Virgin's visit is believed to have been a great source of strength for the Christians of the time who faced numerous challenges. It also established Kuravilangad as the pre-eminent center for the Christian community for nearly 1500 hears unifying them under their common Mother. Devotees refer to the Virgin as "Kuravilangad Muthiamma" (Amma being the word for Mother).

Our Lady of the Snows, Italy, 352

> *Date* – 352 A.D.
> *Place* – Rome, Italy
> *Witnesses* – Roman couple, Pope Liberius
> *Enduring Evidence*: St. Mary Major Basilica, Rome

Although this is one of the most ancient of the appearances of the Virgin, the strongest basis for its authenticity is the existence of the largest Marian church in the world, St. Mary Major, one which has been beloved of Popes for centuries.

In the year 352, a wealthy but childless Roman couple, John and his wife, decided to leave their fortune to the Virgin. They often prayed to the Virgin asking for guidance on how their wealth could be put to her use. The Virgin appeared to them on the night of August 4th and told them that she wished a basilica to be constructed on the Esquiline Hill, one of the seven hills of Rome. She would leave snow on the precise area in which she wanted the church - which would be a miracle since August is the hottest time of year in Rome. Liberius, the Pope at the time, also received the same message from the Virgin.

On the morning of August 5, a large part of the Esquiline Hill was covered with snow. Both John and his wife and Pope Liberius came to the Hill. After they had measured out the area covered by snow, which was to be the area for the basilica, the snow disappeared. The Pope ordered immediate construction of the basilica and St. Mary Major was completed in 360.

The Theotokos of Protection/Pokrov, Turkey, 912

Date – circa 912
Place – Constantinople (Istanbul, Turkey)
Witness – St. Andrew the Blessed and St. Epiphanius
Enduring Evidence – A twelfth century Russian book called the Prologue recounts the origin of the feast: "For when we heard, we realized how wondrous and merciful was the vision... and it transpired that Your holy Protection should not remain without festal celebration, O Ever-Blessed One!" https://www.oca.org/saints/lives/2000/10/01/102824-the-protection-of-our-most-holy-lady-the-mother-of-god-and-ever
Feast Day – October 1

Image source –
https://en.wikipedia.org/wiki/Intercession_of_the_Theotokos#/media/File:Icon_of_theotokos_pokrov_naive.jpg

By the turn of the first Christian millennium, Constantinople had become the largest and most glamorous city in the Western world. Even before that, it had become the relic-house of Christendom. The glory that was Byzantium lasted for nearly ten centuries starting with the fifth century. The most prestigious church in Constantinople was called the Blachernae church. Often, the faithful of the city would pray for protection at this church when faced with dangerous threats ranging from enemy armies to plagues. During one such occasion, the faithful gathered there with a holy man of the time, St. Andrew the Fool for Christ and his disciple St. Epiphanius. As they implored the assistance of heaven in an all-night vigil, the two of them are said to have seen the dome of the church open up to reveal the Virgin Mary surrounded by saints. In tears she was observed praying for the protection of the people. She then spread her veil over all the gathered people. According to one account, a plague that afflicted the populace came to an end after this encounter. St. Andrew is said to have told St. Epiphanius: "Do you see, brother, the Holy Theotokos, praying for all the world?" Epiphanius answered, "Yes, Holy Father, I see it and am amazed!" This intervention of the Virgin is commemorated every October under the title "The Theotokos of Protection or Pokrov." Theotokos is a traditional title of Mary and means Mother of God or God-bearer.

Churches with the name Protection (*Pokrov*) of the Theotokos are found all across Russia. The original Blachernae church had burned down and was replaced several times and today there is only a small church where once there was once an enormous basilica. The feast of the Protection of the Theotokos is celebrated with great splendor by the Eastern Orthodox and Byzantine Catholic Churches.

Our Lady of Walsingham, England, 1061

Date – 1061
Place – Walsingham, Norfolk, England
Witness – Lady Richeldis de Faverches
Enduring Evidence – Ancient remnant of the Slipper Chapel and historical records of the Holy House of Walsingham

It may be hard to believe today, but one of the holiest places in Europe at one time was Walsingham, a village in Norfolk, England. Walsingham was known as the Nazareth of England for it was the site of a supernaturally reconstructed replica of the house of Nazareth to which kings and commoners from all over Europe used to make pilgrimages.

Accounts of the apparition behind Walsingham appear in a fifteenth century ballad that claimed to record the authentic tradition. The widowed Lady Richeldis de Faverches of Walsingham had prayed for a way in which she could honor the Blessed Virgin. One night in the year 1061 the Virgin asked her to build a replica of the House of Nazareth. The Virgin wanted the re-construction of the house because she wished to commemorate the Annunciation and also to assist those who sought her help. Lady Richeldis was mystically transported to Nazareth where she was shown the original home and given the exact dimensions required. The Lady began work on the construction of the house and at various stages received supernatural assistance.

The house became the destination for pilgrimages the year after it was completed. A church was built around the house to protect it. A chapel, called the Slipper Chapel, was built a mile away from it so that pilgrims could leave their shoes in this chapel and travel the last mile on foot. Edward the Confessor, who ruled England during the construction of the house, offered England to the Virgin as her Dowry. All the kings of England from Henry II to Henry VIII made special pilgrimages to Walsingham.

At the express order of Henry VIII, the Shrine of Walsingham and the chapels around it were destroyed and the defenders of the Shrine executed during the English Reformation. After 1829, when Catholics were allowed to practice their faith again in the UK, the Shrine at Walsingham was re-consecrated (the Slipper Chapel managed to survive the destruction). Today there is an Anglican shrine of Our Lady of Walsingham and Walsingham itself has become a center of Christian unity.

Two things about Walsingham are worthy of notice: it fits the pattern of most Marian apparitions in which the Virgin asks for the construction of a church or chapel (*Revelation* 11 and 12 show her first as the Ark of the Covenant in the Sanctuary in Heaven and then as the Woman Clothed with the Sun when she appears on earth); secondly, even non-Christians who visit Walsingham are moved by its "atmosphere". Its particular emphasis is on the mystery of the Annunciation.

The Lady Richeldis witnessed three appearances of the Virgin during which she was told, "Let all who are in any way distressed or in need seek me there in that small house that you maintain for me at Walsingham. To all that seek me there shall be given succor. The small house at Walsingham shall be a remembrance of the great joy of my Salvation, when St. Gabriel the Archangel announced that I should become the Mother of God's Son through humility and obedience to his will."

R.A. Varghese

Our Lady of Good Counsel, Italy, 1467

Date – April 25, 1467
Place – Genazzano, Italy,
Witnesses – The townspeople of Genazzano
Enduring Evidence – "One striking aspect of the fresco [with the image of Our Lady of Good Counsel], which has lent a certain credence to the legends surrounding it, is that the upper portion of the image is separated from the wall so that much of the fresco is just a thin sheet of plaster. Yet the image of Our Lady of Good Counsel has survived for centuries in this precarious state, through the rebuilding of the main walls of the church, through a number of earthquakes, and even through the aerial bombardment of Genazzano during World War II. Because of this condition, the restoration undertaken in 1957 was a delicate task."[1]
Feast day – April 26

Image source –
https://en.wikipedia.org/wiki/Our_Lady_of_Good_Counsel#/media/
File:OurLadyGenazzano02.jpg

Genazzano is a city about thirty miles south of Rome. In the fourth century a church was built there in honor of the Virgin Mary under the title of Mother of Good Counsel. In subsequent centuries, the church fell into ruin. In 1356, the Augustinians were asked to tend to it. In the fifteenth century, a widow named Petrucia donated most of her money to help restore the church. But this enabled only some preliminary construction. Then, during the celebration of the feast of St. Mark, on April 25, 1467, the townspeople reported heavenly music and the appearance of a cloud that descended onto an unfinished wall of the church. When the cloud vanished, there appeared on the wall a wafer thin painting of the Virgin and Son. From that time, the church and the fresco became a great pilgrimage destination for popes and the people. The church itself was rapidly restored. The painting is 18 inches high and 12 inches wide. Two Albanians who came into town soon after the event said that the picture had been celestially transported from Scutari, Albania in view of its imminent conquest by Islamic invaders. In recent years, art experts have claimed that it was the painting of the Italian artist Gentile de Fabriano and that the fresco was revealed when the plaster covering it fell off. Regardless of its origin, the painting itself has become reputed for the miracles associated with it.

"Prelates reported that 171 miracles were recorded in the months following the icon's appearance. The pope's commission also found that there was an empty space on the church wall at Scutari. An icon that had been venerated there for centuries was, indeed, missing.

The image was painted on a sheet of plaster so thin that it would have been impossible for any human hand to remove it without damage. It had survived the subsequent centuries through the tumult of several earthquakes and withstood the bombing during World War II. Several altars were destroyed, walls caved in, and the roof was crushed. The icon, only yards away from the explosion, remained intact."[2]

NOTES

[1]http://www.augustinianfriends.org/saints/goodcounsel.htm

[2]https://www.clavermissionarysisters.org/?page_id=289

Our Lady of Consolation, Poland, 1578

Date –1578
Place – Lezajsk, Poland
Witness – Thomas Michalek
Enduring Evidence – Basilica at site and continuing miracles

Image source –
https://www.wikidata.org/wiki/Q30005158

In the year 1578, Thomas Michalek of Lezajsk, Poland, saw a bright light in a forest where he was collecting wood. From the light there emerged a woman who identified herself as the Blessed Virgin Mary. She told him, "Thomas, I have chosen this place; on it my Son shall be honored, and everyone who shall invoke me here shall experience my intercession. Go to the rulers of the city and tell them that it is my will and command, and also that of my Son, that they build here a church dedicated to me." Thomas did not act on this very specific request and she appeared two times more asking him to follow through. Finally, he got to work and tried to build a church on the site. Neither his bishop nor his parish priest believed him and he was thrown into prison for his pains. Eventually, after the death of the priest, a wooden chapel was built on the site of the appearances. It soon became renowned for the favors received there. A larger church replaced the chapel and Our Lady of Consolation of Lezajsk was honored by kings and popes.

A basilica stands at the site of the apparitions. Because of the miracles reported there, it has become a prominent pilgrimage destination.

Our Lady of Good Event (Buen Suceso) of the Purification, Ecuador, 1594

Place – Quito,
Date – February 2, 1594 and after
Witness – Mother Mariana de Jesus Torres
Enduring Evidence – Statue of Our Lady of Buen Suceso, built after the apparition, is still at the monastery. The body of the witness, Mother Mariana de Jesus Torres, was found to be incorrupt when her tomb was opened in 1906 after three centuries.

The apparition of Our Lady of Buen Suceso in Ecuador is remarkable for its prophetic messages. The prophecies made in the 16th century especially concerned the 19th and 20th centuries and beyond.

The Virgin, enveloped in light and holding her Infant, appeared to the Abbess of a monastery of contemplative nuns in Quito, Mother Mariana de Jesus Torres. She said, 'I am Mary of Buen Suceso, the one whom you have invoked with such tender affection. Your prayer has greatly pleased me. Your faith has brought me here. Your love has invited me to visit you." She asked that a statue be made of her as she looked which is still to be found in the monastery.

She appeared to the Abbess from1594 and 1634. During this time she made several prophecies. She said that a President of Ecuador would consecrate the country to the Sacred Heart of Jesus and that he would later be assassinated. Both happened. It was prophesied that the Immaculate Conception and the Assumption of Mary would be defined as dogmas – and they were.

Most disturbing of all were the detailed warnings of the moral breakdown of society starting in the 19th century and reaching a crescendo in the 20th century and beyond.

> "Thus, I make it known to you that from the end of the 19th century and from shortly after the middle of the 20th century … the passions will erupt and there will be a total corruption of customs, for Satan will reign almost completely."

Also emphasized was the profanation of the sacraments and the corruption of many of the clergy during this time.

> "The Christian spirit will rapidly decay, extinguishing the precious light of faith until it reaches a point that there will be an almost total and general corruption of customs."

She was also shown three swords that represented punishments that would come starting in the 20th century: (1) "I will punish heresy"; (2) "I will punish blasphemy"; and (3) "I will punish impurity."

In the official documents of the time, the then bishop of Quito, Bishop Salvador de Ribera, testified to the miraculous completion of the statue of Our Lady of Buen Suceso of Quito and anointed and consecrated the statue on February 2, 1611. His successor, Bishop Pedro de Oviedo (1630-1646), approved and promoted both the apparition and the associated devotions.

Third decade – Asia/Africa/America

Our Lady of Akita, Japan, 1973

"The Father is Preparing to Inflict a Great Chastisement on All Mankind."

Place – Akita, Japan
Dates – Started June 12, 1973, ended September 15, 1981.
Witness – Sister Agnes Sasagawa
Enduring Evidence – Wooden statue of the Virgin that exuded blood, sweat and tears; stigmata on visionary; deaf visionary regains hearing.
Theme – Prophecy, Admonitions on sin and reparation

Image source –
https://en.wikipedia.org/wiki/Our_Lady_of_Akita#/media/File:Virgin_Mary_of_Akita_Japan.jpg

Sister Agnes Sasagawa (born 1931) entered the convent of the Institute of the Handmaids of the Eucharist in Akita, Japan, on May 12, 1973. Not long before she had lost her hearing. A month after joining the order, she came to the convent chapel to adore the Eucharist. On opening the tabernacle door, she was astounded to see a light brighter than the sun coming from within and prostrated herself before it. She witnessed the same phenomenon on several subsequent occasions when she came to the chapel; she also saw "spiritual beings" worshipping the Eucharist. She reported these experiences to Bishop John Ito, the bishop of Niigata, the Diocese to which Akita belonged, and he advised her to be open but cautious.

Later in the month, Agnes discovered that she was receiving the stigmata. On Thursdays, the palm of her left hand would start to hurt and on the next day a red cross would form on it. On Sunday, she would be healed and the pain would go away.

At 3:00 a.m. on the morning of July 6, she saw a beautiful person in the chapel, her guardian angel, who told her, "Be not afraid. Pray with fervor not only because of your sins, but in reparation for those of all people. The world today wounds the most Sacred Heart of Our Lord by its ingratitudes and injuries. The wounds of Mary are much deeper and more sorrowful than yours. Let us go to pray together in the chapel."

After the angel disappeared, Agnes saw that a three foot high wooden statue of the Virgin in the chapel was blazing with light. The statue was modeled on the image of the Virgin as she is said to have appeared in Amsterdam in 1945. The statue spoke to Agnes and asked her to pray in reparation for the sins of humanity and to follow her superior. After this apparition, Agnes and the other nuns found that there was a wound in the palm of the statue that continued to bleed until Sunday.

On July 26, the pain from Agnes' wound was almost unbearable. Again, she heard from her angel, "Your sufferings will end today. Carefully engrave in the depth of your heart the thought of the blood of Mary. The blood shed by Mary has a profound meaning. This precious blood was shed to ask your conversion, to ask for peace, in reparation for the ingratitude and the outrages against the Lord. As with devotion to the Sacred Heart, apply yourself to devotion to the most Precious Blood. Pray in reparation for all men. Say to your superior that the blood is shed today for the last time. Your pain also ends today. Tell them what happened today. He will understand all immediately. And you, observe his directions." The angel then disappeared and Sr. Agnes noticed that the pain from her wound had subsided.

On August 3, Agnes again heard from the statue. The Virgin told her that the Heavenly Father was preparing a great chastisement for the world. She also asked for prayer and penance.

On September 29, the statue stopped bleeding but tears started flowing down its cheeks.

On October 13, Sister Agnes received her last message from the Virgin. She was told that the Father would inflict a terrible punishment on humanity, that fire would fall from the sky and wipe out a good portion of humanity, that the Devil would infiltrate the Church.

In May 1974, her angel told Agnes that her hearing would be temporarily restored and then permanently cured later. On October 13 of that year, Agnes regained her hearing but by March of 1975 she had lost it yet again. At the end of 1975, the angel told her, "Do not be so surprised to see the Blessed Virgin weeping. She weeps because she wishes the conversion of the greatest number. She desires that souls be consecrated to Jesus and to the Father by her intercession. He who directs you told you during the last sermon today: Your faith diminishes when you do not see. It is because your faith is weak. The Blessed Virgin rejoices in the consecration of Japan to her Immaculate Heart because she loves Japan. But she is sad to see that devotion is not taken seriously. Even though she has chosen this land of Akita to give her messages, the local pastor doesn't dare to come for fear of what one would say. Do not be afraid. The Blessed Virgin awaits you all."

Meanwhile the statue continued to weep on certain given days and by September 15, 1981, the last time this happened, it had shed tears a total of 101 times. On September 28, 1981, her guardian angel showed Agnes a vision of a Bible and asked her to read Genesis 3:15: "I will place enmity between thee (Satan) and the woman (Mary), between thy seed and hers. She will crush thy head and thou shalt lie in wait for her heel." (This was the rendition of the verse in the modern Japanese translation.) The angel then explained the relation between this verse and the fact that the statue had wept 101 times: "There is a meaning to the figure one hundred and one. This signifies that sin came into the world by a woman and it is also by a woman that salvation came into the world. The zero between the two signifies the Eternal God who is from all eternity until eternity. The first one represents Eve, and the last, the Virgin Mary."

Fr. Thomas Teiji Yasuda, Sr. Agnes' spiritual director, interpreted the verse and the message in this manner: "The passage from the Scripture elucidated the profound meaning of the angel's message regarding the 101 weepings. Here in Akita, God himself sent the angel to reveal the profound meaning of the message 'by the authority of the Bible', the words of God. In Genesis Chapter 3, verse 15, the Sovereign God, the Absolute Being, makes the prophetic announcement to Satan of the combat, in which the Blessed Virgin Mary and Her seed will oppose and confront Satan throughout the ages. It is in union with the Church, the Mystical Body of Christ, that the Virgin Mary has received, from the Eternal Father, the mission of fighting against and crushing Satan and his cohorts until the end of the world. The miracles of the bleeding and weeping of the statue of the Blessed Mother in Akita were brought about by God in order to illustrate the truth of Mary's role as Coredemptrix."

Theresa Chun, a Korean lady who was diagnosed with a brain tumor, placed an image of Our Lady of Akita under her pillow and prayed to her for a miraculous healing. On August 4, 1981, the tumor was found to have disappeared. In May 1982, her angel told Agnes that her hearing would be permanently restored that month and on May 30 the deafness was cured (tests performed on Agnes at the Akita Municipal Hospital in 1975 had confirmed that she was deaf and it was noted that the deafness was incurable).

The acceptance of Akita faced three obstacles: scientific, theological and ecclesiastical.

On the scientific front, the results were quite remarkable. The actual weeping of the statue was witnessed not just by the local bishop but was shown on national Japanese TV. On December 8, 1979, a television team filmed the tears in real-time and broadcast it to 12 million viewers across Japan. The tears, sweat and blood from the statue were sent for laboratory analysis in January 1975. The first tests on the samples sent were performed by Professor Eiji Okuhara, a Catholic physician in the Akita University Department of Biochemistry and a former Rockefeller Foundation fellow. Professor Okuhara, who had witnessed the weeping of the statue himself, also passed the samples on to a non-Christian forensic specialist, Dr. Kaoru Sagisaka. The scientists confirmed that the blood, sweat and tears were of human origin.

A subsequent test was performed after Dr. Sagisaka became a professor at Gifu University since it was said that there might have been some contamination of the initial samples by the handlers (in the first report, Dr. Sagisaka had written that "at the time the specimen was taken, or by the time the examiner received the specimen, it could have been contaminated by a minute amount of body fluid of type A or type AB.") The report from the new tests, performed on samples extracted after the required precautions were in place, came out on November 30, 1981. Dr. Sagisaka's medical appraisal certificate stated, "I certify that human body fluid is adhering to the specimen and that the blood type of the specimen is type O."

The theological verdict on Akita was left in the hands of an implacable foe of the apparitions, Fr. Garcia Evangelista, a Mariologist from Tokyo who headed up an investigative commission in 1975. Fr. Evangelista rejected the authenticity of the apparitions and claimed that the blood, sweat and tears pouring forth from the statue came from the "ectoplasmic powers" of Sister Agnes by which she could manifest her bodily fluids through the statue. This conclusion caused confusion for the followers of Akita for many years but it was easily refuted:

(a) Agnes had blood type B but the different analyses of the fluids from the statue showed types A, AB and O (b) the critic said ectoplasmic powers are exercised when the primary agent is fifteen meters away from the statue but the blood, sweat and tears continued when Agnes was visiting her relatives 250 miles away (an American medical doctor Dr. Theresa Wei, who once witnessed the statue shedding tears said that at that precise time Agnes was working in the kitchen - and she could not focus her will power on two things at the same time). When the writer

Francis Mutsuo Fukushima confronted Evangelista with these responses, Evangelista admitted that he could not account for the differences between the blood types from the statue and those of Sister Agnes. He then speculated that there were probably other nuns in the convent who had ectoplasmic powers and "sent" tears through the statue. But then it was shown that there were no nuns with the blood type AB at the time of the 1975 analysis.

Despite the evident error of his arguments, a cloud settled on Akita because of Evangelista's prestige and his negative conclusions. The bishops of Japan were divided among themselves on the authenticity of Akita (we cannot forget that the Akita messages were quite forceful in criticizing the lapses of the clergy). In 1979, Bishop Ito visited the Congregation for the Doctrine of the Faith in Rome and was told that the investigation was under his jurisdiction - and therefore he could deal with it as he saw fit. The bishop then set up a new commission of inquiry and on September 12, 1981, the commission issued a report stating that the events at Akita were indeed supernatural. The last tears of the statue came on September 15, 1981, the Feast of Our Lady of Sorrows.

In a pastoral letter in 1984, Bishop Ito wrote, "After the investigation conducted up to the present day, I recognize the supernatural character of a series of mysterious events concerning the statue of the Holy Mother Mary which is found in the convent of the institute of the Handmaids of the Sacred Heart of Jesus in the Holy Eucharist at Yuzawadai, Soegawa, Akita. I do not find in these events any elements which are contrary to Catholic faith and morals." Although Bishop Ito's declaration settled the question of ecclesiastical approval for the immediate future, the importance and evident supernatural origin of Akita could be rejected in the future because of the severity of its messages.

Messages

First Message from the Virgin
"My daughter, my novice, you have obeyed me well, abandoning all to follow me. Do you suffer much because of the handicap which deafness causes you? You will be assuredly healed. Be patient. It is the last trial.

Does the wound in your hand give you pain? Pray in reparation for the sins of humanity. Each person in this community is my irreplaceable daughter.

"Pray very much for the pope, bishops and priests. Since your baptism you have always prayed faithfully for them. Continue to pray very much. Tell your superior all that passed today and obey him in everything that he will tell you. Your superior is wholeheartedly seeking prayers now."

Second Message from the Virgin
"My daughter, my novice, do you love the Lord? If you love the Lord, listen to what I have to say to you.

"It is very important. Convey it to your superior.

"Many men in this world grieve the Lord. I seek souls to console Him. In order to appease the wrath of the Heavenly Father, I wish, with my Son, for souls who will make reparation for sinners, and the ungrateful by offering up their sufferings and poverty to God on their behalf.

"In order that the world might know the wrath of the Heavenly Father toward today's world, He is preparing to inflict a great chastisement on all mankind. With my son, many times I have tried to appease the wrath of the Heavenly Father. I have prevented the coming of the chastisement by offering Him the sufferings of His Son on the Cross, His Precious Blood, and the compassionate souls who console the Heavenly Father. A cohort of victim souls overflowing with love.

"Prayer, penance, honest poverty, and courageous acts of sacrifices can soften the anger of the Heavenly Father. I desire this also from your community; please make much of poverty, deepen repentance, and pray amid your poverty in reparation for the ingratitude and insults toward the Lord by so many men. Recite the prayer of the Handmaids of the Eucharist with awareness of its meaning; put into practice; offer your life to God in reparation for sins. Let each one endeavor by making much of one's ability and position, to offer oneself entirely to the Lord.

"Even in a secular institute, prayer is necessary. Already souls who wish to pray are on the way to being gathered in this community. Without attaching too much attention to the form, pray fervently and steadfastly to console the Lord.

"Is what you think in your heart true? Are you truly prepared to become the rejected stone: My novice, you who wish to become the pure bride of the Lord. In order that you, the bride, become the spouse worthy of the Holy Bridegroom, make your vows with the hearty readiness to be fastened to the Cross with three nails. These three nails are honest poverty, chastity and obedience. Of the three obedience is the foundation. With total obedience follow your superior. Your superior will understand you well and guide you."

Third Message from the Virgin
"My dear daughter, listen well to what I have to say to you. And relay my messages to your superior.

"As I told you, if men do not repent and better themselves, the Heavenly Father will inflict a great punishment on all humanity. It will definitely be a punishment greater than the Deluge, such as has never been seen before.

"Fire will plunge from the sky and a large part of humanity will perish ... The good as well as the bad will perish, sparing neither priests nor the faithful. The survivors will find themselves plunged into such terrible hardships that they will envy the dead. The only arms which will remain for you will be the Rosary and the sign left by My Son (Eucharist).

"Each day recite the prayers of the Rosary. With the Rosary pray for the bishops and priests. The work of the devil will infiltrate even into the Church. One will see cardinals opposing other cardinals, and bishops confronting other bishops.

"The priests who venerate me will be scorned and opposed by their confreres; churches and altars will be sacked. The Church will be full of those who accept compromises and the demon will tempt many priests and consecrated souls to leave the service of the Lord.

"The demon is trying hard to influence souls consecrated to God. The thought of the perdition of so many souls is the cause of my sadness. If sins continue to be committed further, there will no longer be pardon for them.

"With courage, convey these messages to your superior. He will tell each one of you to continue prayers and acts of reparation for sins steadfastly while ordering all of you to pray fervently. Pray very much the prayers of the Rosary. I alone am able still to help save you from the calamities which approach. Those who place their total confidence in me will be given necessary help."

Our Lady of Soufanieh, Syria, 1982-1990

"Announce My Son the Emmanuel.
He Who Announces Him is Saved."

Place – Damascus, Syria

Dates – Started November 22, 1982. Ended November 26, 1990.

Witness – Myrna Nazzour

Enduring Evidence – Olive oil with healing properties oozing from a statue of the Virgin and from the visionary. Stigmata (wounds) appeared on the visionary's forehead, hands, feet and side.

Themes – Healing, Unity of the Christian Community, Stigmata, Suffering

Description of the Virgin – The "large, luminous, white globe like a large diamond ball ... opened, splitting from the top and dividing into two half-moons. As the halves opened, a bow of light appeared over the top, and inside was the same Beautiful Lady. As the ball disappeared, the Lady seemed to be standing on the branch of the tree. She had a white veil that covered her hair. The veil was part of her dress. Over her right shoulder was a sky-blue cape that wrapped around her back and over her left side. The white dress covered her feet, and only her hands could be seen. The dress and cape seemed to be made of white and blue light. From her right hand, between the second and third fingers, hung a long Rosary."

The Damascus Experience of St. Paul is the most famous metaphor for extraordinary conversions to the Christian Faith. This metaphor found a literal contemporary translation in the apparitions of Myrna (for Mary) Nazzour of Damascus. Myrna, who lives a few blocks away from the house of Ananias where St. Paul spent three days when he was blinded after seeing Jesus, was also blinded for three days during the course of her apparitions when she beheld and heard Jesus on May 31, 1984.

Myrna, a Melkite Catholic, married Nicholas Nazzour, who was Eastern Orthodox, in May 1982. Neither of them were particularly "religious" and in fact quite enjoyed their social life. Then in November of that year,

Nicholas' sister Layla fell seriously ill. While Myrna was praying by her side along with two other women, olive oil started oozing from her fingers. At the suggestion of one of the women present, Myrna applied the oil to Layla who was instantly healed. On November 27, an icon of Our Lady of Soufanieh in the Nazzour home began to exude large quantities of olive oil (which was chemically tested and found to be pure); the oil resulted in many healings. These phenomena mystified the couple who gathered with other family members to pray for discernment. While they were praying, Myrna suddenly found she could not hear them and instead heard an enchanting voice calling her, "Mary, do not be afraid. Open the doors and do not deprive anyone from seeing me." (Myrna, as noted, meant Mary).

As both Myrna and the image of Our Lady continued to exude oil, both scientists and the local police investigated the phenomenon. The investigations only confirmed that oil was indeed coming from the image and not from the frame, that even when Myrna had washed her hands she would exude oil when she started praying. The clergy were also convinced that fraud could be ruled out.

The next definitive phase in the phenomenon took place on December 15, 1982 when Myrna was led by an invisible escort to her roof garden. Once she was there, she saw the Virgin who was shining "as if she were covered with diamonds." Terrified, Myrna ran away. After being counselled by a clergyman experienced in supernatural phenomena, she developed a more receptive state of mind. Three days later, she was again taken to the roof, this time accompanied by her husband and a number of friends. She saw a globe of light on top of a tree across the street. A beautiful Lady emerged from this globe and then came across the street to Mryna on a "bridge" of light. Speaking in Arabic, the Virgin then gave her first message to Myrna which essentially outlined her program of action for all of the subsequent messages and apparitions:

> My children, Remember God, because God is with us. You know all things and yet you know nothing. Your knowledge is an incomplete knowledge. But the day will come when you will know all things the way God knows me. Do good to those who do evil. And do not harm anyone. I have given you oil more than you have asked for. But I shall give you something much more powerful

than oil. Repent and have faith, and remember me in your joy. Announce My Son the Emmanuel. He who announces Him is saved, and he who does not announce Him, his faith is vain. Love one another. I am not asking for money to give to churches, nor for money to distribute to the poor. I am asking for love. Those who distribute their money to the poor and to churches, but have no love, those are nothing. I shall visit homes more often, because those who go to church, sometimes, do not go there to pray. I am not asking you to build me a church, but a shrine. GIVE. Do not turn away anyone who asks for help.

The command to "Announce My Son the Emmanuel. He who announces Him is saved, and he who does not announce Him, his faith is vain." is especially significant. Evangelization is fundamental to Christianity - but in no other part of the world is evangelization more difficult than in the Middle East.

The Virgin's appearances and messages continued. Over a hundred thousand people had seen the phenomenon of the oil and healings continued taking place, among them such extraordinary events as a blind Moslem woman recovering her sight and a paralyzed boy regaining the use of his limbs. The Eastern Orthodox Patriarch Ignatius IV Hazim met with the Nazzours and after carrying out an investigation approved the authenticity of the phenomenon as a supernatural reality on December 31, 1982. The Roman Catholic Bishop of Damascus, the Most Rev. Paulus Barkash, personally witnessed the phenomenon and wrote the following in his introduction to a book on the apparitions: "Peace and blessing and my prayer for God's redeeming graces to all who will read this interesting book about the supernatural events of Soufanieh, which continue to occur from 1982 until now. I was personally an eye witness to the oil coming from the hands and face of Mirna and from copies of the Soufanieh Icon more than once. We congratulate the writer for publishing the Soufanieh events to the glory of God and for devotion to the Virgin Mary. We encourage the faithful to pray, sacrifice and work with persistence for the unity of the Churches as mentioned in the messages of the Virgin to Mirna. While encouraging the faithful to read this precious book, we assure them that what is written in it as extraordinary events, quotes, messages and events corresponds to the facts. We ask from God blessing and success to the readers of this valuable book and to all those who contributed to its publication." (June 18, 1990). The book received an imprimatur from the Melkite (Greek Catholic) Archbishop of Damascus Boulos Bourkhocke.

On May 31, 1984, the oil exuded from Myrna's eyes - a very painful experience. At this time she went into ecstasy and for the first time saw and heard Jesus. She lost her eyesight for a period of three days after this event. Myrna has also been privileged to receive the stigmata, the wounds of Christ including the wounds from the crown of thorns, on Good Friday. After three hours, however, the wounds stopped bleeding and closed by themselves.

On August 4, 1984, Myrna went into ecstasy at the end of Mass and was told by Jesus that anyone who divides the Church or rejoices in such divisions was guilty of sin. Her whole ministry is focused on the unity of the Churches (here again she follows in the footsteps of St. Paul, the Apostle of Unity) as commanded by Our Lord and the Virgin. A key component of this unity, as shown in the messages, is their request that "the feast (of Easter) is unified."

Even the most skeptical of observers will find it striking that great progress has finally been made on the question of celebrating a common Easter - in a meeting in Syria! The Aleppo Statement of March 1998 that came out of a meeting of Eastern Orthodox, Oriental Orthodox, Catholic and Protestant representatives has come close to an agreement on the norms for a common date by following the norms of the First Ecumenical Council of Nicaea (325): Easter is to be celebrated on the Sunday following the first full moon of spring after the vernal equinox (when the sun crosses the equator and using calculations with Jerusalem as the point of reference) starting in 2001. Remarkably, the agreement, which has ramifications for the entire Christian world, was reached in the very country where Our Lord and the Virgin brought this ancient but vital issue back to the attention of the faithful. The importance of the common Easter is evident from the fact that one of the reasons the Council of Nicaea was called was in fact to resolve the question of a common date for Easter.

The oil from the original icon stopped exuding oil in 2001. The exuding resumed during the Holy Week of 2017. Despite the Syrian civil war and the ongoing crises in the Middle East, Myrna has continued to bear witness to the miracle of Soufanieh.

Messages
[Excerpted from the version in Father Elias Zahlaoui's *Remember God*]

February 21, 1983
My children, Let it be said between us, I have come back here. Do not insult the haughty who are devoid of humility. The humble person craves other people's remarks to correct his shortcomings, while the corrupt and haughty neglects, rebels, becomes hostile. Forgiveness is the best thing. He who pretends to be pure and loving before people, is impure before God. I would like to request something from you, a word that you will engrave in your memory, that you shall always repeat: God saves me, Jesus enlightens me, the Holy Spirit is my life, thus I fear nothing.

Thursday, March 24, 1983
The Church that Jesus adopted is One Church, because Jesus is One. The Church is the kingdom of Heaven on Earth. He who has divided it has sinned. And he who has rejoiced from its division has also sinned. Jesus built it. It was small. And when it grew, it became divided. He who divided it has no love in him. Gather! I tell you: "Pray, pray, and pray again!" How beautiful are My children when they kneel down, imploring. Do not fear, I am with you. Do not be divided as the great ones are. You, yourselves, will teach the generations THE WORD of unity, love and faith.

Thursday, May 31, 1984 (Ascension Day)
Message from Jesus Christ
My daughter, I am the Beginning and the End. I am Truth, Freedom and Peace. My Peace, I give you. Your peace shall not depend on what people say, be it good or bad, and think little of yourself. He who does not seek people's approval, and does not fear their disapproval, enjoys true peace. And this is achieved through Me. Live your life, contented and independent. The pains you have incurred for Me shall not break you. Rather, rejoice. I am capable of rewarding you. Your hardships will not

be prolonged, and your pains will not last. Pray with adoration, because Eternal life is worth these sufferings. Pray for God's will to be done in you, and say: Beloved Jesus, Grant that I rest in You above all things, above all creatures, above all Your angels, above all praise, above all rejoicing and exultation, above all glory and honor, above all Heavenly hosts, For You alone are the Most High, You alone are the Almighty and Good above all things. May You come to me and relieve me, and release me from my chains, and grant me freedom, because without You my joy is not complete, without You my table is empty. Only then will I come to say: Here I am, because you have invited Me.

Tuesday, November 26, 1985
Message from Jesus Christ
My daughter, Do you wish to be crucified or glorified? *Answer: Glorified. Jesus smiles and says*: Do you prefer to be glorified by the creature or the Creator?
Answer: by the Creator.
Jesus: This is realized through Crucifixion. Because each time you look at the creatures, the eyes of the Creator move away from you. My daughter, I want you to apply yourself to praying and to humble yourself. He who humbles himself, God increases him in strength and in greatness. I was crucified out of love for you, and I want you to carry and bear your cross for Me, willingly, with love and patience, and (I want you) to await My arrival. He who participates in My suffering, I shall make him participate in My glory. And there is no salvation for the soul except through the Cross. Do not fear, My daughter, I shall give you from My wounds enough to repay the debts of the sinners. This is the source from which every soul may drink. And if My absence lasts, and the light disappears from you, do not fear, this will be for My glorification.

Friday, August 14, 1987
Message from Jesus Christ
My daughter, She is My Mother from whom I was born. He who honors Her, honors Me. He who denies Her, denies Me. And he who asks something from Her obtains because She is My Mother.

Thursday, November 26, 1987
<u>Message from Jesus Christ</u>
My daughter, I am pleased that you have chosen Me, not only in words. I want you to join My Heart to your gentle heart so that our hearts will unite. By doing so, you will save suffering souls. Do not hate anyone, so that your heart not be blinded by your love of Me. Love everyone as you have loved Me, especially those who have hated you and have spoken evil of you, because in so doing you will obtain glory. Continue in your life as wife, mother and sister. Do not worry about the difficulties and the pains that will afflict you. I want you to be stronger than them because I am with you otherwise you will lose My heart. Go and preach to the whole world and tell them without fear to work for unity. Man is not condemned for the fruit of his hands, but for the fruit of his heart. My peace in your heart will be a blessing for you and for all those who have cooperated with you.

Sunday, August 14, 1988
<u>Message from Jesus Christ</u>
It is easier for Me (to accept) that an infidel believe in My name than that those who pretend to have faith and love swear by My name.

Saturday, November 26, 1988
<u>Message from Jesus Christ</u>
My children, Is everything you do out of love for Me? Do not say: What shall I do, because this is My work. You must fast and pray, because through prayer you face My truth and you confront all enemies. Pray for those who have forgotten the promise they made Me because they will say: Why did I not feel your presence, O Lord, even though You were with me?

Saturday, April 14, 1990 (Holy Saturday)
<u>Message from Jesus Christ</u>
My children, You, yourselves, will teach the generations THE WORD of unity, love and faith. I am with you. But you, My daughter, will not hear My voice until the Feast (of Easter) has been unified.

Monday, November 26, 1990

<u>Message from the Holy Virgin</u>

Do not fear, my daughter, if I tell you that you are seeing me for the last time until the feast (of Easter) is unified. Therefore, tell my children: Do they want or not to see and remember the wounds of my Son in you? If it does not pain them to see that you are suffering doubly, I myself, am a mother, and it pains me to see my Son suffering repeatedly. Remain in peace, remain in peace, my daughter. Come, so that He may give you peace, so that you may spread it among the people. As for the oil, it will continue to manifest itself on your hands to glorify my Son Jesus, whenever He wishes and wherever you go. We are with you and with everyone who wishes the Feast (of Easter) to be One.

Our Lady of Jerusalem, Israel 1954

Place – Jerusalem, Israel
Dates – July 18, July 25, 1954
Witnesses – children at the school of St. Anthony, parishioners of the Coptic Patriarchal Church
Enduring evidence – Thousands visited the St. Anthony church and many miracles were reported.
Description of the Virgin – Dressed in blue and surrounded by luminous aura that glowed white near the body and iridescent blue as it went out.
Link – https://www.youtube.com/watch?v=5mOpmBwflug

The Coptic school of St. Anthony and the Coptic Patriarchal Church of Jerusalem are located within a few hundred yards of what is believed to be the site of Calvary. On July 18, 1954, at 11:00 a.m., looking out of their classroom windows, the fifth grade children at the school saw a woman in blue floating in the sky above the courtyard surrounded by a luminous aura. The children yelled out "El Adra! El Adra!" which meant "The Virgin." Their teacher could not see her. Since the children would not settle down, the school secretary came and ordered them to sit down and locked the door. But shortly after, the Virgin appeared inside the classroom. This time her luminous form became brighter until even the adults could see her. Eventually, she vanished.

On July 25, during evening prayers at the Coptic church, the Blessed Virgin appeared again hovering over the congregation and then moving among them. This time the more than 300 people attending the prayers could see her. Rays of light emanated from the Virgin. She remained there for some 15 minutes. Some reported her waving a white scarf and others said she blessed the people present. Reporters from national and international media reported the vision.

These two events were described in the *Coptic Patriarchal Journal* of the time. The Coptic bishop wrote, "She did not come for our sakes. She came because this place is holy, being within a few yards of Calvary and the Tomb."

In a remarkable parallel, 63 years later the Blessed Virgin is reported to have appeared to a group of schoolchildren while they were praying on their own in a church in Kochi, India, in 2017. Their school too was affiliated with a church. The children included Hindus, Moslems and Christians. Despite their excitement, the children were ordered to come back to class. At that point, the Virgin came and visited them in their classroom. Initially only children could see her but eventually adults also reported seeing her.

Our Lady of Ocotlan, Mexico, 1541

Date – 1541
Place – Ocotlan, Mexico
Witness – Juan Diego Bernardino
Enduring evidence – Statue of Our Lady of Ocotlan, discovered after the apparition, which continues to manifest miraculous properties. Healing spring.

Nuestra Señora de Ocotlán, Tlax.

Another remarkable apparition of Mary took place in Mexico just ten years after Guadalupe. This apparition of Our Lady of Ocotlan is known for two fascinating features: its supernaturally revealed healing spring and a miraculous statue of herself bestowed by the Virgin in the same mysterious fashion as at Guadalupe. The following account is based on the official history of the Shrine of Our Lady of Ocotlan.

"The visionary, Juan Diego Bernardino, no relation of Juan Diego of Guadalupe, lived in Tlaxcala, Mexico. Many of his fellow-villagers had been stricken by an incurable plague and on February 27, 1541, Juan set out to bring water from a nearby river to help alleviate their suffering. On returning from the river, he passed through a forest near a cliff where he encountered a beautiful lady who said: "God be with you, my son. Where are you going?" When Juan explained that he had gone to bring water for the suffering villagers, the lady appeared pleased and said, "Come with me! I will give you a different water that will cure the sicknesses of your people. Not only your relatives and friends will be healed, but also all those who drink it." The Lady took him to a cliff where a fountain of water was gushing forth and said, "My heart always desires to help those who are suffering. My heart cannot bear to see so much pain and anguish among people without healing them. Drink as much water as you desire. Upon drinking just one drop, the sick will not only be cured, but they will receive perfect health!" The Lady also gave him a message for the Franciscan monks who lived in a nearby monastery: "Tell the monks that in this place, they shall find an image of me, which not only will represent my perfection, but also, through it, I will bring forth my mercy and blessings. I want the image to be placed in the chapel of Saint Lawrence."

"The water from the fountain not only cured the stricken villagers but has been a source of healing for thousands of others through the centuries. The second part of the story is the statue. After hearing Juan's story, "the Franciscans, accompanied by a group of people from the village, entered the forest one night and headed towards the fountain of water. Suddenly, they were blinded by a great light spewing huge flames of fire into the sky and onto the trees. Miraculously, the trees in the forest did not burn. One tree seemed to stand out from the rest. They marked that tree and returned to the monastery because it was late at night. Early the next morning, the group, armed with axes, returned to that particular pine tree to split it open. Inside a cavity in the tree, they found a wooden statue of the Blessed Virgin Mary. It was "burnt" into the tree. The Franciscans carried the statue of Our Lady on their shoulders to the nearby chapel of St. Lawrence."

"The magnificent statue is beautifully dressed and about 5 feet tall (the average height for women of that region). Its hands are held in a prayerful position. (Fr. Bachill Laoyzaga, an 18th century historian, wrote, "Spacious forehead, beautiful as a sun-lit sky, lovely rosy cheeks, carmine lips and her eyes a bluish green.) During certain religious festivities the countenance of the face changes color from red rose to pale and back again."

Many people through the centuries and even in modern times have witnessed this miracle and other phenomena, for instance, its mysterious luminosity, the sweat that sometimes appears on it, and so on. The tilma of Guadalupe was made from cactus fibers that ordinarily decay in two to three decades. The wood from which the statue of Ocotlan is made should have decomposed long ago. But to this day it continues to bear witness to its supernatural origin as forcefully as the tilma.

R.A. Varghese

Our Lady of Aparecida, Brazil, 1717

Date – October 12, 1717
Place – Sao Paulo
Witnesses – Domingos Garcia, Joao Alves and Felipe Ramos
Enduring Evidence – Image of Nossa Senhora Aparecida

Nossa Senhora Aparecida is the Queen and Patroness of Brazil. The origin history of this devotion below was provided by Ms. Rocilda Oliveiro of Brazil:

> In 1717, the village of Guaratingueta, Sao Paulo, was waiting for a very important visitor, the Count of Assumar, the Governor of Sao Paulo. The day of his arrival was a day of abstinence and so the hosts needed to have fish at the reception.
>
> The local fishermen were asked to go fishing in the Paraoba River. Domingos Garcia, Joao Alves and Felipe Ramos were three of these fishermen. Although they tried hard they could not catch any fish and they were beginning to lose all hope.
>
> At this point, when Joao Alves pulled up the empty net, he saw something inside it. It was the body of a small statue made from obarro (a black material); the statue had no head. The surprised men rowed down the river and tried to fish once more. Again they found something caught in their net. It was the head of the statue.
>
> The astonished fishermen recognized at once that it was the image of Our Lady of Conception (Nossa Senhora da Conceicou) and called her "Nossa Senhora da Conceicao Aparecida" (Our Appeared Lady of Conception).
>
> They let the net down again. Although they had toiled all day they had not gotten anything. But this time, when they hauled up the net, they found they had caught a great multitude of fish.
>
> As in Luke 5, when the presence of Our Lord in Peter's boat filled the ships to the extent that it began to sink, likewise the presence of Our Appeared Lady of Conception did the same to their boat.
>
> Once the statue was brought to the village, many miracles took place and graces seemed to proliferate exponentially throughout the country. Princess Isabel, who initially refused to free the slaves, signed a paper freeing the slaves. Princess Isabel also offered Our Lady of Conception a precious gold crown. This image was later honored by many Popes.

There is a deeper dimension to the discovery of this particular image which pertains to the theological truth it embodies – the truth of the Immaculate Conception. This was powerfully highlighted in a recent perceptive article:

> The posture of the Virgin of Aparecida is typical of images of Mary portraying the Immaculate Conception. That she was discovered in 1717 (137 years before the formal definition of the Dogma of the Immaculate Conception) reveals that the devotion and belief in the dogma was already widespread. Furthermore, her dark complexion, her posture of prayer, and her position on the crescent moon is the same as the miraculous image of Our Lady of Guadalupe. Even more interesting, the United States is also under the patronage of the Immaculate Conception, to which the great shrine in Washington, DC stands as witness.
>
> The main importance of the Virgin of Aparecida is ... the fact that her image is that of the Immaculate Conception. This connects her to that great Marian image in Mexico as well as to the Patroness of the United States. It is no coincidence that this dogma of the Church surged into prominence and importance in the 16th and 17th centuries, culminating in the definition of the dogma in 1854. This was the age of revolution and reform that saw the rise of rationalism and secular humanism.
>
> Why is the Immaculate Conception important? The dogma of the Immaculate Conception of the Blessed Virgin Mary is the belief that God interrupted the flow of human history by a special act and preserved Mary from the stain of original sin from the first moment of her conception. This action of God reminds us of two important truths – truths which have been obliterated in the rationalist, secular-humanist modern world.
>
> The first is that God is alive and at work in the world. He has not abandoned the human race, but he cares enough to be involved. Through a special act he preserved the Virgin Mary from the stain of original sin, and through this unique action he reminds us that he is still engaged with the human race in our eternal struggle.... The miraculous is still alive in the world.

Secondly, the Immaculate Conception reminds us that human life is sacred from the first moment of conception. We are taught by divine revelation and by divine interaction with the world that the first moment of human life is the moment of conception....

Finally, it is no mistake that the Immaculate Conception is the primary image of the Americas. The Americas are the ultimate battleground in the war between secular, godless humanism and the divine mercy of God in the world.[1]

NOTES

[1]https://aleteia.org/2013/07/25/whats-so-important-about-the-virgin-of-aparecida/

R.A. Varghese

Our Lady of Ransom, India, 1752

Date – 1752
Place – Vallarpadam, Kerala, India
Witness – Meenakshi Amma
Enduring Evidence – Image of Our Lady of Ransom. Continuing miracles at the church built near the site.

THE MIRACULOUS PICTURE OF 'VALLARPADATHAMMA' PLACED AT THE
TOP OF THE ALTAR OF THE CHURCH OF OUR LADY OF RANSOM

The island of Vallarpadam is located next to the port city of Kochi in the state of Kerala in India. Kerala is notable for having a community of Jews who lived there even before the birth of Christ. It was a commodity trading hub that attracted not just the Jews but Babylonians, Sumerians, Greeks, Romans, Phoenicians, Egyptians, Arabs and Chinese. In later centuries, the Portuguese, Dutch and British became part of the history of Kerala. The Apostle Thomas, we have seen, set up a Christian community in Kerala. Over the centuries this community entered into relationships with Christians in Persia, Portugal, Italy and Syria.

In 1524, the Portuguese explorer Vasco Da Gama and his entourage brought a spectacular painting of the Virgin and Infant under the title of Our Lady of Ransom that was installed in the church in Vallarpadam. In 1676, a flood destroyed the church. The picture was found floating in the water and was recovered with the help of the Hindu prime minister of the local king. The same prime minister donated the land for the building of a new church as well as the sanctuary lamp there (his descendants continue to keep the lamp burning).

Then in May 1752, Meenakshi Amma, a lady from a noble Hindu Nair family set sail in a boat with her son to another island. A sudden storm overturned the boat. Some of those on the boat were able to swim to shore. As she started sinking into the murky depths, Meenakshi Amma prayed then to the Virgin Mary pledging that she and her son would serve her for the rest of their lives if she saved them. That same night, the priest at the Vallarpadam church had a dream where the Virgin Mary asked him to rescue a lady and her son submerged in the water. He dismissed it as just a dream. But then he had the same dream the next night and this time the Virgin was more insistent. The priest realized something was going on and organized professional fishermen to launch a search mission. Given the number of days that had transpired since the storm, no one expected to find the missing pair. But then on the third day, the fishermen, on dropping their net, lifted what seemed like a heavy load. It was Meenakshi Amma and her son.

She told them what happened: "When the winds were raging and we were drowning, I looked towards the shrine of Our Lady and made an oath that I would live a slave to her all my life. Then, holding my baby tightly, I fell into the water and went unconscious. In a vision, I saw the Virgin enveloped in golden rays with her divine baby in her hands.

I experienced a bliss I have never known in my life. I kept gazing on her divinely alluring countenance, and we were in a state of oblivion. Now, she has brought us safely to her church. I have no words to express my gratitude!"[1]

They changed their names to Mary and Jesudas and spent the rest of their lives serving the church. In fact, the pictures of the two of them are now always included in the images of Our Lady of Ransom of Vallarpadam. Devotees call the Virgin "Vallarpadathamma" which means "Mother of Vallarpadam." The rescue of the mother and son was just the first of miracles and miracles continue to be reported at the church.

The church in Vallarpadam was made into a basilica by papal decree. Miracles continue to be reported there to this very day and pilgrims of every religion visit the shrine.

NOTES

[1] https://www.mariantimesworld.org/the-amazing-story-of-our-lady-of-vallarpadam/

Our Lady of Coromoto, Venezuela, 1651

Date – 1651
Place – Guanare, Venezuela
Witness – Cacique (Chief) of the Cospes Indians
Enduring Evidence – "The relic the Blessed Virgin left with the chief is the most authentic link we have to the apparitions themselves. The image was thoroughly analyzed during a process of restoration in 2009. Indigenous symbols found in the image, such as the style of the crowns worn by the Blessed Mother and Jesus, are authentic to the culture and time period of the Coromoto people in 17th-century Venezuela. How the image itself was created remains mysterious and is believed to be miraculous. While the picture appears to have been drawn on the paper, the paper does not seem to have absorbed any ink or other such substance. In this way, it resembles the apparition of Our Lady of Guadalupe, which likewise looks to be painted on the tilma but seems to mysteriously hover just above the cloth without actually affixing to it."[1]
Feast Day – September 8

© Public Domain

The story of the Virgin of Coromoto is a story of an apparition, an image and the evangelization of a non-Christian population - much like Guadalupe.

In 1591, the Spaniards arrived in Guanare in Venezuela. The indigenous tribe in the region, the Coromoto, had no interest in living with the Spaniards and moved to the forests in the north. The two groups co-existed separately but peacefully. Then, sixty years later, in 1651, the Chief of the Coromoto happened to be at a nearby creek with his wife when a radiant young lady holding her child appeared to them on the water. Smiling at them, she told the Chief:

'Go to where the white men are to receive water on your head so you can go to heaven.'

The Chief consented and went with his tribe to the Spaniards who introduced them to Christianity. But a year later, the Chief tired of the life in the settlement created for them and announced that he would be leaving with his tribe to the forests. Those who had become Christians planned to stay behind.

After this announcement, on September 8, the Chief and his family returned to his hut. But they were stunned a second time when the same radiant lady entered their hut asking the Chief to remain. But he was in no mood to listen. He tried to threaten her with his weapons and then grabbed her. When he took hold of her, however, she disappeared and left a tiny image of her and her Son in the Chief's hands.

Although bewildered, the Chief remained adamant. The next day he left with most of the tribe. Those who had become Christians stayed behind. During the journey to the forests, the Chief was bitten by a venomous snake. Knowing that he would soon die, the Chief asked to be baptized and this was administered. Following his baptism the others in his tribe also embraced the new faith.

The tiny image showed miraculous properties and is today enshrined in a church at the site of the second apparition:

> "The Virgin of Coromoto is a tiny relic that measures 27 millimeters high and 22 millimeters wide. The Virgin is painted seated, and

on her lap sits the Child Jesus. It seems to have been drawn with a fine pen, sketched as a portrait done in Indian ink with dots and dashes. The Virgin and Child are looking straight ahead; their heads erect with royal crowns upon them. The back of the throne which supports them has two columns joined together by an arch. The Virgin's shoulders are covered by a crimson cloak with dark purple reflections, and a white veil falls symmetrically over her hair. She wears a straw colored tunic and the Child a white one."[2]

"Nancy Jimenez, responsible for restoring the Act of Independence of Venezuela, was one of those that participated in the study and conservation treatment of the Holy Relic. She had impressive detail: "When the picture was clean and clear, we begin to see amazing details: In such a small image, perfectly blurred in one eye, [we see] the image of the Indian Coromoto trying to get at the Virgin Mary … In the Holy Relic, the Virgin appears smiling and the ink that draws it looks like it was printed yesterday."[3]

The Virgin of Coromoto was declared the national patroness of Venezuela.

NOTES

[1]https://aleteia.org/2018/09/11/has-our-lady-left-us-another-image-of-herself-besides-guadalupe/

[2]https://faithofthefathersapparitions.blogspot.com/2005/12/our-lady-of-coromoto.html

[2]https://virgencoromotopatronavenezuela.wordpress.com/2014/07/20/holy-image-of-the-virgin-of-guadalupe-in-mexico-and-the-virgin-of-coromoto-in-venezuela-are-the-only-ones-in-the-world-coming-from-heaven/

R.A. Varghese

Our Lady of the Rosary of the Rocks (las Lajas), Colombia, 1754

> *Date* – 1754
> *Place* – Las Lajas, Colombia
> *Witness* – María Mueses de Quiñones and her daughter, Rosa,
> *Enduring Evidence* – Scientifically inexplicable images of the Virgin and her Son and of two saints imprinted in the rocks
> *Feast day* – September 16

Maria Mueses de Quiñones, an Amerindian/mestizo lady from Potosi, Colombia, and her deaf-mute daughter Rosa were walking through a rocky area called Las Lajas (for its rocks). When she sat down to rest, her daughter Rosa was playing among the rocks. Then Rosa called out to her saying that there is a woman here with a boy in her arms. Maria was astounded because Rosa had never spoken before. And she could not see any woman.

A few days later, Rosa disappeared from their home. Maria guessed that she was in Las Lajas because Rosa had said before that the woman was calling her. On reaching the rocks, Maria this time saw Rosa kneeling before the lady and playing with her son. She realized it was the Virgin and the Infant Jesus. She was discreet about the encounter for fear of ridicule.

Some time later, Rosa fell ill and died. Maria took her body to Las Lajas and asked the Virgin to intercede on behalf of the child. Her prayers were answered and Rosa came back to life. This time all the villagers became aware of what was going on and headed to Las Lajas. On reaching there they saw a miraculous image of the Virgin and the Infant imprinted in the rocks. The image showed Mary giving the rosary to St. Dominic and Jesus giving the scapular to St. Francis. A shrine was rapidly built there and today there is a church built around the image which attracts pilgrimages from all across the country.

Much like the tilma of Guadalupe, the image of Las Lajas is scientifically inexplicable.

> "The image is not painted, but mysteriously imprinted in the rock. The colors are not applied on a surface layer of paint or other material but penetrate deep into the rock."
> Prof. Plinio Corrêa de Oliveira, *Our Lady of Las Lajas*.
> "Geologists from Germany bored core samples from several spots in the image. There is no paint, no dye, nor any other pigment on the surface of the rock. The colors are the colors of the rock itself and run uniformly to a depth of several feet."
> Michael O'Neill, *Guáitara Canyon, Columbia (1754): Our Lady of Las Lajas*.

The incident and the shrine is mentioned in a book written by the Franciscan Juan de Santa Gertrudis recounting his journeys in the region from 1756 to 1764.

R.A. Varghese

Our Lady of Cuapa, Nicaragua, 1980

"If You Do Not Change, You Will Hasten the Arrival of a Third World War."

Dates – May 8 - October 13, 1980; subsequent apparitions and locutions
Place – Cuapa, Nicaragua
Witness – Bernardo Martinez, adult peasant of 50, later a priest
Enduring Evidence – Luminous phenomena witnessed by onlookers. Fulfilled prophecies.
Theme – Admonitions to pray the Rosary and follow the Word of God

---

15. Another statue of Our Lady of Cuapa also carved from the tree over which the Blessed Virgin Mary appeared in 1980 in Cuapa, Nicaragua. This particular statue belongs to Sister Paula Hildalgo, a Nicaraguan nun active in several Nicaraguan orphanages and a close friend of Bernardo Martinez. This statue has been shown to the Holy Father, Pope John Paul II. A total of four statues of Our Lady of Cuapa were carved from the tree over which the Blessed Virgin Mary appeared in 1980 in Cuapa. (Taken 9/92; Photograph courtesy of Joseph Cassano.)

The information in this chapter is primarily derived from the witness himself, Fr. Bernardo Martinez, and from the book *Let Heaven and Earth Unite* by his friends Miriam and Stephen Weglian.

Cuapa is a town of 5,000 people in Nicaragua. Fr. Andres Rongier, S.J., a Jesuit missionary from Mexico, is said to have prophesied in the 1880's that Cuapa would become famous in the future as the site of apparitions of the Blessed Virgin Mary. In the Native Indian language Nahuatl, the word Cuapa means "crushing the serpent's head with a blow" - from CUA for "serpent" and PA for "on." Intriguingly, Guadalupe, if pronounced in the original Nahuatl sounds like "Cuapa" because there are no "g" or "d" sounds in this language; one interpretation of the meaning of Guadalupe in the native language, we have seen, is the one "who will crush, stamp out, abolish, and eradicate the stone serpent." It might be said here that the Cuapa visionary, Bernardo Martinez, bears several similarities to Juan Diego of Guadalupe: both were humble peasants who had consecrated their lives to working for the Church and who were privileged to witness apparitions of the Virgin in their middle age; both told the Virgin they were unworthy to perform the mission she assigned to them but to both of them she said that they had been chosen; when they did not perform the tasks she had assigned to them, they both tried to avoid her by going to a different location but she intercepted them there.

Bernardo was born on August 20, 1931. He grew up with his grandmother and studied up to the sixth grade after which he went to a vocational training school where he learnt various manual trades (he went back to high school in later life and completed it in 1989). After school, he supported himself by working on a farm.

Bernardo, who had always wanted to be a priest, was the main assistant to the pastor of the local church in Cuapa. In April 1980, Bernardo was puzzled to find that the statue of the Virgin in the chapel was lighting up on its own. This phenomenon, and the soul-searching it caused him, prepared Bernardo for the events that were soon to take place. For starting in May of that year, he was blessed to witness numerous apparitions of both the Virgin Mary and Jesus. The principal apparitions lasted from May to October 1980 but Bernardo was the recipient of several subsequent apparitions and locutions.

In 1982, Bishop Bosco M. Vivas Robelo, then auxiliary bishop and vicar general of Managua, and now Bishop of Leon, the diocese to which Fr. Martinez belongs, declared, "I, the undersigned, Auxiliary Bishop and Vicar General of the Archdiocese of Managua, authorize the publication of the narration of the apparitions of the Blessed Virgin Mary in Cuapa." On November 13, 1982, Bishop Pablo Antonio Vega M., Prelate Bishop of Juigalpa, the diocese in which the apparitions took place, released this statement, "It has been nearly three years now, since one of the peasants from the area arrived communicating a message which he said he received from Mary in a series of dreams and apparitions. ... Because of the duty and the obligation to protect the wholesome piety of the faithful and for the truth of those events, in my capacity as Bishop of the area, I find an obligation to assure the authenticity of the events in order to be able to assist in discerning the true value of the alluded to message. ... The 'report' that we present retains the accurate content and language used by the individual who received the visions." *Let Heaven and Earth Unite!* an account of the apparitions by Stephen and Miriam Weglian, received the following authorization from Bishop Robelo, Bishop of Leon on June 10, 1994: "I hereby authorize the publication of the Story of the Apparitions of the Blessed Virgin Mary in Cuapa and the Messages given to Bernardo Martinez under the title *Let Heaven and Earth Unite!* May this publication help those who read it to have an encounter with Jesus Christ in the Church through the mediation of the Mother of our Lord." The Bishops Conference of Nicaragua also approved the apparition and in fact the bishops presented Pope John Paul II with a statue of Our Lady of Cuapa on his last visit to Nicaragua.

After the principal apparitions, Bernardo was allowed to attend a minor and then a major seminary. On March 19, 1995, he was ordained a deacon and on August 20, 1995, he was ordained a priest. He continued to have encounters with the Virgin until he passed away in 2000.

The Appearances and Messages

Below are excerpts from Bernardo's account of the appearances of the Virgin.

May 8, 1990

After a sleepless night, Bernardo went fishing at a river near Cuapa. In the afternoon he gathered various fruits from surrounding trees. Around three o'clock, he started on his way back to town.

> Suddenly I saw a lightning flash. I thought and said to myself, 'It is going to rain.' But I became filled with wonder because I did not see from where the lightning had come. I stopped but I could see nothing - no signs of rain. Afterwards, I went over near a place where there are some rocks. I walked about six or seven steps. That was when I saw another lightning flash, but that was to open my vision, and she presented herself.

> I was then wondering whether this could be something bad, whether it was the same statue as in the chapel. But I saw that she blinked and that she was beautiful. She remained above the pile of rocks as if on a cloud. And there was a little tree on top of the rocks and over that tree was the cloud. The cloud was extremely white. It radiated in all directions rays of sunlight. On the cloud were the feet of a very beautiful lady. Her feet were bare. The dress was long and white with a celestial cord around the waist, and it had long sleeves. Covering her was a veil, a pale cream color, with gold embroidery along the edge. Her hands were held together over her breast. It looked like the statue of the Virgin of Fatima. I was immobile ...

> And when I removed my hands from my face I saw that she had human skin and that her eyes moved and blinked. I then said, in my thoughts because I could not move my tongue - I said, 'She is alive .. she is not a statue! She is alive!' My mind was the only thing that I could move. I felt numb, my lower jaw stiff and my tongue as if asleep; everything immobilized, as I said, only the ideas moved in my head. I was in those thoughts when she extended her arms - like the Miraculous Medal which I had never seen but which

later was shown to me. She extended her arms and from her hands emanated rays of light stronger than the sun and the rays that came from her hands touched my breast.

When she gave out her light is when I became encouraged to speak. Although somewhat stammering, I said to her, 'What is your name?' She answered me with the sweetest voice I have ever heard in any woman, not even in persons who speak softly. She answered me and said that her name is Mary. I saw the way she moved her lips. I then said, 'She is alive! She spoke! She has answered my question!' I could see that we could enter into a conversation, that I could speak with her. I asked her then, where she came from.

She told me with the same sweetness, "*I come from Heaven. I am the Mother of Jesus.*"

At hearing this, I immediately ... asked her, "What is it you want?"

She answered me, "*I want the Rosary to be prayed every day.*"

I then interrupted and said to her, "Yes, we are praying it ...."

She told me: "*I don't want it prayed only in the month of May. I want it to be prayed permanently, within the family .... including the children old enough to understand ... to be prayed at a set hour when there are no problems with the work in the home.*"

She told me that the Lord does not like prayers we make in a rush or mechanically. Because of that she recommended praying of the Rosary accompanied with the reading of biblical citations and that we put into practice the Word of God. When I heard this I thought and said, "How is this?" Because I did not know the Rosary was biblical. That is why I asked her and said, "Where are the biblical citations?" She told me to look for them in the Bible and continued saying:

"*Love each other.*
Fulfill your obligations.
Make peace. Don't ask Our Lord for peace because, if you do not make it, there will be no peace."

Afterward she told me:
"Renew the five first Saturdays. You received many graces when all of you did this."

... Then she said:
"Nicaragua has suffered much since the earthquake. She is threatened with even more suffering. She will continue to suffer if you don't you change."

And after a brief pause she said:

"Pray, pray, my son, the Rosary for all the world. Tell believers and non-believers that the world is threatened by grave dangers. I ask the Lord to appease His justice, but, if you don't change, you will hasten the arrival of a Third World War."

After she had said these words, I understood that I had to tell this to the people, and I told her, "Lady I don't want problems. I have many in the Church. Tell this to another person."

She then told me: *"No, because Our Lord has selected you to give the message."*

When she told me this, I saw that the cloud which was holding her was rising, ... and I told her, "Lady don't go because I want to go and notify Senora Consuelo because she told me that she wanted to see you."

She said to me, *"No. Not everyone can see me. She will see me when I take her to Heaven, but she should pray the Rosary as I ask."*

And after telling me this the cloud continued to rise. She raised her arms to Heaven as in the statue of the Assumption, which I have seen so many times in the Cathedral at Juigalpa. She again looked upward toward Heaven, and the cloud that held her slowly elevated her as if she was in a ray of light. When she reached a certain height she disappeared.

May 16, 1980

I saw her in the same way as I had seen her on the 8th of May, with her hands together, and then she extended them. And on extending her hands, the rays of light came toward me. I remained watching her. I remained silent, but I said to myself, "It is she! .." I though she had come to complain about all that she had told me to say. I felt guilty for not having spoken as she had asked, and at the same time, in my mind, I said, "I don't go to the place where she appeared because she appears there, and now, she appears to me here. I will be a fine state, she will be following me wherever I am."

It was with this in mind, when she told me with her voice soft, but with a tone as of in reprehension, *"Why have you not told what I sent you to tell?"*

I then answered her, "Lady, it is that I am afraid. I am afraid of being the ridicule of the people, afraid that they will laugh at me, that they will not believe me. Those who will not believe this will laugh at me. They will say that I am crazy."

She then said to me, *"Do not be afraid. I am going to help you, and go tell the priest."* Saying this, there was another flash of lightning and she disappeared.

June 8, 1980

During the night, in dreams she presented herself. It was the same as during the day - I was at the same place where I saw her the first time. I prayed the Rosary. Upon finishing the Rosary, I again saw the two lightning flashes and she appeared. In my dream, she gave me the same message as she had done the first time. ....

Raising her right hand, she pointed toward [a large open] space and said, *"Look at the sky."*

I looked at that direction. A tree that is in front, between the two palms, did not impede my ability to see because it has few branches and it is low. She presented something like a movie in that space I mentioned. I saw a large group of people who were dressed in white and were walking toward where the sun rises. They were bathed in light and very happy; they sang. I could hear them, but I could not understand the words. It was a celestial festival. It was such happiness ... such joy ... which I had never ever seen. Not even in a procession had I seen that. Their bodies radiated light. I felt as if I were transported. Nor can I myself explain it ... in the midst of my admiration I heard her tell me:

"Look. These are the very first communities when Christianity began. They are the first catechumens, many of whom were martyrs. Do you people want to be martyrs? Would you yourself like to be a martyr?"

In that instance I did not know exactly what the meaning of being a martyr was - I now know, because I have been asking, that it is he who professes Jesus Christ openly in public, he who is a witness to Him including the giving of his life - but, I answered, "Yes."

After that I saw another group, also dressed in white with some luminous rosaries in their hands. The beads were extremely white and they gave off lights of different colors. One of them carried a very large open book. He would read, and after listening they silently meditated. They appeared to be as if in prayer. After this period of prayer in silence, they then prayed the Our Father and ten Hail Marys. I prayed with them. When the Rosary was finished, Our Lady said to me:

"These are the first ones to whom I gave the Rosary. That is the way I want all of you to pray the Rosary."

I answered the Lady that, yes, we would. (Some persons have told me that this possibly has to do with the Dominicans.)

Afterward I saw a third group, all of them dressed in brown robes. But these I recognized as being similar to the Franciscans. Always the same, with rosaries and praying. As they were passing after having prayed, Our Lady again told me:

"These received the Rosary from the hands of the first ones."

After this, a fourth group was arriving. It was a huge procession. This group was dressed as we dress. It was such a big group that it would be impossible to count them. In the earlier ones I saw many men and women; but now, it was like an army in size, and they carried rosaries in their hands. They were dressed normally, in all colors. I was very happy to see them. ... I felt at once that I could enter into that scene because they were dressed the same as I was. But ... I looked at my hands and saw them black. They, in turn, as the previous ones, radiated light. Their bodies were beautiful. I then said, "Lady, I am going with these because they are dressed as I am."

She told me, "*No. You are still lacking. You have to tell the people what you have seen and heard.*" And she added:

"*I have shown you the Glory of Our Lord, and you people will acquire this if you are obedient to Our Lord, to the Lord's Word; if you persevere in praying the Holy Rosary and put into practice the Lord's Word.*"

After having said this to me the Vision of the Glory of God disappeared, and the cloud that was sustaining her elevated her toward Heaven. She looked like, as I said, the statue of the Assumption. And in that way, with the cloud lifting her, she disappeared.

September 8, 1980

I saw her as a child. Beautiful! But little! She was dressed in a pale cream colored tunic. She did not have a veil, nor a crown, nor a mantle. No adornment, nor embroidery. The dress was long, with long sleeves, and it was girdled with a pink cord. Her hair fell to her shoulders and it was brown in color. The eyes, also, although much lighter, almost the color of honey. All of her radiated light. She looked like the Lady, but she was a child.

I was looking at her amazed without saying a word, and then I heard her voice as that of a child ... a child of seven ... eight ... years. In an extremely sweet voice she gave me a message - totally identical. ... I then told her, "Let yourself be seen so that all the

world will believe. These people who are here want to meet you."
.... But after listening to me she said:

"No. It is enough for you to give them the message because for the one who is going to believe that will be enough, and the one who is not going to believe though he should see me is not going to believe."

... I no longer insisted that she allow herself to be seen, but rather I talked to her about the church that the people wanted to build in her honor. She answered me saying:

"No, the Lord does not want material churches. He wants living temples which are yourselves. Restore the sacred temple of the Lord. In you is the gratification for the Lord."

She continued, saying:
"Love each other. Love one another.
Forgive each other.
Make peace. Don't just ask for it. Make peace."

[When asked what to do with the money donated by people for a church] She told me to donate them for the construction of the chapel in Cuapa, and added:

"From this day on do not accept even one cent for anything."

... I did not know whether or not to continue in the catechumenate. I did it to see what she would advise me. She told me:

"No. Don't leave. Always continue firmly in the catechumenate. Little by little you will comprehend all that the catechumenate signifies. As a community group, meditate on the Beatitudes, away from all the noise."

Later she added:

"I am not going to return on the 8th of October, but on the 13th."

When we finished the Rosary, we sang "Holy Queen of Heaven." We were repeating the part that says, "Shining Day Star, grant me grace to be able to sing the Ave Maria," when all of a sudden a big luminous circle formed over the ground. Everyone, without a single exception, saw it. It was like a single ray that fell and marked this luminous circle on the ground. The light came from above. The light that came was like a spotlight that, on touching the ground, was scattered. Seeing how this light fell over the heads of everyone who was there, I again looked upward and saw that a circle had also formed in the sky, as when we say, "There's a ring around the moon.," or "There's a ring around the sun." This circle gave off lights in different colors, without coming from the sun. It was not at that spot as the sun was already setting. ...

All of a sudden a lightning flash, the same as the other times; then, a second one. I lowered my eyes and I saw the Lady. This time the cloud was over the flowers we had brought and upon the cloud the Lady's feet. Beautiful! She extended her hands and rays of light reached all of us.

I, at seeing the Lady there with her arms extended, said to the people, "Look at her! There she is!"

No one answered anything. I then told the Lady to let herself be seen, that all the people present wanted to see her. She said, "*No. Not everyone can see me.*" ... I again insisted to the Lady that she allow herself to be seen, and she again told me, "No." ... I then told the Lady, "Lady, let them see you so that they will believe! Because many don't believe. They tell me that it is the devil that appears to me, and that the Virgin is dead and turned to dust like any mortal. Let them see you, Our Lady!"

She did not answer anything. She raised her hands to her breast in a similar position to the statue of Our Lady of Sorrows - the statue that is carried in procession during Holy Week - and the same as that statue, her face turned pale, her mantle changed to a gray color, her face became sad, and she cried. I cried too. I trembled to see her like that. I said to her, "Lady, forgive me for what I have said to you! I'm to blame. You are angry with me. Forgive me! Forgive me!"

She then answered me saying: "*I am not angry nor will I get angry.*"

I asked her, "And why are you crying?"

She told me:

"*It saddens me to see the hardness of those persons' hearts. But you will have to pray for them so that they will change.*"

I could not speak. I continued to cry. I felt that my heart was being crushed. I felt very sad as if I were going to die from the pain right there. My only relief was through crying. I no longer continued insisting that she let herself be seen. I felt that I was to blame for having said this to her. I could not endure seeing her cry. As I continued to cry, she gave me a message:
"*Pray the rosary; meditate on the mysteries.*
Listen to the Word of God spoken in them.
Love one another. Love each other.
Forgive each other.
Make peace. Don't ask for peace without making peace because if you don't make it, it does no good to ask for it.
Fulfill your obligations.
Put into practice the Word of God.
Seek ways to please God.
Serve your neighbor, as that way you will please Him."

When she had finished giving her message, I remembered the requests from the people of Cuapa. I said to her, "Lady I have many requests, but I have forgotten them. There are a great many. You, Lady, know them all."

Then she said to me:
"*They ask of me things that are unimportant.*
Ask for faith in order to have the strength so that each can carry his own cross.

The sufferings of this world cannot be removed. Suffering is the cross that all of you have to carry.
That is the way life is. There are problems with the husband, with the wife, with the children, with the brothers. Talk, converse so that problems will be resolved in peace. Do not turn to violence. Pray for faith in order that you will have patience."

In this manner she has given me to understand that, if with faith we ask to be free from a suffering, we will be free if that suffering is not the cross we are to carry; but when the suffering is that person's cross, then it will remain as a weight of glory. That is why she tells us to ask for faith in order to receive fortitude and patience.

Afterward she told me, *"You will no longer see me in this place."*

I thought that I would definitely never see her again and I began to shout:

"Don't leave us, my Mother!

I was speaking for those who were not speaking. She then said to me: *"Do not be grieved. I am with all of you even though you do not see me. I am the Mother of all of you, sinners.*
Love one another. Forgive each other. Make peace, because if you don't make it there will be no peace. Do not turn to violence. Never turn to violence.

Nicaragua has suffered a great deal since the earthquake and will continue to suffer if all of you don't change. If you don't change you will hasten the coming of the third world war.

Pray, pray, my son, for all the world. Grave dangers threaten the world.

A mother never forgets her children. And I have not forgotten what you suffer. I am the Mother of all of you, sinners. Invoke me with these words: 'Holy Virgin, you are my Mother, the Mother to all of us, sinners."

And after having said this three times, she was elevated as if the cloud were pushing her. When she was in the direction of the branches of the cedar, she disappeared.

Accounts of subsequent appearances and locutions of the Virgin and visions and locutions of Jesus to Bernardo are narrated in *Let Heaven and Earth Unite!* by Stephen and Miriam Weglian. The book also includes an interview with the visionary and descriptions of healings and fulfilled prophecies.

In an apparition on March 8, 1987, she spoke of the coming "*destruction of atheistic communism in Russia and the whole world.*" She also said, "*I want you to propagate the devotion to the shoulder wounds of my Son*" and "*If you change and convert, soon, very soon, you will see an end to your sorrows.*" Then she added, "*Repeat with me this prayer (and she said it slowly): Saint Mary of Victory. Favorite Daughter of God the Father, give me your faith; Mother of God the Son, give me your hope; Sacred Spouse of God the Holy Spirit, give me your charity and cover us with your mantle.*"

R.A. Varghese

Our Lady of the Rosary of San Nicolas, Argentina, 1983-1990

Dates – Started September 25, 1983. Ended February 11, 1990.
Witness – Gladys de Motta
Enduring Evidence – Healing, Conversion
Theme – Admonition, Prophecy, the Virgin's role as Ark of the Covenant
Description of the Virgin – The Virgin's figure glowed with light. She had a blue gown and a veil and held the baby Jesus in her arms along with a large rosary. She bore a close resemblance to a statue of Our Lady of the Rosary that had been left to languish in the belfry of a nearby cathedral.

MARIA DEL ROSARIO DE SAN NICOLAS
Imagen bendecida por León XIII (1884)

The material below was provided courtesy of Patrizia de Ferrari Coronado of Argentina:

Since the creation of the Parish of San Nicolas de los Arroyos in the vicinity of Buenos Aires, Argentina, there has been a deep devotion to Our Lady of the Rosary. On September 25, 1983, San Nicolas played host to a phenomenon that aroused nationwide and even international attention: Gladys de Motta, an ordinary housewife, a mother and grandmother who had no formal education (she had studied only up to the fourth grade) and no knowledge of either the Bible or theology, announced that she had seen the Holy Virgin on that day. The phenomenon lasted from the first apparition which was silent to almost daily apparitions with messages (most of them from the Virgin and sixty eight from her Son) until February 11, 1990.

The bishop of the diocese, Monsignor Domingo Salvador Castagna, instituted an investigation of the phenomenon which concluded that the visionary was of sound mental health and that her messages were doctrinally sound. The bishop approved the devotions associated with the apparition and authorized the construction of the Sanctuary requested by the Virgin. From March 25, 1986 the bishop accompanied the procession held on the 25th of each month. At one such procession, up to one hundred thousand people are present. On July 25, 1990, the bishop said, "Undoubtedly this event of grace will continue to grow; it has proved its authenticity by its spiritual fruits." An image with a likeness to the Virgin as she appeared to Gladys is kept at the Cathedral. San Nicolas is the source of many conversions, healings, vocations, and many groups of prayer in the country. Numerous healings, including the cure of a boy with a brain tumor, have been reported and documented.

On May 22, 2016, the then-Bishop of San Nicolas, Bishop Hector Cardelli, who had been investigating the content of the apparitions through 1990, announced final Church approval of the authenticity of the encounter. Bishop Cardelli said:

> "(I)n my twelfth year of pastoring San Nicolas and, having followed with faith and responsibility the Marian events that I have known about since the very beginning, I have reached the decision to recognize them for my diocese. I recognize the

supernatural nature of the happy events with which God through his beloved daughter, Jesus through his Most Holy Mother, the Holy Spirit through his beloved spouse, has desired to lovingly manifest himself in our diocese."

The Bishop said that two principles were deployed in making the judgement: "Positive and negative, and in both cases there were not, nor are there errors." Three questions had to be addressed: "Were the events of natural origin? Could it be a work of the Enemy? Are they of supernatural origin? The answers to these questions gave me the certainty that the fruits are real and positive and go beyond mere human action."

A chronology of the phenomenon is given below.

1983

September 25: First appearance of the Virgin to Gladys Quiroga de Motta
On October 7, 1983, Gladys asked the Virgin what she wanted. Gladys: "I saw her and I asked her what she wanted of me. Then her image faded away and a chapel appeared. I understood that she wanted to be among us."
October 12: Gladys discusses her experiences with a priest
October 13: The Holy Virgin talks to her for the first time
November 17: Gladys sprinkles holy water on the apparition.
November 19: Gladys informed of mission: "You will become a bridge of union. Proclaim my words."
November 24: A shaft of light in the darkness shows Gladys where the Church should be built - on a wasteland called Campito on the banks of the Parana river (the ray of light is seen by one other witness, a nine year old girl).
November 27: Gladys recognizes the apparition when she sees an image of Our Lady of the Rosary relegated to the belfry of the diocesan Cathedral because of damage. The Virgin referred to Exodus 25:8 in describing the church to be built. This passage says, "They shall make a sanctuary for me, that I may dwell in their midst." The significance of this passage is that it contains the instructions given by God to the Israelites for building the Ark of the Covenant by means of which Yahweh would be present to them. The New Testament and the early Church had consistently understood Mary to be the New Ark of the Covenant who was the dwelling place of

the Holy Spirit and the Bearer of the Son. At San Nicolas, the Virgin was restating this ancient teaching.

1984

November: Gladys is welcomed by the new Bishop of San Nicolás, Domingo Salvador Castagna. The bishop has an audience with Pope John Paul II at which he discusses the phenomenon.

1985

April: A Commission of Inquiry is named

1986

February 25: First pilgrimage and celebration of the Holy Mass in El Campito, the location for the new Sanctuary.
May 25: Spreading of a Medal introduced by the Virgin in the apparitions
September 25: Placing of the foundation stone of the Sanctuary.

1987

April 11: Bishop Castagna has an audience with Pope John Paul II in Rosario, the main city in his diocese. The Bishop promises the Pope that he will direct a study of San Nicolas.
October 13 : The building of the Sanctuary begins.

1989

March 19: Moving of the Image from the Cathedral and blessing and opening of the Sanctuary.
November: Bishop Castagna has another audience with the Pope.

1990

February 11: The end of the catechesis of Our Lady of San Nicolas.
August 25: Bishop Castagna consecrates the Sanctuary and the pilgrims to God through the Immaculate Heart of Mary.

The Bishop of the Diocese announces final Church approval of the apparitions.

Over 1,800 messages were received over the course of the apparitions. Some distinctive features of this apparition and its messages: the Virgin often included specific scriptural references in her messages; the visionary Gladys "saw" the apparition of the Virgin when she closed her eyes after receiving a supernatural signal (unlike most other apparitions where the visionaries saw the Virgin physically in front of them and were oblivious to their external surroundings); Gladys could hardly read or write before the phenomenon began but she was able to document the many messages she received with great clarity and precision; Gladys was the recipient of the stigmata (the wounds of Christ) on her wrists (with stigmata also on her feet, side and one shoulder) and has been a "victim soul" uniting her suffering to that of the Lord. In some of the apparitions, the Virgin confirms that she is the New Ark of the Covenant as well as the Woman Clothed with the Sun of Revelation 12. In his messages, the Lord confirms that his Mother is the new Ark of the Covenant and states that acceptance of the Virgin and her messages is necessary for the world.

Messages from the Virgin

(Initial commentary on the messages provided courtesy of Patrizia de Ferrari Coronado; the text of the messages are taken from *Messages of Our Lady at San Nicolas* produced by Faith Publishing company)

Here is a synthesis of the 1800+ messages that were given almost daily for a period of nearly seven years:

Our Lady prepares Gladys for her mission. She teaches her a pedagogy of prayer and Christian Life and asks that the Sanctuary be a place of ecclesial gathering. She promotes a prophetic catechism for the people of today, with their anguish and sufferings, in order to give them back hope supported in Jesus Christ, the Savior. The words of Jesus (78 messages) are associated with the words of Mary (1816 messages) to create a dynamic of conversion and spiritual force. The Virgin invites everyone to restore their life with God inside the Church with the essential means of faith and the sacraments, the love and sacrifice they promote and the development of the Christian virtues. She invites her children to go back to all that the Church had received from God. She invites us to consecration, the seeds of which have been received from God in Baptism but which are blocked by materialism and secularism, because this "divinization" must take over all of our being and life. This is emphasized specially in her last messages such as the invitation she makes on February 2, 1990, where she explains the real nature of the consecration:

> Gladys, I want my consecrated children to give the Mother whatever she asks: To dedicate at least one hour a day to prayer. To go to communion every day. To be humble. To be at the total service of Mary. To thank God for every day of consecration lived. To be united to the Son's Love. To ask the grace of living under the Light of the Holy Spirit. The consecration must be made on a special day of the Mother. This is the consecration that I ask at my Sanctuary.

Five messages of special significance are cited here.

December 12, 1983

> "Father deliver us from all evil. With Your holy wisdom, Lord, save us from all sin. In the name of all those who love You, Lord, lead us on the right road. Amen. Read: Proverbs 2:1-11. He who says this prayer during nine consecutive days, together with a Rosary, will receive a very special grace from me."

December 2, 1984

> "You must have a medal cast with my image of the advocation of Mary of the Rosary of San Nicolas, and on the other side the Blessed Trinity with seven stars."

September 25, 1986:

> "My daughter, I will tell you the meaning of the seven stars. They are seven graces that my Son Jesus will grant to those who wear it on their breast. Praise be to the Lord."

December 15, 1986

"My daughter, because of a few good people, many bad people will be saved. I mean that with prayer, with the continual prayer of true Christians, many will reach salvation. Here, I explain the reason for my presence and the remaining of my messages, that are in the final instance, the Lord's word. There must be conversion for the salvation of the soul to be possible."

February 6, 1987

"My daughter, in this time, I am the Ark, for all your brethren! I am the Ark of peace, the Ark of salvation, the Ark where my children must enter, if they wish to live in the Kingdom of God. There is no obstacle for this Mother, and there will be none for the children."

Fourth decade – Europe

Our Lady of Czestochowa, Poland, 1382, 1920

Date – 1382, 1920
Place – Częstochowa, Poland
Enduring Evidence – Image of the Black Madonna. Miraculous interventions in the history of Poland

The Queen of Poland is the Black Madonna, the Virgin depicted in the famous portrait of Czestochowa. This great icon has preserved the faith of the Polish people and is believed to be responsible for miraculous interventions in the history of Poland. It is an image of the Virgin reputedly painted by St. Luke and first displayed in Constantinople.

The traditional accounts of the origin of the Black Madonna were usefully outlined by Professor Anna Hamlin at the 2017 International Academic Forum:

> It is believed that the figure of Matka Boska Częstochowska was painted by Luke the Evangelist on a table top which was built by Jesus himself. It was discovered in the Holy Land by St Helen, the mother of Emperor Constantine and a collector of Christian relics. The piece was enshrined in Constantinople, where it remained for the next 500 years (Maniura, 2004, p. 67). The painting was then given as a wedding present from the Byzantine emperor to a Greek princess marrying a Ruthenian nobleman in 803 (Maniura, 2004, p. 98) before it eventually arrived in Poland in 1382. The Polish historian Jan Dlugosz wrote in his fifteenth-century work *Liber Beneficiorum* that the work of art was brought to the Pauline monastery at Częstochowa by Prince Wladyslaw Jagiello from a castle at Belz, Russia. Prince Jagiello invited monks from Hungary into Poland to safeguard the holy picture. Four years later, in 1386, at the monastery of Jasna Góra in the small town of Częstochowa, these monks established a shrine for the sacred painting. When the Hussites (the Czech forerunners of the Protestant reformation) attacked Jasna Góra in 1430, they damaged the work with arrows and by slashing the Virgin's face with a sword. The legend continues with the monks rescuing the painting from a bed of mud, where a miraculous fountain appeared, which then they used to carefully clean the painting. It was said to have been repainted in Krakow, but the arrow marks and the gash from the sword remained and are clearly visible to this day.

With such a rich history the Black Madonna of Częstochowa is also famous for the miraculous liberation that occurred when Swedish troops were set to invade the city in 1655. With the Swedish army pressing around them a group of Polish soldiers prayed desperately at the feet of their revered icon for deliverance from the approaching threat. Miraculously, despite their overwhelming strength, the invading army retreated. In 1656, a year after the failed invasion, King Kazimierz of Poland declared *Our Lady of Częstochowa* to be "Queen of Poland" and made the city the spiritual capital of the nation. Thus, she became a symbol of protection and created a specific national identity that impacted on the entire population of Poland. In 1717, Pope Clement XI officially recognized the miraculous nature of the image (Maniura, 2004, p. 123).

The Virgin helped Poland again in 1920, when the Soviet Red Army massed for an attack on Warsaw at the banks of the Wisla River. In this case, the entire nation prayed to *Our Lady of Częstochowa* and, on September 15, on the Feast of Our Lady of Sorrows, the Virgin is said to have appeared in the clouds above Warsaw. The Russians were soon defeated in a series of relentless battles that later became referred to as the "Miracle at the Wisla River". In 1925 Pope Pius XI designated May 3 a feast day in honour of the Black Madonna of Częstochowa.

During the Nazi occupation of Poland (1939–1945) Hitler prohibited pilgrimages to Jasna Góra, but many Poles continued to make the journey in secret. On September 8, 1946, a year after the liberation of Poland, huge crowds of people gathered at Częstochowa and expressed gratitude to the Virgin Mary. Because of its strongly held devotions and the high number of followers during the communist era in Poland, Jasna Góra, the home of the Black Madonna, became known as the centre of anti-government resistance (Maniura, 2004, p. 138).[1]

NOTES

[1]https://think.iafor.org/the-power-of-an-image-the-black-madonna-of-czestochowa/

R.A. Varghese

Our Lady of Šiluva, Lithuania, 1608

Date – 1608
Place – Šiluva, Lithuania
Witnesses – Shepherd children and villagers

Image source –
https://en.wikipedia.org/wiki/Our_Lady_of_%C5%A0iluva#/media/
File:Siluvos_baznycia2._2007-04-21.jpg

Like many of the other notable encounters, the appearances of the Blessed
Virgin in Šiluva, Lithuania, falls into its own unique category. Lithuania
turned to Christianity in 1251. In 1457, a diplomat from the country
built a church in Šiluva and installed a Madonna and Child painting
he brought there from Rome. During the Protestant Reformation, the
governor of the region and other local leaders became Calvinists and took

over the churches. The Catholic pastor in the village put the image and various religious items and documents in a box and buried it near a rock. Within eighty years later all traces of the Catholic faith had disappeared.

Then, one summer day in 1608, some village children were tending sheep outside the village when they heard the sound of someone crying. It turned out to be a lady with a child who was weeping profusely. She had brown hair and she and her child seemed enveloped in light. They reported the vision to the villagers but no one believed them. The Calvinist pastor rebuked them saying they were victims of a diabolic illusion.

But the children returned to the site along with the villagers. The pastor too joined them so as to stamp out the superstition. Suddenly all present too saw the weeping lady. The pastor asked her why she was crying. In response, she said, "There was a time when my beloved Son was worshipped by my people on this very spot. But now they have given this sacred soil over to the plowman and the tiller and to the animals for grazing." And then she disappeared. With this event many of the villagers returned to the faith of their fathers.

Upon hearing of all that happened, a 100 year old blind man told the villagers about the burial of the church treasures. They were, in fact, buried in the vicinity of the appearance and he had himself helped the priest bury the church treasures. Hearing this, the villagers took him to the site of the appearance. At that moment, he regained his sight and was able to point them to the location of the buried treasure which was then retrieved.

This single event led to a revival of faith in the entire nation.

Our Lady of the Miraculous Medal, France, 1830

"Those Who Wear It Will Receive Great Graces"

Dates – July 18 and November 27, 1830 then three further apparitions in December 1830, March, 1831 and September, 1831.

Place – 12, Rue de Bac, Paris

Witness – Catherine Laboure, 24

Theme – Prophecy, Miraculous Image that is an instrument of grace for all recipients.

Enduring Evidence – the Miraculous Medal, prophecies that were fulfilled, incorrupt body of St. Catherine Laboure

Description of the Virgin – "The Virgin was standing. She was of medium height, and clothed all in white. Her dress was of the whiteness of the dawn, made in the style called "*a la Vierge*," that is, high neck and plain sleeves. A white veil covered her head and fell on either side of her feet. Under the veil her hair, in coils was bound with a fillet ornamented with lace, about three centimeters in height or of two fingers' breadth, without pleats, and resting lightly on the hair. Her face was sufficiently exposed, indeed exposed very well, and so beautiful that it seems to me impossible to express her ravishing beauty."

Feast Day – November 27

The apparition of Our Lady of the Miraculous Medal at the Rue du Bac in Paris was the first of the great modern apparitions of the Virgin. Paris had become the greatest enemy of Christianity in Europe and the Virgin chose to begin her counter-attack in that very city. It was one of the only Marian apparitions in which the visionary's identity was never disclosed to the public until after her death.

Catherine was the daughter of a farmer in a tiny village near Dijon. Her mother died when she was nine and in her grief she embraced a statue of the Virgin and said, "Now, dear Blessed Mother, you will be my mother." At the age of eighteen, she had two dreams of an old priest from whom she fled when he beckoned to her. She felt called to join a religious order but was forbidden to do so by her father. She was sent to work in Paris after which she attended a finishing school. She was miserable in both places but while she was at the latter she happened to go to the visitor's parlor of a hospital and saw there a portrait of the old priest. He was none other than St. Vincent de Paul, the founder of the Sisters of Charity, and Catherine was convinced that she was called to join this order.

By the time she was twenty three, her sister-in-law managed to persuade her father to allow her to become a Sister of Charity. Despite her lack of a sound education, she was admitted into the order in January 1830 and in April was sent to the novitiate of the order at 140 rue du Bac in Paris. From the time she came to the novitiate, Catherine received various visions, of St. Vincent de Paul, of Jesus present in the Eucharist. The climax of these visions came with the apparitions of the Virgin on July 18 and November 27 1830. Here is Catherine's own account of the experience:

> "And then came the feast of St. Vincent. On the eve, Mother Martha gave us an instruction on devotion to the Saints, and in particular the Blessed Virgin. For so long a time I had desired to see her. I went to sleep thinking that St. Vincent might obtain this grace for me. About half past eleven, I heard myself called by my name. I looked in the direction of the voice and I drew the curtain. I saw a child of four or five years old dressed in white who said to me, "Come to the chapel; the Blessed Virgin is waiting for you". Immediately the thought came to me: "But I shall be heard". The child replied: "Be calm, it is half past eleven, everyone is asleep; come, I am waiting for you". I hurriedly dressed and went to the side of the child. I followed him wherever he went. The lights were lit everywhere. When we reached the Chapel, the door opened as soon as the child touched it with the tip of his finger. The candles were burning as at midnight Mass. However I did not see the Blessed Virgin. The child led me to the sanctuary and I knelt down there. Towards midnight, the child said, " Here is the Blessed Virgin!". I heard a noise like the rustle of a silk

dress... a very beautiful lady sat down in Father Director's chair. The child repeated in a strong voice,"Here is the Blessed Virgin". Then I flung myself at her feet on the steps of the altar, and put my hands on her knees. I do not know how long I remained there; it seemed but a moment, but the sweetest of my life. The holy Virgin told me how I should act towards my director, and confided several things to me." These messages concerned future events and are quoted below under the Messages section. After she had given the messages, "The Virgin disappeared like a light that is extinguished." Catherine believed that the child was her guardian angel.

In this first apparition, Catherine was told that God wished to give her a mission but she was not informed about the nature of this mission. It was on November 27th of the same year that the Virgin told her what the mission was to be. Again, Catherine's own words will serve best in telling her story:

"It was a Saturday before the first Sunday of Advent, at half past five in the evening. In the silence, just after the point of meditation had been read [in the chapel], I seemed to hear a noise at the side of the tribune. When I looked in that direction, I saw the Blessed Virgin. She was standing, dressed in a white robe of silk, like the dawn, her feet resting on a globe, only half of which I could see. There was also a serpent green in color with yellow spots. In her hands, held at the level of her breast, she held a smaller globe, her eyes raised towards heaven ... her face was beautiful, I could not describe it... Then suddenly, I saw rings on her fingers, covered with jewels, some large and some small, from which came beautiful rays ... At this moment, when I was contemplating the Virgin, she lowered her eyes and looked at me, and an interior voice spoke to me: "This globe that you see represents the entire world, particularly France ... and each person in particular". I cannot explain here what I felt and what I saw, the beauty and the light of the rays was so magnificent!. The voice spoke to me again: "This is a symbol of the graces which I shed on those who ask me". At this moment, where I was or was not I do not know, an oval shape formed around the Blessed Virgin, and on it were written these words in letters of gold: 'O MARY CONCEIVED WITHOUT SIN, PRAY FOR US WHO HAVE RECOURSE TO THEE'. Then a voice was heard to say: 'Have a medal struck after this model. Those who wear it will receive great graces; abundant graces will be given to those who have confidence'. Some of the precious stones gave forth no ray of light. 'Those jewels which are in shadow represent the graces which people forget to ask me for'. Suddenly the oval seemed to turn. I saw the reverse of the medal: the letter M surmounted by a cross, and below it, two hearts, one crowned with a crown of thorns, and the other pierced by a sword. I seemed to hear a voice which said to me:'The M and the two hearts say enough'." After this the Virgin disappeared "like a candle blown out."

In May of 1831, with the permission of Catherine's spiritual director, Fr. Aladel, and the director general of the Sisters of Charity, the medal prescribed in the apparition was produced by a Monsier Vachette. The Sisters of Charity began distribution of the medal and from the very beginning many of those who wore it around their necks reported conversions, cures and other miracles. It became known as the Miraculous Medal. Fifty thousand were given out in 1832 and 1833 and millions more every year after that so that today well over a billion of these medals have been distributed around the world.

The official inquiry into the apparition began in 1836 but Catherine declined to testify during the investigation. The appearance was approved as authentic by Archbishop de Quelen of Paris. Catherine lived on for another forty six years during which time she mainly did menial tasks in one of the Sisters' hospices. Her identity as the visionary was kept a secret. Six months before her death in 1876, she was distressed that the Virgin's request for the construction of a statue of herself as the "Virgin of the Globe" had yet to be executed. Neither of her spiritual directors had implemented this request and one of them had died and the other had been transferred. Catherine approached the Superior General of the Order with the request but was refused. She then went to her own Superior and revealed her identity as the visionary of the Miraculous Medal and asked for her help in the construction of the statue. The model for the statue was finished just before she died. Catherine's body did not decay after her death and is now displayed beneath the altar built on the spot where the Virgin appeared to her. She was canonized in 1947.

Messages

July 18, 1830
"My child, the good God wishes to charge you with a mission. You will have much to suffer, but you will rise above these sufferings by reflecting that what you do is for the glory of God. You will know what the good God wants. You will be tormented until you have told him who is in charge with directing you. You will be contradicted, but do not fear, you will have grace. Tell with confidence all that passes within you. Tell it with simplicity. Have confidence. Do not be afraid.

"The times are very evil. Sorrows will befall France; the throne will be overturned. The whole world will be plunged into every kind of misery.

"But come now to the foot of this altar; there, graces will be poured on all those who ask for them with confidence and fervor. They will be poured out on the great and the humble. Grave troubles are coming. There will be great danger, for this, the [novitiate] and other communities. At one moment when the danger is acute, everyone will believe all to be lost; you will recall my visit and [the novitiate] will have the protection of God. But it will not be the same for other communities."

['With tears in her eyes, the Virgin then said,'] "Among the clergy of Paris there will be victims - Monseigneur the Archbishop will die, my child, the cross will be treated with contempt, they will hurl it to the ground and trample it. Blood will flow. The streets will run with blood. Monseigneur the Archbishop will be stripped of his garments." Some of these events were to take place quite soon and the others "in about forty years."

"My eyes will be ever upon you. I shall grant you graces. Special graces will be given to all who ask them, but people must pray."

These prophecies were fulfilled quite rapidly: "the throne" of King Charles X was "overturned" in the latter part of July 1830, riots broke out all over Paris and churches were desecrated, the archbishop was beaten and stripped of his clothes. Some of the buildings housing religious communities were burned down but though angry crowds gathered outside the novitiate of the Sisters of Charity at the rue du Bac, it was unharmed, as promised by the Virgin. By 1870, forty years after the first apparition, all the prophecies given at the time were fulfilled. Two subsequent archbishops of Paris were murdered during this period.

November 27, 1830
"Have a medal struck after this model. Those who wear it will receive great graces; abundant graces will be given to those who have confidence."

(The other messages of November 27 have already been cited in the narrative.)

Our Lady of Zion, Italy, 1842

Date – January 20, 1842.
Place – Church of Sant' Andrea delle Fratte, Rome.
Witness – Marie-Alphonse Ratisbonne
Enduring Evidence – The congregations started by Alphonse and his brother continue to bear fruit. The site of the apparition is a pilgrimage center visited by popes and is now a basilica.

Image source –
https://en.wikipedia.org/wiki/Marie-Alphonse_Ratisbonne#/media/
File:Ratisbonne's_tomb.jpg

Alphonse Ratisbonne belonged to a prominent Jewish banking family in France. His older brother Theodor shocked the whole family when he converted to Catholicism. Alphonse and his family cut off all relations with Theodor after his conversion. Alphonse himself became vehemently anti-Catholic despising it for its superstitions. In 1842, he was engaged to be married and also to take a position in the family's banking business. Just before entering this new chapter, he took a trip to Rome and other parts of Italy.

In Rome he ran into a Protestant friend of his from France. The friend introduced him to his brother, a baron, who had become a Catholic. Alphonse did not hold back on his hostility to Catholicism. They then got into a discussion on religious matters. Alphonse's sarcasm and blasphemous statements tried the baron's patience. But he finally proposed a challenge. He asked if Alphonse would dare to wear a miraculous medal (from the apparition to Catherine Laboure) and recite the ancient Memorare prayer ("Remember O most gracious Virgin Mary"). Alphonse scornfully agreed to take up the challenge. On January 20, he was to attend the funeral of a friend of the baron's, another member of the French aristocracy, at the Church of Sant' Andrea delle Fratte.

While the baron went about making arrangements, Alphonse was waiting in the church. Then IT happened. In Alphonse' words: "I was scarcely in the church when a total confusion came over me. When I looked up, it seemed to me that the entire church had been swallowed up in shadow, except one chapel. It was as though all the light was concentrated in that single place. I looked over towards this chapel whence so much light shone, and above the altar was a living figure, tall, majestic, beautiful and full of mercy. It was the most holy Virgin Mary, resembling her figure on the Miraculous Medal. At this sight I fell on my knees right where I stood. Unable to look up because of the blinding light, I fixed my glance on her hands, and in them I could read the expression of mercy and pardon. In the presence of the Most Blessed Virgin, even though she did not speak a word to me, I understood the frightful situation I was in, my sins and the beauty of the Catholic Faith."[1]

Expanding further, he noted, "It is well known that I never opened a religious book and had never read a page of the Bible, and that the dogma of Original Sin, which it is either denied or forgotten by modern Jews, had never for a single moment occupied my thoughts—indeed, I doubt I had ever heard its name. How did I arrive at a knowledge of it? I know not. All I know is that when I entered that church I was profoundly ignorant of everything, and that when I came out I saw everything clearly and distinctly."[2]

When the baron returned, he was shocked to find Alphonse kneeling in prayer. In tears, Alphonse asked the baron to take him to a priest to be baptized immediately. After his baptism, where he added the name Marie to his name, Alphonse became a Jesuit and later joined his brother to start a congregation specifically directed to the evangelization of the Jewish people. He set up two convents and a monastery in Jerusalem. It was here that he died.

With regard to the truth of his encounter with the Virgin, Alphonse (who was disowned by his family after the incident) wrote,

> "O my God.... I who only a half hour before was still blaspheming! I who felt such a deadly hatred of the Catholic religion! And all who know me well enough that, humanly speaking, I have the strongest reasons for remaining a Jew. My family is Jewish; my bride is Jewish; my uncle is a Jew. In becoming a Catholic, I sacrifice all the interests and all the hopes I have on earth; and yet I am not mad. Everyone knows that I am not mad, that I have never been mad. Surely they must receive my testimony."[3]

> "A man has a claim to be believed, when he sacrifices everything to a conviction that must have come from Heaven. If all that I have said is not rigorously true, I commit a crime, not only the most daring, but the most senseless and motiveless."[4]

NOTES

[1] https://stphilipcc.org/our-lady-of-zion

[2] "The Conversion of Ratisbonne" Roman Catholic Books, p.71 (2000)

[3] Ibid., p.71

[4] Ibid., p.36-37

Our Lady of La Salette, France, 1846

"If My People Will Not Obey,
I Shall be Compelled to Let Go of My Son's Arm"

Date – A single apparition on September 19, 1846
Witnesses – Melanie Mathieu, 14, and Maximine Giraud, 11
Enduring Evidence – Fulfilled prophecies, healing spring
Themes – Prophecy, Healing, Call to Conversion, Secrets
Description of the Virgin – Melanie, 1853: "The clothing of the Most Holy Virgin was silver white and quite brilliant. It was quite intangible. It was made up of light and glory, sparkling and dazzling. There is no expression nor comparison to be found on earth. The Most Holy Virgin had a yellow pinafore.

"What am I saying, yellow? She had a pinafore more brilliant than several suns put together. It was not of tangible material; it was composed of glory, and this glory was scintillating, and ravishingly beautiful.

"The crown of roses which she placed on her head was so beautiful, so brilliant, that it defies imagination. The different colored roses were not of this earth; it was a joining together of flowers which crowned the head of the Most Holy Virgin.

"The Most Holy Virgin was tall and well proportioned. She seemed so light that a mere breath could have stirred her, yet she was motionless and perfectly balanced. Her face was majestic, imposing. The voice of the Beautiful Lady was soft. It was enchanting, ravishing, warming to the ears.

"The eyes of the majestic Mary appeared thousands of times more beautiful than the rarest brilliants, diamonds and precious stones. They shone like two suns; but they were soft, softness itself, as clear as a mirror.

"The Holy Virgin had a most pretty cross hanging around her neck.

"The Holy Virgin was crying nearly the whole time she was speaking to us. Her tears flowed gently, one by one, down to her knees, then, like sparks of light they disappeared. They were glittering and full of love. I would have liked to comfort her and stop her tears."

The apparition of La Salette is significant in many ways, not least because it is the first of Mary's apparitions to children in modern times and the first modern apparition with both short-term and apocalyptic prophecies (the Rue du Bac prophecies were more near-term in nature).

Melanie and Maximine, neither of whose parents were practicing Catholics, were tending sheep for different masters on a mountainside near the village of Ablandins in the parish of La Salette. After eating lunch they took a nap. When they woke up, they saw a glowing globe of light that seemed to outshine the sun. The frightened children were about to run away when the globe opened and they saw a weeping lady seated with her head in her hands. Gradually she arose, faced them with her hands crossed across her chest and asked them kindly to come to her. She spoke in French and not in the patois with which they were more familiar. The children could see the crystal-like tears on her cheeks. The lady then spoke (in their patois) of the different ways in which people were offending her and her Son and of the calamitous consequences of these offenses. She warned of famines ahead, of the failure of the potato crop and of grapes rotting and the walnuts turning bad. She gave each of them separately a "secret" and then said that the calamities ahead could be averted if the people repented. She asked the children to say their prayers and to make what she had said known to all her people. After this she turned away and the globe of light around her grew brighter and then disappeared.

When the children returned to the village, Maximin first reported the events they had experienced and Melanie confirmed his account. The parish priest accepted their testimony without further ado for which he was later reprimanded by his bishop. The civil authorities interrogated the children and tried to catch them in a lie with no success. The children were twice taken up to the site of the apparitions. On the second visit, a man broke off a piece of the rock on which the lady had been sitting and found a spring gushing next to it. Almost immediately the water from this spring was found to heal people who were desperately ill. The bishop of the diocese began an official inquiry into the phenomenon and appointed several commissions of investigators while asking his priests to maintain silence about the apparition in the pulpit. The government in Paris now also got involved and tried to suppress the "pretended apparition."

Although skeptics hotly rejected the apparition account, people in surrounding villages began to reform their lives while hundreds of pilgrims began the trek up the mountains. Fifty to sixty thousand people came to the location of the apparition on the first anniversary of its occurrence. Twenty three cures attributed to the mountain spring in the first year were widely accepted. Although the main commission appointed by the bishop ruled in favor of the apparition, the bishop assigned a new team to continue the investigation. The "secrets" given to the children were written down and sent to the pope who was reportedly deeply impressed by them.

In November of 1851, five years after the incident took place, the local bishop accepted the authenticity of the apparition of Our Lady of La Salette and announced that the Apparition "has within itself all the characteristics of the truth, and that the faithful are justified in believing it beyond doubt and for certain." A basilica was subsequently built on the mountain of La Salette and hundreds of miraculous cures were reported there. The prophecies of Our Lady of La Salette - which were widely circulated by October 1846 - turned out to be remarkably accurate. By December of the year of the apparition, most of the popular crops were disease-stricken and in 1847 a famine swept all of Europe claiming a million lives, including one hundred thousand in France. Potatoes were not available because they had rotted in the ground, grape diseases caused the closure of most of the vineyards in France and the walnut crop also failed. Cholera was prevalent in various parts of France and caused the deaths of many children (as predicted) and entire families.

Messages

The central message was: Turn away from sin and do penance or undergo terrible suffering.

"Come, My children, do not be afraid: I am here to tell you something of the greatest importance."

"If my people will not obey, I shall be compelled to let go of My Son's arm. It is so heavy, so pressing, that I can no longer restrain it. How long have I suffered for you! If I do not wish my Son to abandon you, I must take it upon myself to pray for this continually. And the rest of you think little of this! In vain will you pray, in vain will you act, you will never be able to make up for the trouble I have taken for you all!

"I gave you six days to work, I kept the seventh for myself and no one wishes to grant me that one day. This it is that causes the weight of my Son's arm to be crushing. Those who drive carts cannot swear without adding My Son's name. These are the two things which causes the weight of my Son's arm to be so burdensome.

"If the harvest is spoiled, it is your own fault. I made you see this last year with the potatoes; you took little account of this. It was quite the opposite when you found bad potatoes; you swore oaths, and you included the name of my Son. They will continue to go bad; at Christmas there will be none left.

"If you have corn, you must not sow it. The beasts will eat all that you sow. And all that grows will fall to dust when you thresh it. A great famine will come. Before the famine comes, children under the age of seven will begin to tremble and will die in the arms of those who hold them. The others will do penance through hunger. The nuts will go bad, the grapes will become rotten."

"If the people are converted, the stones and rocks will change into heaps of wheat, and potatoes will be found sown in the earth."

"Do you say your prayers properly, my children?"
"No, Madame, hardly at all."
"Ah! my children, you must say them morning and evening. When you can do no more, at least say an 'Our Father' or a 'Hail Mary,' and when you have the time to do better, you will say more."

"Only a few old women go to Mass; in the summer, the rest work all day Sunday and in the winter, when they do not know what to do, they only go to Mass to make fun of religion. During Lent, they go to the butchers like hungry dogs!"

"Have you ever seen spoilt wheat, my children?"
"Oh! no, Madame."
To Maximin: "But you, my child, you must have seen some once near Coin, with your father. The farmer said to your father: 'Come and see how my wheat has gone bad!' You both went to see. Your father took two or three ears in his hand, rubbed them, and they fell to dust. Then, on your way back, when you were no more than half an hour away from Corps, your father gave you a piece of bread, and said: 'Take it, eat while you can, my son, for I don't know who will be eating anything next year if the wheat is spoiled like that.'

Maximin: "That's quite true, Madame; I didn't remember." (This was an incident Maximin had forgotten about; when he narrated it to his unbelieving father, it had a profound effect on him since only the two of them knew about it).

"Well, my children, you will make this known to all my people."

The Secrets

"The priests, ministers of my Son, the priests, by their wicked lives, by their irreverence and their impiety in the celebration of the holy mysteries, by their love of money, their love of honors and pleasures, the priests have become cesspools of impurity. Yes, the priests are asking vengeance, and vengeance is hanging over their heads."

"God will strike in an unprecedented way. Woe to the inhabitants of the earth! The chiefs, the leaders of the people of God have neglected prayer and penance, and the devil has dimmed their intelligence. God will abandon mankind to itself and will send punishments which will follow one after the other. The society of men is on the eve of the most terrible scourges and of gravest events. Mankind must expect to drink from the chalice of the wrath of God."

"May the curate of my Son, Pope Piux IX, never leave Rome again after 1859; I will be at his side. May he be on his guard against Napoleon; he is two-faced, and when he wishes to make himself pope as well as emperor, God will soon draw back from him." [At the time when this prophecy was made, no one expected another Napoleon to come to power. By November 1852, Napoleon III became Emperor. Pope Pius IX had been driven from Rome in 1848 and came back with the support of Napoleon who seemed to have designs on the papacy.]

"The earth will be struck by calamities of all kinds, in addition to plague and famine which will be widespread. There will be a series of wars until the last war. Before this comes to pass, there will be a kind of false peace in the world. People will think of nothing but amusement. The wicked will give themselves over to all kinds of sin. But blessed are the souls humbly guided by the Holy Spirit! I shall fight at their side until they reach the fullness of years."

Concerning the Secrets, Pope Pius IX said, "These are the secrets of La Salette: Unless the world repent, it shall perish!"

Our Lady of Hope, France, 1871

"My Son Allows Himself to Be Moved"

Place – Pontmain, France

Date – A single apparition on January 17, 1871.

Witnesses – Eugene Barbedette, 12, Joseph Barbedette, 10, Francoise Richer, 11, Jeanne-Marie Lebosse, 9, Eugene Freiteau, 6.

Enduring Evidence: Protection from the advancing Prussian Army

Theme – Consolation, Power of Prayer, Protection from Danger.

Description of the Virgin – She wore a blue robe embroidered with numerous golden stars. On her head she had a black veil and a gold crown and on her feet blue shoes with gold ribbons. The Lady was tall and beautiful and looked about eighteen; "smiles of ineffable sweetness played about her mouth." When the cross with Christ appeared in her hands, Joseph Barbedette recalled that "Her face was marked with a deep sorrow ... the trembling of her lips at the corners of her mouth showed deep feeling ... But no tears ran down her cheeks ..."

The Pontmain apparition is above all a "sign" for the world that those with a special devotion to the Virgin will be protected during times of tribulation. It is also a testimony to the power of prayer.

War had broken out between France and Prussia and things were going badly for the French with the Prussians under Otto von Bismarck swiftly advancing across France. Paris was surrounded and bombarded daily and the Emperor Napoleon was imprisoned by the Prussians. To the west of Paris was the city of Laval which was on the verge of falling. Pontmain, a village belonging to the region of which Laval was the capital, was one of the few places in France where the local population practiced their faith and showed great devotion to the Virgin under the leadership of a devout parish priest Abbe Guerin. Thirty eight men from Pontmain had been conscripted into the French army and the townspeople were concerned about their safety. Among the thirty eight was Auguste, the older brother of Eugene and Joseph Barbedette. At Mass on the morning of January 17, 1871, the Abbe Guerin prayed, "Let us add penance to our prayers, and then we may take courage. God will have pity on us; his mercy will surely come to us through Mary."

That same evening the boys had been helping their father in the barn when a family friend dropped by. While she was talking to their father, Eugene stepped outside and to his astonishment saw a beautiful lady of about eighteen suspended in the air above a house across from them. The lady wore a blue robe covered with golden stars. On her head was a gold crown and under the crown and over the forehead was a black veil. She wore blue shoes adorned with gold ribbons. He called out to the others but when they came out, only Joseph could see the lady in the sky. There were three bright stars around the lady's crown and this even the adults could see. When the mother of the boys came out she refused to believe them. But two other children who came by, Francoise Richer and Jeanne-Marie Lebosse, also saw the lady. Sister Marie Edouard, a nun in the crowd, began to believe that this may be an apparition of the Virgin Mary since children were often able to see the Virgin even when adults could not. She called for yet another child, Eugene Freiteau, who also saw the lady as did a two year old baby.

As Sister Marie led the crowd in prayer, the apparition went through five changes. The first stage was the initial motionless state which continued for two hours. The second stage began when Sister Marie started the rosary. A small red cross appeared over her heart and a blue oval frame with four candles appeared around her while the stars in her robe seemed to increase. When Sister Marie began the Magnificat, the Lady elevated her hands with the palms outward apparently in a gesture of protection. A white scroll appeared under the Lady's feet and words of gold started to form on them: "But pray my children." In the next phase, a larger cross appeared in her hands and a banner with the name of Christ hung from it. Yet another sentence appeared on the scroll: "God will soon grant your request." In the final phase, a third sentence appeared on the scroll, "My Son allows Himself to be moved." An image of Christ appeared on the cross and then the cross vanished. The candles in the oval frame were lit by a star and when the Lady lowered her hands two white crosses appeared on her shoulders. When the parish priest began his prayers, a white veil rose from beneath her feet and covered her until she disappeared.

Amazingly, at precisely the time at which the apparition began (about 5:30 p.m.), the victorious Prussians halted their advance. Historians have no ready explanation for the decision to halt but it is reported that some Prussian soldiers claimed to have seen an image of the lady in the sky. The Prussian commander, General Schmidt, is even quoted as saying, "We cannot go farther. Yonder, in the direction of Brittany, there is an invisible Madonna barring the way." A peace treaty between Prussia and France was signed eleven days later. All the soldiers from Pontmain returned unharmed.

Pilgrims arrived to pray at Pontmain the day after the apparition and in February 1875 Bishop Wicart of Laval declared: "We judge that the Immaculate Mary, Mother of God, has truly appeared on January 17, 1871, to Eugene Barbadette, Joseph Barbadette, Francoise Richer, and Jeanne-Marie Lebosse, in the hamlet of Pontmain."

Messages:

"Pray my children."

"God will soon grant your request."

"My Son allows Himself to be moved."

Our Lady of Knock, Ireland, 1879

Date – August 21, 1879
Place – Knock, Ireland
Witnesses – Eighteen townspeople
Enduring Evidence – Healing miracles. Basilica of Our Lady Queen of Ireland at the site of the apparitions

Image source –
https://en.wikipedia.org/wiki/Knock_Shrine#/media/File:Statue_of_Our_Lady_Knock_Shrine.jpg

On August 21, 1879, Ireland played host to a heavenly tableau straight out of the *Book of Revelation*. The site of this apparition was the humble town of Knock (Cnoc is Gaelic for "hill"). The apparition itself was different from most of the Marian apparitions of the 19th and 20th centuries in the following respects: no words were spoken, everyone present was able to see the Virgin and not just a group of visionaries, those who witnessed the apparition did not enter into a state of ecstasy.

The day had been stormy and the pastor of Knock's small church, Archdeacon Cavanagh, was thoroughly soaked by the time he returned home after visiting his parishioners. His housekeeper, Mary McLoughlin, built a fire for him and then went to visit her friend Margaret Beirne (known locally as the widow Beirne). On the way, as she passed the church, she noticed a few figures outside the church gable on the south end that she took to be statues. After meeting with the Beirnes, Mary returned to the presbytery accompanied by the Widow Beirne's daughter, Mary Beirne.

This time, as they passed the church, they observed that the figures she thought were statues were actually people, namely the Blessed Virgin Mary, accompanied by St. Joseph and St. John the Evangelist. Behind them was a Lamb resting above an altar. The supernal spectacle was lit by a bright light that lit up the gable wall of the church and was visible miles away. Despite the heavy rain, the figures remained entirely dry. As Mary McLoughlin kept watch, Mary Beirne ran to her house and summoned her mother, her sister Margaret, her brother Dominick and a niece named Catherine Murray, aged eight. She also brought some neighbors. All those who arrived at the church - eighteen in all - saw the heavenly display. The witnesses included three men, six women, two teenage boys and a girl, and two children. Archdeacon Cavanagh, however, did not take the reports seriously and so did not come out to see what was going on. A little over two hours after they first saw the spectacle, all of those present either went about their chores or had gone to help with a lady whose mother was on her deathbed. When they returned to the church, they saw that the apparition had disappeared.

This is Mary Beirne's description of the apparition:

> "At the distance of three hundred yards or so from the church, I beheld all at once, standing out from the gable, and rather to the west of it, three figures which, on more attentive inspection, appeared to be that of the Blessed Virgin, of St. Joseph, and St. John. That of the Blessed Virgin was life-size, the others apparently either not so big or not so high as her figure; they stood a little distance out from the gable wall, and as well as I could judge, a foot and a half or two from the ground.

> "The Virgin stood erect, with eyes raised to heaven, her hands elevated to the shoulders or a little higher, the palms inclined slightly toward the shoulders or bosom; she wore a large cloak of a white color, hanging in full folds and somewhat loosely around her shoulders and fastened to the neck; she wore a crown on the head - a rather large crown - and it appeared to be somewhat yellower than the dress or robes worn by Our Blessed Lady.

> "In the figure of St. Joseph, the head was slightly bent, and inclined toward the Blessed Virgin, as if paying her respect; it represented the saint somewhat aged with gray whiskers and grayish hair. The third figure appeared to be that of St. John the Evangelist; I do not know, only I thought so, except the fact that at one time I saw a statue [of St. John] at the chapel of Lekanvey, near Westport, County Mayo, very much resembling the figure which now stood before me.

> "Above the altar, and resting on it was a lamb, standing with face toward St. John, thus fronting the western sky. I saw no cross or crucifix. On the body of the lamb and around it, I saw golden stars, or small brilliant lights, glittering like jets or glass balls, reflecting the light of some luminous body.

> "I remained from a quarter past eight to half past nine o'clock."

Shortly after the apparition, two blind men regained their sight there. Knock soon became a center of pilgrimage and healing. Over three hundred miraculous cures have been reported there and at least a million pilgrims now visit Knock every year.

The ecclesiastical authorities did not respond as rapidly to Knock as did the faithful. Although Archdeacon Cavanagh believed in the authenticity of the apparition, the local bishop, the Archbishop of Tuam, appointed an investigative Commission to study the phenomenon. A scientist from Maynooth did experiments with a magic lantern to show that the display seen by the witnesses could not have been created by a photographic image on the gable wall. Although the Commission concluded that the witnesses were trustworthy and satisfactory, the bishop, who was ninety, did not publish their report or say anything further about Knock. Nevertheless, bishops from other countries came to Knock and some of them reported cures they attributed to Knock. By 1929, the Archbishop of Tuam was participating in the ceremonies at Knock. He instituted a new investigative Commission in 1936 - and this Commission also came back with a positive verdict. In the first gesture of recognition from the Vatican, Pope John Paul II visited Knock in 1979, the centenary year of the apparitions. On March 19, 2021, Pope Francis formally elevated Knock to the status of an International Sanctuary of Special Eucharistic and Marian Devotion.

Although there was no verbal communication at Knock, the silent tableau spoke to the hearts and minds of the faithful most eloquently and effectively simply through its silence. Knock was a call to contemplation and a reminder of the reality of the Eucharist and the communion of saints.

Our Lady of the Golden Heart, Belgium, 1932

"I Will Convert Sinners"

Dates – Started November 29, 1932. Ended January 3, 1933. A total of thirty three apparitions.
Place – Beauraing, Belgium
Witnesses – Fernande, Albert and Gilberte Voisin; Andree and Gilberte Degeimbre
Enduring Evidence – Healings, luminous phenomena seen by those present
Theme – Healing, Conversion, Secrets
Description of the Virgin – As in all other cases, the visionaries were most moved by the beauty of the Virgin. She looked eighteen and had deep blue eyes. Rays of light from the head. Wore a flowing white gown which radiated a "kind of blue light", stood on a cloud, had a rosary on the right arm, displayed a golden heart surrounded by rays of light.

Albert and Fernande Voisin, brother and sister, left on the evening of November 29 with Andree and Gilberte Degeimbre to pick up their sister also named Gilberte (the younger Gilberte) from an Academy run by the Sisters of Christian Doctrine in the little railroad town of Beauraing. The parents of the Voisins were no longer practicing Catholics and the father, Hector Voisin, was even a member of the Marxist Labor party. The mother of the Degeimbres, Germaine, was a widow who was infrequent in church attendance. When the four children reached the Academy, Albert (who was the prankster in the group) happened to turn around and saw "the Virgin in White" walking over a bridge that went over the convent adjoining the Academy. The other three did not believe him but at his insistence they looked back and also beheld a luminous woman clearly walking over the bridge. When the younger Gilberte joined them, she too saw the lady. The nun who received them, however, was unable to see the apparition. The children saw the same apparition again the following day but neither the parents nor the nuns believed the accounts of the children. When the children returned the next day, December 1, Germaine Degeimbre and some adults accompanied them. This time the children saw the apparition in the courtyard of the convent. On that day, they saw the Lady four times mainly over a rose hawthorn bush in the courtyard. On December 2, the Mother Superior had locked the gates to the Convent but the Lady appeared to them as usual and for the first time spoke to them answering their questions.

Over the next few days too, the Virgin appeared to the visionaries daily - from December 4, they noticed that she had a rosary hanging from her right arm and on December 8 she appeared to them in the presence of at least ten thousand spectators. It was during the December 8 apparition that, for the first time, the visionaries entered a state of ecstasy in which they were demonstrably impervious to any external stimuli (doctors who were present burnt them, pricked them with knives, etc. without any reaction from the visionaries or any physical injury). The Virgin continued appearing to them on different days. During the December 29 apparition, the children saw that she had a golden heart surrounded by rays of light. The last apparition took place on January 3 before thirty thousand people. Each of the visionaries was given a secret. The last one to get a message was Fernande: observers saw a ball of fire suddenly descend on the hawthorn bush and heard a thunderclap while Fernande immediately dropped to her knees and was given a final message by the Virgin.

After the apparitions were over, two people who had personally come to the visionaries with petitions about their ailments were healed, one from a bone disease and the other from a tubercular condition. Numerous other cures were reported. Another person, Tilman Come, who was healed of a disease of the spinal vertebrae in the summer of 1933 was privileged to witness several additional apparitions of the Virgin with the Golden Heart.

One of the Virgin's chief messages was that she would convert sinners. The Beauraing phenomenon certainly had this effect on many who came into contact with it ranging from the parents of the visionaries to the editor of a Belgian Communist newspaper who actually saw the Virgin at Beauraing and spent the rest of his life promoting Marian devotion.

In a July 2, 1949 document the bishop of the diocese to which Beauraing belongs wrote, "We are able in all serenity and prudence to affirm that the Queen of Heaven appeared to the children of Beauraing during the winter of 1932-33 especially to show us in her maternal Heart the anxious appeal for prayer and the promise of her powerful mediation for the conversion of sinners." In subsequent years, over a million pilgrims a year visited Beauraing.

Messages

December 2: Alberte: "Are you the Immaculate Virgin?" to which she nodded

Albert: "What do you want?" The Virgin: "Always be good." The Virgin asked later on that day: "Is it true you will always be good?" Andree: "Yes! We will always be good."

December 5: The visionaries ask for a sign to which the Virgin gives no response.

December 17: [The visionaries:] "At the request of the clergy, we ask you what you want of us." The Virgin tells them she wants a chapel to which the visionaries say: "Yes, we will have it built here."

December 21: [Several of the children:] "Tell us who you are." [The Virgin:] "I am the Immaculate Virgin."

December 23: In response to Fernande's question on why she had come there, the Virgin said, "That people might come here on pilgrimages."

December 28: "Soon I shall appear for the last time."

December 30: "Pray. Pray very much." From December 31, all the visionaries saw the Virgin with her golden heart, a reminder of the doctrine and devotion of the Immaculate Heart.

January 1: [To Gilberte Voisin:] "Pray always."

January 2: "Tomorrow I will speak to each one of you separately."

January 3: [To Gilberte Voisin:] "This is between you and me, and I ask you to speak of it to no one."

[To Gilberte Degeimbre:] "I will convert sinners." This is the famous promise of the Virgin of Beauraing. She then entrusted her with a secret and said "Goodbye".

Albert was given a secret and then told "Goodbye".

[To Andree:] "I am the Mother of God, the Queen of Heaven. Pray always."

[To Fernande:] "Do you love my Son?" Fernande: "Yes"

"Do you love?" Fernande: "Yes"

"Then sacrifice yourself for me."

The Virgin then said "Goodbye" before Fernande could ask any further questions.

The Virgin of the Poor, Belgium, 1933

"Believe in Me, I Will Believe in You"

Dates – Started January 15, 1933, ended March 2, 1933.
Place – Banneux, Belgium
Witness – Mariette Beco, eleven years old
Enduring Evidence – Healing spring
Theme – Consolation, Prayer
Description of the Virgin – Extraordinarily beautiful, enveloped in a "great oval light," wore a long white gown with a sash of an "unforgettable blue" and a white, transparent veil covering head and shoulders. Right foot was visible and "crowned with a golden rose" between the toes. Rosary on the right arm with diamond-like beads and a golden chain and cross. Stood on a cloud with the head and shoulders bent slightly to the left.

Image source –
https://en.wikipedia.org/wiki/Our_Lady_of_Banneux#/media/
File:Banneux_Maagd_der_armen.jpg

Mariette was the oldest of seven children. Her father was a lapsed Catholic living in a poverty-stricken socialist part of Belgium. Her mother was not a practicing Catholic and Mariette had stopped going to church and receiving instruction in the faith. On the night of January 15, she was looking out of the window for her younger brother Julien and saw a beautiful and luminous young lady who was beckoning to her. Her mother did not believe Mariette's account but on looking out saw a figure of light outside. She would not allow Mariette to go out for fear of witchcraft. Mariette's father tried to explain away the phenomenon as having been caused by light reflections but could not give a demonstration to establish his claim. Mariette's friend took her next day to the parish priest who was skeptical and thought her account was simply a copycat version of the just-finished Beauraing apparitions. At the next apparition, the Virgin led Marietta from her house to a spring which she said would bring healing to all nations. She also asked for construction of a chapel. There were eight apparitions in all. The parish priest was initially skeptical but eventually accepted the authenticity of the apparitions. In 1949, the bishop of the region officially approved the apparitions upon completion of extensive investigations.

Some distinctive features of the apparitions: people were converted in large numbers simply by listening to accounts of the apparitions (Mariette's father was one of the converts); the path from Mariette's house to the spring is now open to the public and is the only place in the world which traces a route taken by the Virgin; Mary's self-description was "Virgin of the Poor" and this was especially significant since the world had just gone through a devastating economic depression and Banneux was one of the poorest areas in Belgium; the Virgin said the spring was for "all nations," a prophecy since over 500,000 pilgrims from around the world visit the spring every year and over 50 miraculous cures have been documented; over three thousand monuments and shrines, three hundred chapels and twenty five churches around the world are dedicated to the Virgin of the Poor.

The apparitions of Banneux, along with those of Beauraing, took place just before the onset of the Second World War and signified the Virgin's empathy with a world soon to witness terrible suffering. As noted earlier, both towns are located in the Ardennes, the site of the Battle of the Bulge, the single most devastating battle of the Second World War.

Messages

Second apparition, January 18, 1933:
Upon reaching the spring, the Virgin told Mariette, "Place your hands in the water," which she did. Mariette then repeated the Virgin's words, "This stream is reserved for me. Good evening. *Au revoir.*"

Third apparition, January 18, 1933:
Mariette: "Who are you, lovely Lady?" The Virgin: "I am the Virgin of the Poor."
The Virgin's reply to the next question indicated that Mariette had misunderstood her statement of the previous day.
Mariette: "Beautiful Lady, yesterday you said, 'This spring is reserved for me.' Why for me?"
The Virgin: "This spring is reserved for all nations - to relieve the sick." (The Virgin appeared to be amused by this misunderstanding). "I shall pray for you. *Au revoir.*"

Fourth apparition, January 20, 1933
Mariette: "What do you wish, my beautiful Lady?"
The Virgin: "I would like a small chapel."
After this the Virgin blessed her with the sign of the cross and Mariette collapsed (without any resultant harm).

Fifth apparition, February 11, 1933
The Virgin: "I come to relieve suffering."
Sixth apparition, February 15, 1933
Mariette: "Blessed Virgin, the chaplain told me to ask you for a sign?"
The Virgin: "Believe in me, I will believe in you. Pray much. *Au revoir.*"
This was one of the most intriguing replies in the literature of Marian apparitions. Many times the recipients of Marian apparitions were asked for signs and many times the Virgin furnished unmistakable signs of her presence. But here we see that Heaven operates by its own rules: Heaven's "sign" was the miraculous spring that would draw millions of pilgrims, a "sign" that would be shown in good time. The true miracles of God are always subtle - although they elicit faith, they are displayed only when they serve a clear and permanent purpose. But a sincere faith had to come first.

Seventh apparition, February 20, 1933
The Virgin had a grave expression and said, "My dear child, pray much. *Au revoir.*"
Eight apparition, March 2, 1933
In her final apparition, the Virgin was grave and sorrowful, "I am the Mother of the Savior, Mother of God. Pray much."
She blessed Mariette and said, "*Adieu* - till we meet in God."
In French, au revoir means "see you again" and "adieu" is "goodbye."

Mariette was also given a "secret" at one of the apparitions which has never been disclosed.

Our Lady of Hrushiv, Ukraine, 1914, 1987

*"The Times are Coming Which Have Been Foretold
as Being Those in the End Times"*

Dates – May 12, 1914; April 27, 1987; numerous sightings in 1987-88.
Place – Hrushiv, Ukraine
Witnesses – First apparitions witnessed in 1914 by 22 people, then witnessed again in 1987 by a 12 year old girl Marina Kizyn. Subsequently witnessed and heard by hundreds of thousands of people.
Enduring Evidence – Apparitions were visible to hundreds of thousands of people.
Theme – Consolation, Repentance for sin
Description of the Virgin – Before she arrived, a bright light covered the church and surrounding areas (this light was even seen in a television program). The Virgin appeared from within the light and floated above the church.
Link – https://www.youtube.com/watch?v=GR25elE6BEU

On May 12, 1914, two weeks before the First World War, 22 people in the village of Hrushiv who were mowing fields near the local church witnessed an apparition of the Virgin. The Virgin told them: "There will be a war. Russia will become a godless country and the Ukraine, as a nation, will suffer terribly for 80 years and will have to live through the world wars, but it will be free afterwards." Then on April 27, 1987, exactly one year after the Chernobyl nuclear reactor disaster, the Virgin appeared to Marina Kizyn above a small church. Subsequently, nearly 500,000 people witnessed the apparition as the Virgin appeared daily until August 15, often before crowds of tens of thousands at a time. The Virgin said "I have come on purpose to thank the Ukrainian people because you have suffered most for the church of Christ in the last seventy years. I have come to comfort you and to tell you that your suffering will soon come to an end. Ukraine will become an independent state." Ukraine had been consecrated to the Virgin in 1058 A.D.

Messages

About the Chernobyl catastrophe she said, "Do not forget those who have died in the Chernobyl disaster. Chernobyl is a reminder and a sign for the whole world."

"Forgive your enemies. Through you and the blood of the martyrs will come the conversion of Russia. Repent and love one another. The times are coming which have been foretold as being those in the end times. See the desolation which surrounds the world ... the sin, the sloth, the genocide. Pray for Russia. Oppression and wars continue to occupy the minds and hearts of many people. Russia, despite everything, continues to deny my Son. Russia rejects real life and continues to live in darkness ... If there is not a return to Christianity in Russia there will be a third world war and the whole world faces ruin."

"Teach the children to pray. Teach them to live in truth and live yourselves in truth. Say the Rosary. It is the weapon against Satan. He fears the Rosary. Recite the Rosary at any gathering of people.

"I have come to comfort you and to tell you that your suffering will end soon. I shall protect you for the glory and the future of God's kingdom on earth, which will last for a thousand years. The Kingdom of Heaven and Earth is close at hand. It will come only through penance and the repentance of sin.

"This wicked world is feasting on depravity and impurity. Many lies are proclaimed against the Truth. The innocent are condemned. Many come as false messiahs and false prophets. Be diligent. Be on your guard.

"Happy are they whose lives are blameless and who walk in fear of the Lord.

"My children, all of you are dear to me and please my heart. I make no distinction of race or religion. You here in Ukraine have received the knowledge of the One, True Apostolic Church. You have been shown the door to Heaven. You must follow this path, even though it may be painful.

"The Eternal God is calling you. This is why I have been sent to you. You in the Ukraine were the first nation to be entrusted to me. Throughout your long persecution you have not lost faith, hope or love. I always pray for you, my dear children, wherever you are."

Fifth decade – Global

Our Lady of the Guard, Italy 1490

Dates – 1490
Place – Genoa, Italy
Witness – Benedetto Pareto
Enduring evidence – A plaque dating from 1530 gives a description of the incident as recounted by three individuals who had met Benedetto and knew what had transpired. A second plaque from 1818 says, "In these rubble you can see the remains of the residence where Benedetto Pareto was staying, to whom the Queen of Heaven appeared on 29 August 1490 and gave the grace to erect in her name the church that towers at the top of the Figogna." Healings at the church were recorded at least from the 18th century.
Feast Day – Second Sunday of September

Image source –
https://it.wikipedia.org/wiki/Nostra_Signora_della_Guardia#/media/File:Abbazia_di_San_Fruttuoso_di_Camogli-DSCF0687.JPG

In several Marian apparitions (think of Guadalupe), the Blessed Virgin appears to a man of modest means and asks him to build a church in the specified location. The man declines the offer but then eventually does the job. This is what happened in the case of Benedetto Pareto of Genoa in 1490.

He had scaled Monte Figogna, a local mountain, collecting hay when a beautiful woman appeared to him and introduced herself as the Virgin Mary. She asked him to build a church at a specific location on the mountain. She said she would help get him the support to do this. Although he initially said Yes, Benedetto had second thoughts and gave up the idea after discussing it with his wife, fearing the ridicule of his fellow peasants. Later, he took a severe fall from a fig tree and was given the last rites. At that moment, the Lady appeared and through her intercession he was healed.

His healing convinced the others who were with him that something supernatural had happened and they assisted him in building a small wooden chapel. It soon became a prominent pilgrimage site in Genoa and a larger church was later built there.

The apparition is called Our Lady of the Guard because Monte Figogna was an observation point for ships.

Our Lady of the Miracles of Caacupé, Paraguay, 1500s

Date – 1500s
Place – Caacupé. Paraguay
Witness – Indio Jose, a member of the Guarani tribe
Enduring Evidence – the Shrine with the Image of Our Lady of Miracles is the spiritual capital of Paraguay. One million pilgrims come there on the feast day. Many claim miracles.
Feast Day – December 8

Image source –
https://oracionesalavirgenmaria.blogspot.com/2014/03/a-la-virgen-de-caacupe-suplica-en-una.html

Franciscan missionaries came to Paraguay in the 1500s. An indigenous tribe called the Guarani accepted the new faith. But others like the Mbayo fiercely resisted and rejected all conversions.

During this time, a Guarani Christian named Indio Jose was in a forest when he was surrounded by the hostile Mbayo. He hid in the trunk of a large tree and prayed to the Virgin Mary for her protection promising that he would carve an image of her. According to one tradition, Jose was enveloped by a pillar of light and the Virgin appeared to him and promised to ensure his safety. Jose then carved two statues, using the wood of the tree in which he hid, one for the Franciscan mission in the village of Tobati and the other for his personal devotion.

Years later, in 1603, there was a major flood in the area destroying everything in its wake. All the inhabitants of the area led by the Franciscans prayed for relief from the destruction. When the raging waters receded, they found the image of the Virgin carved by Jose floating on Tapaicuá Lake with no damage. Ever since it has been called the Virgin of Miracles.

The image is now in the Basilica of Caacupé.

Our Lady of Lichen, Poland, 1813, 1850

Date – 1813, 1850
Place – Lichen, Poland
Witnesses – Tomasz Kłossowski and Mikołaj Sikatka
Enduring Evidence – Icon of Our Lady of Lichen and continuing miracles

Image source –
https://en.wikipedia.org/wiki/Our_Lady_of_Sorrows,_Queen_of_Poland#/media/File:Liche%C5%84_-_Cudowny_Obraz_Matki_Bo%C5%BCej_Liche%C5%84skiej.JPG

The encounter with the Virgin in Lichen involved two individuals, one a soldier and the other a peasant. Lichen is known for its healing miracles and the foundation stone for the basilica built there was, in fact, laid by Pope John Paul II.

The history of the first apparition, as described in the Basilica website, was quite straightforward.

> Tomasz Kłossowski (1780-1848) "fought in the Battle of Leipzig in 1813 where he was badly injured. When he was praying for his life to be saved, Mary appeared to him with a crown on her head and holding an eagle in her arms. Our Lady promised Tomasz that he would be cured and would return to his Motherland. She wanted him to find an image faithfully representing her and to place it in public view. He came back to Izabelin and worked as a blacksmith. Folk tradition has it that in 1836 he found such an image in Ligota, near Częstochowa, when he was coming back home from one of his pilgrimages.
>
> The icon shows the sorrowful Blessed Virgin Mary with a bowed head, looking at the eagle placed on her chest. On her vestment there are symbols of the Lord's Passion.... It was made as a copy of the icon of Rokitno around the second half of 18th century in Greater Poland (Wielkopolska). For a short time the image was kept at Tomasz Kłossowski's home. Before he died, he hung it on a pine tree in Grąblin Forrest.[1]

The second apparition took place in 1850

> In 1850 the Holy Virgin revealed herself to the shepherd Mikolaj Sikatka who was pasturing cattle near the image in the forest. In her message to Mikolaj, Our Lady summoned people to conversion, to break with greed and licentiousness. She exhorted them to pray the rosary and reminded them to participate in celebration of the Sunday liturgy. She asked priests to celebrate the liturgy worthily. Finally, she also requested that her image be moved to a more fitting place. She promised that those who earnestly prayed before it would escape death during the plague, which was to be the punishment for the lack of conversion of sinners. Furthermore,

the Holy Virgin predicted the foundation of the sanctuary and the monastery in Lichen, from where her glory would be made known. Mikolaj, the poor shepherd, started to spread Our Lady's message, but he was persecuted and imprisoned by the Russian invaders. At first, people wouldn't believe him. Only two years later, when, according to Mary's prophecy, the cholera epidemic broke out, they remembered her warning. Then people flocked to the image of the Holy Virgin to pray the rosary for the sick and dying.

A special episcopal committee examined the apparition. At the request of the parish priest, Florian Kosinski, the committee decided to move the portrait to the parish church in Lichen. This took place on September 29, 1852. Until 1939, three-thousand answers to prayers were recorded, among them miraculous recoveries.... The number of pilgrims has been increasing ever since. During their stay in Lichen, the majority of pilgrims go to confession, for the mission of this pilgrimage place seems to be reconciliation with God.... [Pope John Paul II consecrated a new church built in Lichen in 1999]. The church, modeled after Saint Peter's Basilica in the Vatican, is the seventh largest in Europe.[2]

NOTES

[1]http://www.lichen.pl/en/115/the_apparitions

[2]https://udayton.edu/imri/mary/o/our-lady-of-lichen.php

R.A. Varghese

Our Lady of All Help, France, 1652

Date – 1652
Place – Querrien, France
Witness – Jeanne Courtel
Enduring Evidence– Multitudes of pilgrims come to visit the ancient statue which is known as "Our Lady of Eternal Aid." Miracles reported through the ages.

Image source –
http://www.missionnaires-st-jacques.org/2019/06/07/pelerinage-de-la-communaute-pastorale-a-notre-dame-de-toute-aide/

Jeanne Courtel, a deaf-mute 12 year old shepherdess, was tending her flock of sheep when the Virgin appeared to her with the Child Jesus in one arm. This happened on August 15, 1652, in the region of Querrien in northwestern France. The Virgin said, 'I choose this place to be honored. Build for me a chapel in the middle of this village and many people will come.' When she heard these words, Jeanne realized she could now hear. The Virgin also said "To prove that the message comes from heaven's command, I tell you that you will discover a few steps from the fountain of Saint-Gal ... an image that was honored in ancient times."

Over a thousand years before then, St. Gal had built a now-destroyed hermitage in the area. As promised, a statue of the Blessed Virgin sculpted for that house of prayer was found in the pond. Although submerged for centuries, it was undamaged. The Virgin repeated her request for a church.

Jeanne's father conveyed the request to the local bishop who visited the village. He approved the apparition after an investigation and sanctioned the building of the church. It was completed in 1656.

Our Lady of Happy Meetings, France, 1664

Date – 1664
Place – Laus, France
Witness – Benoîte Rencurel
Enduring Evidence – Tens of thousands of pilgrims come to the church in Laus every year and it is known both for the resulting conversions and physical healings.
Link – http://www.sanctuaire-notredamedulaus.com/en/message-and-places/benoite-rencurel-messenger-reconciliation.html

Image source –
https://immaculate.one/our-lady-of-the-day-august-4-our-lady-of-laus-saint-etienne-le-laus-france#.X_JUUthKiUk

Benoîte Rencurel of Saint-Etienne-d'Avançon in the Southern Alps lost her father at the age of seven. The family fell into poverty and she had to help with their sustenance by working as a shepherdess. Although illiterate, she led a life of prayer. One day, St. Maurice, a popular saint of the region, appeared to her and said she would receive a visit from the Virgin Mary.

Shortly after, in the Vallon des Fours she met a beautiful lady. They spoke over a period of four months at the end of which, the lady said, "I am Lady Mary, the Mother of my very dear Son." She later asked Benoîte to go to a chapel that "exhales good odours" in the nearby village of Laus. Inside the church, the Virgin told her: "I have asked my Son for this place for the conversion of sinners and He granted it to Me." She told Benoîte that the goal was to build a church there and a sanctuary for priests where people could come for reconciliation.

The church was built by 1669 and soon multitudes of pilgrims came there for confession and penance. Benoîte herself lived nearby tending to the pilgrims with her gifts of "reading souls" as a third-order Dominican. The Virgin continued to appear to Benoîte for 54 years.

Our Lady of Good Help, USA, 1859

"I am the Queen of Heaven who prays for the conversion of sinners, and I wish you to do the same."

Date – 1859
Place – Champion, Wisconsin, USA
Witness – Adele Brise
Enduring Evidence– Protection from the Peshtigo Fire

Image source –
https://www.catholicfoundationgb.org/shrine-of-our-lady-of-good-help/

Our Lady of Good Help is the first Marian apparition to be approved in the United States. The Virgin appeared to Adele Brise, a Belgian immigrant in a village in Wisconsin now called Champion.

In October 1859, Adele had a vision of a lady in white with a yellow sash and a crown of stars. On October 9, she saw her again and this time the lady said: "I am the Queen of Heaven who prays for the conversion of sinners, and I wish you to do the same. You received Holy Communion this morning and that is well. But you must do more. Make a general confession and offer Communion for the conversion of sinners. If they do not convert and do penance, my Son will be obliged to punish them." She was asked "to gather the children in the wild country to teach them what they needed to know for their salvation.' Specifically, she was to 'teach the children their catechism, how to 'make the sign of the cross' and how to 'approach the sacraments.' In conclusion she said: 'That is what I wish you to do. Go and fear nothing, I will help you.'

Adele spent the rest of her life carrying out the mission entrusted to her. Her father built a chapel at the apparition site.

Exactly 12 years later, on October 8, one of the greatest fires in American history, the Peshtigo Fire, swept through Wisconsin. It destroyed 1.2 million acres and took 2,500 lives. As the conflagration headed toward them, eviscerating everything in its path, the families with whom Adele worked came to the little chapel to pray the rosary with her. Just when the fire came toward the chapel, a sudden shower put it out.

A priest named Fr. Peter Pernin, who lived through and chronicled the Peshtigo Fire, came to investigate this seeming miracle. In his book *The Finger of God*, he reported: "[All] the houses and fences in the neighborhood had been burned, with the exception of the school, the chapel and fences surrounding the six acres of land consecrated to the Blessed Virgin. (…) [The property] sanctified by the visible presence of the Mother of God now shone out like an emerald island amid a sea of ashes."

The preservation of the chapel and the devotees at the site of the apparition calls to mind the miraculous protection of the priests praying the rosary at the hypocenter of the Hiroshima atomic explosion.

The apparition site soon drew numerous pilgrims drawn by the physical healings, conversions and other miracles reported there.

150 years later, on December 8, 2010, Bishop David Ricken, Bishop of the Diocese of Green Bay, Wisconsin, declared the authenticity of the apparitions of 1859 to Sister Adele Brise. The apparition site is now named The Shrine of Our Lady of Good Help.

In his decree of approval, Bishop Ricken stated, "I declare with moral certainty and in accord with the norms of the Church that the events, apparitions and locutions given to Adele Brise in October of 1859 do exhibit the substance of supernatural character, and I do hereby approve these apparitions as worthy of belief (although not obligatory) by the Christian faithful."

In this age of pandemics, natural disasters, and widespread skepticism, the shrine serves as an enduring witness to the reality and power of Heaven mediated by its Messenger of Good Help.

Our Lady, Help of Christians, Czech Republic, 1866

Date – January 13, 1866
Place – Fillipsdorf, Czech Republic
Witness – Magdalene Kade
Enduring Evidence – Pilgrimages and healings continue at the site of the apparition, the church of Mary, Help of Christians.

Image source –
https://prezi.com/svylryxxicm8/our-lady-of-filippsdorf/

The Mary Help of Christians church in Fillipsdorf has been called the Lourdes of Bohemia. It all began with the visitation of the Virgin to a 31 year old lady. Magdalene Kade, who had been beset by serious illness throughout her life. On the night of January 13, 1866, she was lying in bed unable to speak when she saw a lady in white with a golden tiara.

She told her, "My daughter, now you are healed!" and vanished. At that moment she was totally healed.

Magdalene knew it was the Virgin and announced her healing. Eleven other seriously ill people also reported healings through the Virgin of Fillipsdorf. The local bishop set up a commission to investigate the claims. The commission concluded that medically inexplicable healings had taken place and the event reported by Magdalene was supernatural. A church built there was later dedicated to Mary, Help of Christians by Pope Leo XIII.

The Lady in White of Tra Kieu, Vietnam, 1885

Date – 1885
Place – Tra Kieu, Vietnam
Witnesses – Enemy army

Image source –
https://tuannyriver.com/2019/09/29/marianism-under-fire-the-tra-kieu-festival-in-may-1971/

ĐỨC MẸ TRÀ KIỆU

During colonial times, particularly in non-Christian countries, indigenous Christians were often caught in the crossfire between the colonists and the natives seeking independence. Like it or not, the anti-colonialists identified their fellow natives who were Christians with the enemy. This was the case in 1880s Vietnam where the French colonialists (mostly of Catholic origin) and Vietnamese nationalists were in a state of war.

It was in this setting that a heavily armed militia of Vietnamese anti-colonialists marched toward the village of Tra Kieu made up of unarmed native Catholics. The goal of this movement was of "killing the false religion" which meant wiping out all Catholics. Hearing of the army coming their way, the Catholics turned to their pastor who led them in prayers to the Blessed Virgin imploring her protection. When the militia, which greatly outnumbered the villagers, reached the village and began hostilities, they were astonished to see a Lady in White atop the village. Their bullets hit nothing and their cannon balls kept going off course. They directed their fire at the Lady only to find that these had no effect.

When they tried to march into the village on their elephants, the villagers spooked the animals and the soldiers left in disarray.

Vietnamese Catholics never forgot the Lady in White who saved them and continue to make pilgrimages to the village in gratitude.

The Virgin of Revelation, Italy, 1947

> *Date* – 1947
> *Place* – Rome, Italy
> *Witness* – Bruno Cornacchiola
> *Enduring evidence* – The grotto, which at one time was a place of ill-repute, is now a chapel with regular Masses. It is known for conversions and cures. Miraculous healings have been attributed to the soil from the grotto almost immediately after the apparition. John Paul II called the place 'St. Mary of the Third Millennium at the Three Fountains.'

The statue of the Virgin of Revelation, at the Tre Fontane cave in Rome. (Fczarnowski/Wikipedia)

Rome has been the site of two St. Paul-type conversions – in both cases involving individuals who hated Christianity and who were shocked to their senses by an encounter with the Virgin. The first case was of the French Jew Alphonse Ratisbonne and the second, 105 years later, was of Bruno Cornacchiola.

Bruno was an Italian born in 1913 who became a Protestant while fighting in the Spanish Civil War. On his return to Rome he became an Adventist and had a fervent hatred for the Catholic Church. In fact, he personally planned to assassinate the Pope of his time, Pius XII. His wife, on the other hand, was a devout Catholic, something that greatly irritated Bruno. He not only destroyed her religious pictures but physically abused her. Then, as was the case with Alphonse, Bruno entered into a "challenge agreement" with his wife that resulted in an unexpected outcome.

Bruno's wife's challenge was this. She wanted him to practice the First Friday devotion. This meant receiving communion on the First Friday of nine consecutive months in reparation for the sins committed against Jesus. Jesus had promised, in the Sacred Heart revelation, that he would give the graces necessary for salvation to all who practiced this devotion. Bruno's wife said that if nothing happened after the ninth First Friday, she would herself leave the Catholic Church.

After the nine months, Bruno remained steadfast in his anti-Catholic beliefs and his wife joined his church. Then on April 12 1947, he took his three children, two sons and a daughter, to the Tre Fontane in Rome. This was, in fact, the place where the Apostle Paul is believed to have been beheaded. While he was waiting for a store to open, his children were playing with a ball which they promptly lost. Bruno decided to help them with their search. He was looking for them when he saw his daughter kneeling and repeating the words, "Beautiful lady". Bruno saw nothing but his sons, on coming up there, also saw the lady and knelt. In his confusion, Bruno said, "God help us."

When he said this, two hands reached out and pulled out something from his eyes (as happened to St. Paul). Following this, he saw a light in the cave which grew brighter and then a lady in a white dress with a green mantle and pink band. Speaking to him for the next hour and a half, she said,

> "I am She who is with the Holy Trinity. I am the Virgin of Revelation. You have persecuted me, enough now. Enter into the heavenly fold, which is the heavenly court of God on earth. God's promise is and remains unchanged; you are saved for having observed the nine Fridays dedicated to the Sacred Heart. You observed them, prompted by your faithful, loving spouse before you started on your erring ways!"[1]

Bruno was converted after this encounter and rejoined the Church. He later met with Pope Pius XII from whom he sought forgiveness. He said he had over twenty other encounters with the Virgin during which she warned him about the evils enveloping the world.

The Virgin had also told Bruno: "My body could not decay and did not decay. My Son and the angels took me to heaven." This was before the definition of the dogma of the Assumption, a definition made by the very Pope whom Bruno sought to assassinate!

Among her other messages, she said:

> "Live the divine doctrine. Practise Christianity. Live the Faith"

> "The Hail Marys that you pray with faith and love are like golden arrows that go straight to the heart of Jesus,"

> "Pray much and recite the Rosary for the conversion of sinners, of unbelievers and of all Christians."

> "I promise this special favour: With this sinful soil [of the grotto] I shall perform great miracles for the conversion of unbelievers and of sinners."[2]

NOTES

[1]Msgr. Fausto Rossi, The Virgin of Revelation: Three Fountains – Rome. Translated by Iole Fiorillo Magri. (Roma, Italia: Olimpica Poligrafica, S.r.l., 1994), 19; Saverio Gaeta, Three Fountains: The Apocalyptic Prophecies of the Virgin of Revelation (Sankt Gallen, Switzerland: Lumen Cordium Gmbh, 2019) 13-18. Rossi 14-15; Foley 322; Gaeta 12.

[2]http://www.theotokos.org.uk/pages/approved/appariti/trefonta.html

Flame of Love of the Immaculate Heart of Mary, Hungary, 1960

Date – 1960
Place – Budapest, Hungary
Witness – Elizabeth Kindleman
Enduring Evidence – Elizabeth's messages were endorsed and propagated by bishops including the Cardinal Primate of Hungary. These messages have now created a global Flame of Love movement.

The story of Elizabeth Kindleman is different from most of the Marian apparitions because her encounter with the Virgin came through locutions, a voice speaking to her soul. It is also an inspirational story because Elizabeth responded to her celestial call while living a life of almost unrelenting poverty.

From her earliest days after the death of her father to her life as a widowed mother of six, she faced poverty and hunger, barely hanging on with one low-paying job after another. It was in the midst of this that she received messages from both Jesus and Mary that gave rise to an international movement of love.

On July 13, 1960, she wrote, "I had a wonderful spiritual illumination, which lasted three days from morning to night." She later received this invitation from Jesus and Mary: 'Renounce yourself for We have a great mission for you. You will only be able to do it if you completely renounce yourself. You are free to choose. You will accomplish it only if you want it.'

Elizabeth writes that "After experiencing doubts and torments within my soul, I accepted God's will. My soul was seized with so much grace that I was speechless."[1]

The mission entrusted to her was of spreading devotion to the Flame of Love of the Immaculate Heart of Mary. When she asked "What then is the Flame of Love?", the Virgin replied "The Flame of Love of My Immaculate Heart is Jesus Christ Himself!"

The Flame of Love blinds Satan and enables Jesus through the intercession of his Mother to save souls.

One way to spread the Flame of Love was to add an invocation to the Rosary:

"From now on, any time you pray to Me, add the following request [after the Hail Mary]: ... Holy Mary, Mother of God, pray for us sinners, spread the effect of grace of Thy Flame of Love over all of humanity, now and at the hour of our death. Amen. With this prayer, you will blind Satan."

Other means to spread the Flame are given in her writings and summarized at https://www.theflameoflove.org/survey.html.

The Virgin stressed the urgency of the mission: ""You must strive to participate in the blinding of Satan! I need you, individually as well as collectively. Any delay must be ruled out, for Satan will be blinded to the extent of your participation…individually as well as collectively…. If the whole world is united to Me, the soft light of My Flame of Love will then burn and set the globe aflame."

NOTES

[1]https://www.theflameoflove.org/elizabeth_kindelmann.html

The Message

The Message of the Contact, as is evident from all the encounters we have surveyed, is embodied in the events relating to the offspring of the Woman of Revelation 12. The Devil is waging war on the offspring because they keep the commandments of God and witness to Jesus. As long as they do both they are outside his control and will enjoy eternal union with God – Heaven. Hence his rage. He seeks to draw them to his state of eternal separation from God – Hell.

This is what the Contact is all about. Its single most important goal is to draw all of humankind to salvation, to draw us away from damnation. Every theme in every encounter ties into this overarching goal of salvation. These are the themes –

spreading the Good News;

baptizing, administering the sacraments;

conversion from evil to repentance, penance, purity and prayer;

unveiling Hell, the eternal consequence of sin.

The Mother weeps bitter tears (La Salette, Šiluva) as she sees her children racing toward damnation. She shows them the catastrophic consequences of sin in this world (Akita, Cuapa) and the next (Fatima, Kibeho). She implores all peoples to be baptized and brought to the Faith (Comoto, Good Help, Pilar).

The "End" of the World

A remarkable feature of the encounters that make up the Contact is the congruency of their prophetic messages with the vision of the New Testament and the Fathers of the Church.

The epistle to the *Ephesians* offers a cosmic vision of the mission of Christ: "He has let us know the mystery of his purpose, the hidden plan he so kindly made in Christ from the beginning to act upon when the times had run their course to the end; that he would bring together everything under Christ, as head, everything in the heavens and everything on earth." (*Ephesians* 1:9-10). The Epistle to the *Colossians* continues this theme, "He is the image of the unseen God and the first-born of all creation, for in him were created all things in heaven and on earth: everything visible and everything invisible ... all things were created through him and for him. Before anything was created, he existed, and he holds all things in unity. ... As he is the Beginning, he was first to be born from the dead, so that he could be first in every way; because God wanted all perfection to be found in him and all things to be reconciled through him and for him, everything in heaven and everything on earth, when he made peace by his death on the cross." (*Colossians* 1:15-20).

The Christian message is that all of material creation is finally to be glorified through and in Christ. The Fathers saw a pattern of inverse correspondence in salvation history. They called it "recapitulation" and "recirculation." For instance, the evil done by Eve is remedied by the New Eve. They see the same process at work at all levels of God's creation. In the long run, God's purposes will not be frustrated.

The process of the transfiguration and transformation of the terrestrial order began when God Himself took on human flesh and the process will culminate at the end of history when the whole physical world will be transfigured and transformed by being "taken up into Christ." The model for the transfigured universe is the Risen Body of Christ but this is as far as human imagination can go without being lost in mere speculation.

The New Testament also talks of a time of persecution before the final victory of Christ and this theme too was developed by the Fathers. This is reiterated in the Contact.

As it relates to events in this world, the prophetic message of the encounters with the Virgin echoes three themes: the continuing sinfulness of humanity will cause a new Chastisement from God, the greatest and the last of the chastisements; the Virgin will prepare the faithful for the coming of her Son (before and during the Chastisement) and this will be the Triumph of her Immaculate Heart; her Triumph will be followed by an Era of Peace. All this will be followed by the Second Coming of Christ, the General Judgment of the human race and, finally, eternity.

Although many have speculated about various details of the Era of Peace, it is safe to say that none of the major encounters have given us such details beyond stating the fact that there will be a Chastisement followed by an Era of Peace. The details are perhaps to be found in the "Secrets" but these Secrets will only become known shortly before their fulfillment.

"New" Revelation

To preempt a common concern, we must begin by stating what should be obvious: Marian apparitions neither supplant nor supplement the Gospel. The Virgin's appearances and messages amplify the Word of God and apply it in history and our lives. Just as the Word of God is transmitted through the writings of men, the echoes of his Word are sent to us through the Messenger he had chosen for a singular role in his plan of salvation.

But whereas the written Word is a public and final revelation of God, the messages that come to us via the Contact belong to the domain of private revelation. The public revelation takes precedence over the private at all levels. Nevertheless, the fact that a revelation is private does not imply that it is either untrue or insignificant. If there are good grounds for believing that such a revelation took place then there is also good reason for believing that God wanted us to pay attention to it. The private revelation confirms for both believers and unbelievers the truth of the public. Moreover, a reliable private revelation can give us a reliable explanation of many texts in the public revelation while also showing how we can apply them here and now.

When Christian believers read the Bible they read it with the excitement that comes from knowing that God is speaking through these human words. At times evangelists and preachers may explain or apply the biblical texts so as to deepen our excitement or to offer nuggets of wisdom. We do not normally think of such reflections as substitutes for Scripture or additions to it. Similarly, the Virgin's messages are just examples of explanations and applications of Scripture with the difference that the one who is explaining and applying has been sent by God.

To remind us of his own Teaching about the great questions of life, Jesus sends us, across the world and throughout history, his own Mother whom he named the mother of us all. The community that he founded spread around the world because of the supernatural signs shown by his witnesses, the Apostles and their disciples. This community now is consolidated by the Mother of his witnesses with supernatural signs. And just as Jesus chose people from the humblest walks of life as his witnesses, his Mother too, in her appearances, works through the lowest levels of society. God does not intimidate us into faith by irresistible displays of his Glory and that is why it was possible for many who saw and heard the human Jesus to reject him although he gave them sufficient evidence for acceptance. Likewise, Marian apparitions give just enough evidence to suggest that they are from a supernatural source - but the phenomenon is never coercive.

Supernatural signs have an effect not simply on one's faith but on history itself. For instance, whatever else you might say about it, the reported resurrection of Jesus had a material effect on history. The changed lives changed the history of the world. The transformation of the Apostles led to the transformation of empires and civilizations. The same kinds of things can be said about the apparitions of Mary. Guadalupe led to the conversion of millions of Aztecs. Lourdes, Fatima and other apparitions were also responsible for millions of conversions. Other than the resurrection, no other claims of supernatural occurrences have had the kind of effect on history that we associate with Marian apparitions. Even if we say that the apparitions are illusions, we have to admit that they had a very real effect on history. Moreover, whatever we might say about the biblical background of Marian apparitions, we cannot deny that these apparitions have concretely fulfilled two biblical prophecies: one, that all generations will call her blessed and, second, that she will be present with those who witness to Jesus.

To adopt a familiar vocabulary, we might say that the Virgin appears in history to conduct ongoing "revivals" at which one undergoes a conversion experience and makes a resolution to lead a life of holiness. Heaven and

Hell and sound doctrine are also persistent themes at the revival events run by humanity's mysterious companion in all cultures and ages. Sometimes, instead of a sermon on fire and brimstone, the helpers at the revival have been given a vision of Hell in all its fury.

The Virgin's message through her Contact reinforces the reality of Heaven and Hell, the urgency of conversion, the terrible tragedy that is sin and its horrific consequences even in this world, the necessity of prayer, penance and reparation for sin, and the obligation to turn to the means of grace offered by God. These are the teachings of Jesus in the Gospel and St. Paul in his epistles.

There are two approaches taken by the Virgin in her message: on the one hand she exhorts and encourages us in the journey to holiness; on the other, she warns us in the severest terms of the consequences of sin in history. These approaches are not only compatible but are different sides of the same coin. Jesus too was relentless in his calls to holiness – and his severe warnings of the punishment of Hell for those who die unrepentant are echoed in the admonitions of the Virgin.

The Queen of Peace, Medjugorje-Bosnia, 1981-Present

Visionaries – Mirjana Dragicevic, 17, Ivanka Ivankovic, 16, Vicka Ivankovic, 17, Ivan Dragicevic,16, Marija Pavlovic, 17, Jackov Cholo, 10

Dates – Started June 24, 1981. Daily apparitions continue for Vicka, Ivan and Marija and have ceased for the other three.

Message – Conversion, Mortification, Prayer, Reconciliation, Healing, Secrets

Status – In 1986, in an unprecedented move, Pope John Paul II removed the investigation of Medjugorje from the jurisdiction of the local diocese. In 2010, Pope Benedict XVI formed a commission under Cardinal Camillo Ruini to investigate Medjugorje. The Ruini Commission completed its investigation in 2014. In 2017, the Ruini Commission report was made public. It recommended that the first seven apparitions be approved and that Medjugorje be made a pontifical sanctuary. Pope Francis thereafter appointed Archbishop Henryk Hoser as the papal envoy and later Apostolic Visitor to Medjugorje. The papal nuncio to Bosnia celebrated Mass at Medjugorje more than once – another mark of Vatican recognition. Archbishop Hoser declared that "it is possible to recognize the authenticity of the first [seven] apparitions as proposed by the Ruini commission." About the visionaries, the Archbishop said, "What they say has been consistent. They are not mentally incompetent. A strong argument for the authenticity of the apparitions is their faithfulness to the doctrine of the Church ... In any event, this movement will not stop and should not be stopped, because of the good fruit that grows out of it." The Vatican permits public Church-sponsored pilgrimages to Medjugorje and the Vatican Press office said that part of the role of the papally-appointed Apostolic Visitor is to ensure "a stable and continuous accompaniment to the parish community of Medjugorje and to the faithful who go there as pilgrims, and whose needs require particular attention."[1]

Description of the Virgin – "She has black hair, a bit curly, blue eyes, rosy cheeks, slender, beautiful." She has a beautiful smile and her voice has been compared to music. She is three-dimensional and has often been embraced. She wears a grayish gown but on feast days she wears a gold gown. There is a crown of twelve stars over her head and she appears on a cloud.

24.6. MEDUGORJE 1981

After Fatima, Medjugorje became the most influential Marian phenomenon of the 20th century. Two items are of particular import here. The parish records of St. James Catholic Church in Medjugorje show that over 50,000 priests and religious - among them hundreds of bishops and cardinals - have come to Medjugorje inspired by their belief in the presence of the Virgin. It has been rightly said that, other than Guadalupe, no other Marian apparition in history has been the direct cause of as many conversions as Medjugorje. Guadalupe brought about the conversion of eight million Aztecs. Medjugorje has now attracted over thirty million pilgrims, a good number of whom have had their lives transformed or touched by their encounter with the Queen of Peace (not to speak of the tens of millions of others who have never visited Medjugorje but have been third party recipients of the Medjugorje message).

The significance of these two facts will be evident to anyone who has studied the Church's time-tested canons for the discernment of supernatural phenomena. The Church's great doctors of the spiritual and the mystical life have said for centuries that an authentic supernatural revelation will bear two marks: it will attract the religious and it will cause conversions. Satan posing as an angel of light can bring about many extraordinary signs and wonders but the one thing he cannot and will not do is bring about a conversion. Judged by these two criteria of an authentic supernatural revelation, Medjugorje bears the mark of all the great apparitions: it has attracted tens of thousands of priests and religious and it has caused hundreds of thousands, perhaps millions, of conversions (along with unprecedented levels of reception of the sacraments of Reconciliation and the Eucharist).

These two facts about Medjugorje no one can dispute since they have been so publicly chronicled. It is also to be noted that there are over a thousand documented cures attributed to Medjugorje.

The phenomenon began much like many of the other famous apparitions of the last one and a half centuries. On June 24, 1981, two peasant girls, Mirjana Dragicevic and Ivanka Ivankovic, were walking from their village of Bijakovici past the hill of Podbrdo when Ivanka saw a luminous figure, a lady bathed in light, on the hill. She told her companion Mirjana to look at the Gospa, Croatian for "Our Lady," but Mirjana thought she was joking and refused (similarly the Beauraing visionaries initially dismissed Albert's urgent pleas to look at the apparition of the Virgin as a prank). Nevertheless, Ivanka persisted and when they reached the Pavlovic house, she persuaded Mirjana to return to the hill with Milka Pavlovic, 13. They had tried to bring their friend Vicka Ivankovic as well but was told by her mother that she was asleep. When they reached Podbrdo all three now saw the Lady. They were soon joined by Vicka who was too frightened to look but summoned two boys, Ivan Dragicevic and Ivan Ivankovic, 20. Ivan Dragicevic, later to become one of the six principal visionaries, fled without looking but the other five now saw a beautiful lady with black hair and a grey gown holding a baby and gesturing to them to come to her. The children were too scared to go up but prayed for some time and then returned home.

Although their friends and families were skeptical, Mirjana, Ivanka and Vicka returned to Podbrdo the next evening at about 6 p.m. along with the younger Ivan, Milka's sister Marija and her cousin Jackov Cholo. Neither Milka nor the older Ivan came with them. A few curious villagers followed them. They saw the Lady again and this time accepted her invitation to come closer. Although the adults present could not see the Lady, they were astonished by the speed with which the visionaries ascended the mountain. As soon as they reached the Lady, they were on their knees praying the Lord's Prayer; the adults noticed that they were all spontaneously looking in the same direction. Ivanka's mother had died quite recently and she asked the Lady if she was in Heaven. The Lady said yes and told her that her mother wanted her to be obedient to her grandmother. She told them to pray seven "Our Fathers", "Hail Marys" and "Glory Bes" and the Creed daily. Like many visionaries before her, Mirjana said that they found it hard to convince people of the Lady's presence to which she simply smiled. (On the 28th, when the visionaries asked why she wouldn't appear in the church so that everyone could see her, she said, "Blessed are they who have not seen and who believe.") She then said "Go in God's peace" and left.

On the 26th, thousands of people assembled at Podbrdo - not just from the five villages that made up the parish of Medjugorje but from neighboring towns. The visionaries and some of the others who had gathered there saw a glowing light at the top of the hill at 6:15 p.m. and on reaching the top saw the Lady there. Vicka brought some holy water which she sprinkled on the Lady who smiled. When they asked her who she was, she replied that "I am the Blessed Virgin Mary." They asked why she had come there and she said, "I have come here, because there are many devout believers here. I have come to tell you that God exists, and He loves you. Let the others who do not see me, believe as you do." She also said, "Peace, peace, peace. Be reconciled."

The Communist authorities were now becoming concerned about the situation. They interrogated the visionaries on the 27th and the 28th and had them evaluated by a psychiatrist who pronounced them normal and of sound mental health. Communist regimes often imprisoned dissenters in psychiatric wards on trumped up charges of mental instability. But this stratagem could not be applied here because of their own psychiatrist's report. On the 30th, two Communist social workers abducted the visionaries just before the time of the now-daily apparition. Although the visionaries could not therefore be at Podbrdo, they forced the workers to stop the car at the time of the apparition. They saw a light far away on Podbrdo. The light came to the roadside and the Gospa appeared to them there.

There is a curious footnote to this story: one of the most prolific critics of Medjugorje, who furnished the source material for most of the other critics, was a Croatian priest in the US whose cousin was one of these social workers; moreover his nephew was the high-level Communist official sent to Medjugorje with express orders to end the "disturbance"; apart from the conflict of interest issue here, apparently much of this Croatian critic's source material came from these two hostile "sources".

As if the visionaries didn't have enough problems with the civil authorities, they were soon to run into even worse problems with the clergy. Their parish priest, Fr. Jozo Zovko, was a skeptic from the beginning - and remained a skeptic although his bishop, the bishop of Mostar, the diocese to which Medjugorje belonged, urged him to believe. There was soon to be a role reversal. On the 30th, the authorities arrested their friend Marinko for helping with the crowds. On the same day the visionaries asked Fr. Jozo if the apparitions could be held in the church but he turned them down.

On the next day, July 1, the authorities moved in. The police blocked off access to Podbrdo and then came to Bijakovici to arrest the visionaries. The visionaries made a quick getaway and headed for the parish church of St. James. Meanwhile, Fr. Jozo, who was praying in the church, heard a voice telling him, "Protect the children." This was the sign from Heaven he had been praying for and stepping outside he saw the terrified visionaries running towards the church. He took them to the rectory where the apparition took place on that day. Following the apparition, he celebrated Mass. Thus began a new era in the history of the Medjugorje apparitions. From that day, a regular pattern was established: the apparitions would be in the church or on church property following which there would be the celebration of Mass.

Fr. Jozo, however, had to pay a price for the "protection" of the children. As at Lourdes, Fatima and Marpingen and in so many other sites of Marian apparitions, the civil authorities decided to fight fire with fire: what better way to end an "outbreak" of faith than by persuading the perceived "guardian" of faith to do the dirty work? The initial reaction of the newly installed Bishop of Mostar (he was made bishop in 1980), Bishop Pavao Zanic, to the apparitions was not just positive but exuberant: "the children are not lying," he said, "If there were just one child one could say: 'this kid is so hard-headed that not even the police can make him speak.' But six innocent simple children like these would have told all in half an hour if anybody had been manipulating them." The bishop's train of thought here was and still is formidable (although he himself subsequently abandoned it). But his strong support for the apparitions soon came to the attention of the authorities.

On July 4, 1981, Branko Mikulic, the President of Bosnia-Herzegovina (one of six republics in the erstwhile Yugoslavia), had branded the alleged apparitions as counter-revolutionary. The State Security Police, the UDBA (the Yugoslavian version of the KGB), summoned both the Bishop of Mostar and Fr. Jozo Zovko to their offices in Sarajevo threatening them with imprisonment unless they stopped supporting the apparitions. The two reacted differently to the same threat. Fr. Jozo continued his support, the bishop kept silent. The bishop then called Fr. Jozo to his office and told him both about the threat from the UDBA and a warning he received from his own diocesan priests who said that the bishop's support for the apparitions was elevating the prestige of their rivals, the Franciscans. Fr. Jozo was imprisoned by the UDBA on August 17, 1981 and sentenced to three and a half years of hard labor although this was reduced to a year and a half. Neither during his trial nor his imprisonment did he receive any support or communication from Bishop Zanic. Fr. Jozo's imprisonment convinced the bishop that the UDBA was serious and he began reversing the positive stand he had initially adopted. On his release from prison, Fr. Jozo visited Bishop Zanic at his office. The bishop told him that he had no choice but to back off from Medjugorje in view of the threats from both the state and from his diocesan priests; he said even the local Franciscan authorities were advising silence on Medjugorje because they needed the help of the UDBA.

The bishop's silence about Medjugorje erupted into open hostility when he realized that the phenomenon was beginning to attract thousands of people from around the world and also the support of such eminent theologians as Cardinal Hans Urs Von Balthasar and Fr. Rene Laurentin. Also, the chief champions of the apparitions in Medjugorje were the Franciscans who had engaged in a long and bitter feud with the secular clergy. As bishop, he had two advantages: one, it was he who would ultimately decide on the authenticity of the apparitions; and two, he was both the repository of all data relating to the case and its principals and the disseminator to the world of the interpretations of the data. He issued several statements attacking both the visionaries and the Franciscan supporters of the apparitions. He also instituted a commission made up of individuals he personally appointed to investigate the apparition.

It was well known that the commission's report would be negative but, shortly before the report was published, the Vatican stepped in and removed all affairs relating to the apparition from the jurisdiction of the bishop. Henceforth the view of the Bishop of Mostar on any issue relating to Medjugorje was to be considered nothing more than a private opinion. A letter from the Vatican in 1998 confirmed that this was the case even on the question of whether or not pilgrimages could be made to Medjugorje. The responsibility for investigation of the apparitions was transferred to the Yugoslavian Bishops Conference. In an interim report in 1990, the Conference said that they could not confirm whether or not there was anything supernatural involved at Medjugorje but that they would provide pastoral support for pilgrims to Medjugorje. It was rumored that in a 1991 meeting to be held in Mostar the Conference was going to forbid transmission of the messages from Medjugorje. But this meeting never took place. Shortly before it was to be held, war broke out and Yugoslavia was not only divided into different republics but Bosnia Hercegovina, the republic to which Medjugorje belonged, became the center of some of the most savage and bloody battles in Europe since the Second World War.

Medjugorje itself was miraculously untouched by the violence all around it. A number of media reports noted this puzzling fact: how is it that Medjugorje, which lay at the very center of the bloody war in Bosnia, was entirely untouched by the fire and fury all around it throughout the war? The *Wall Street Journal*, in a November 9, 1992 front page story, reported, "The war has enhanced Medjugorje's fame as an oasis of peace and mystery. ... The sole air raid on the town ended with a few bombs exploding harmlessly. ... 'You have to believe that either we are very lucky,' he [Dragan Kozina, the town's mayor] said, 'or that someone is protecting us.'"

From the first apparitions in 1981, the visionaries continued to see the Gospa daily and were endlessly investigated by scientists and reporters during the apparitions. In judging the authenticity of an apparition, what matters ultimately (in addition to the theological content of the messages) is the actual state of the visionary during the apparition. At the beginning of the typical Medjugorje apparition, the visionaries would suddenly and simultaneously cease whatever they were doing, kneel down and turn their eyes toward the same point on the wall facing them and move their lips without any sound; this naturally inexplicable coordination would be followed by the state of ecstasy. The scientists and psychiatrists who rigorously studied the phenomenon almost from its inception were unanimous on two conclusions: (a) the visionaries are normal people and (b) their physiological processes during the apparitions show no clinical signs of hallucination, hysteria, neurosis, catalepsy or pathological ecstasy. Moreover, the visionaries are insensitive to pain and various other kinds of sensory stimulation during the ecstasy. An April-July 1998 study in Bologna, Italy, included a whole battery of tests from neurological examinations and computerized polygraph tests to numerous other physiological and psychological studies. This latter study confirmed that the visionaries still continued to experience the same state of apparitional ecstasy observed in earlier studies (such as in 1985).

As noted, Medjugorje has been the direct cause of numerous conversions and documented cures. In addition to this, many of the pilgrims have reported a stupendous variety of other supernatural phenomena ranging from rosary links turning to gold to the kind of solar miracles witnessed at Fatima. It would seem that the modern age is so cut off from all sense of the supernatural that Heaven, when it acts decisively, has to bring the full spectrum of signs and wonders to the table. Thus Padre Pio, the saint for the twentieth century, was endowed with every one of the supernatural gifts - the stigmata, reading of souls, bilocation, aroma, healing - whereas saints in previous ages received only one or two of such gifts. Likewise, Medjugorje seems to be "equipped" with all of the charisms that the apparitions of the past possessed singly: conversion and evangelization as in Guadalupe, healing as in Lourdes, penance, mortification and reparation as in Fatima and a host of other apparitions, apocalyptic secrets again as in Fatima and La Salette.

It has often been said that Medjugorje is the fulfillment of Fatima. Whereas Fatima was the herald of the dawn of Communism, Medjugorje was the herald of its dusk. Both apparitions contributed to the demise of Communism, Fatima in unleashing a worldwide campaign of prayer and the subsequent papal consecration of Russia and Medjugorje in bringing about a worldwide religious revival from the middle of a Communist country (many of the most devout pilgrims came from other countries behind the Iron Curtain). The Medjugorje messages made the first direct reference to Fatima after the failed coup of August 22, 1991. In her August 25, 1991, message, the Gospa said, "I invite you to renunciation for nine days so that with your help, everything I wanted to realize through the secrets I began in Fatima may be fulfilled." The relation between Medjugorje and Fatima was most clearly discerned by the countries in which Russia had "spread its errors." Cardinal Frantizek Tomasek, the late Archbishop of Prague and former Communist concentration camp inmate, said Medjugorje "fills me with a great inner joy, fills me with a great inner power." In a 1988 interview with *Medjugorge Gebetsaktion*, he said, "Personally, I am convinced that Medjugorje is the continuation of Lourdes and Fatima. Step by step, the Immaculate Heart of Mary will triumph. And I am also deeply convinced that Medjugorje is a sign for this."

Medjugorje has certainly inspired a torrent of polemic mostly directed at individuals and events that are tangential to the only relevant datum: the phenomenon itself. The generation of such polemic will not surprise those who have studied the history of apparitions. For instance, the Beauraing and La Salette claims spawned storms of controversy both within and outside the Church and succeeded in confusing many of the faithful. The principals of Lourdes and Fatima were both subjected to abuse. It is entirely possible that if the intrepid psychiatrists who conducted such elaborate tests on the visionaries were to study some of the critics they might end up detecting some of the pathologies and neuroses they failed to find in the visionaries!

Concerning the Medjugorje critics, it may be said that they are not developing arguments; they are painting a certain picture, creating a certain history of the events of Medjugorje. If this picture reflects the reality, if this history is true to the facts, then someone who has not studied the sources for himself would understandably be inclined to think that there is a cloud over Medjugorje. What is required is an intellectual exorcism: First, one must lay out one's biases and agendas on the table before beginning the discussion. Second, the narrator must admit that there is more than one **account** of the facts and must attempt to present other accounts. Thirdly, he or she must acknowledge that there is more than one **interpretation** of the facts and here again attempt to present other interpretations. Finally, it must be acknowledged that a presentation of history is not an argument.

If we go by the key criterion instituted by the Congregation for the Doctrine of the Faith, the absence of any "psychopathic tendency in the person which might enter into the alleged supernatural event; no psychosis or collective hysteria of some type," then Medjugorje is an authentic apparition of the Virgin.

The other relevant consideration is the theological content of the messages. Even Bishop Zanic did not criticize the theology of the Medjugorje messages, his only complaint being that they are banal (it might be responded that the repetition of eternal truths is not likely to furnish much in the way of novelty). The Medjugorje messages, in fact, seem so orthodox and sensible that the chief allegation of the critics is that they were doctored by the Franciscans.

The logical structure of the charge of theological editing seems to be the following:

> The messages are theologically sound.
> Therefore they were doctored by the Franciscans.

Now if the messages were coming from the Virgin one would expect them to be theologically sound. So what does this argument prove? Should the messages be theologically unsound so as to prove they are not from the Franciscans? And if they are theologically unsound will the critics accept them as coming from the Virgin? No possible answer will apparently satisfy this class of critic.

Fortunately it is fairly easy to show that - quite apart from the question of theological soundness - the Medjugorje messages could not have originated with the Franciscans. Consider this:

1. Who "created" the original messages from the Gospa? At the beginning of the phenomenon, the parish priest, Fr. Jozo Zovko, did not believe that the visionaries were witnessing an authentic apparition. Both he and his assistant pastor were skeptical - and only the Bishop of Mostar believed the visionaries. So which Franciscans did the editing?

2. Fr. Jozo was imprisoned for a year and a half after he decided to protect the visionaries. So who created the messages during this period?

3. The Franciscans at the parish were regularly transferred - yet the messages have retained a uncanny consistency from the beginning to the present. In other words, the messages before the Franciscans got involved, during the crisis of Fr. Jozo's arrest, during the many transfers of parish priests, during the chaos of the war and to this very day have consistently focused on central Gospel themes.

4. One Franciscan who has been a spiritual adviser to the visionaries, Fr. Slavko Barbaric, came to Medjugorje at the request of Bishop Zanic

in order to investigate the authenticity of the apparition. He came as a skeptical psychiatrist but was so impressed with the evident sincerity and veracity of the visionaries that he remained with them giving them the direction they required for their spiritual formation. Like all human beings, the visionaries also need spiritual directors - as did St. Margaret Mary and many other visionaries of the past.

5. Often the messages of the visionaries were antithetical to the views and background of the Franciscans. For instance, when the visionaries asked the Gospa who was the holiest person in the village, she responded that a good example was a Moslem lady who lived there. Considering the historical animosity between the Franciscans and the Moslems, this could hardly be viewed as a Fransciscan-edited message. On one occasion, the Gospa chided Vicka for asking so many questions about the Franciscans. Moreover, with reference to the war between the Croatians and the Serbs, she said that Satan was on both sides.

6. The visionaries have always said that the Gospa has asked them to respect, love and pray for their bishop, the Bishop of Mostar. Some of the Franciscans, on the other hand, have been less than respectful in their relations with the bishop.

> Here an incident from July 20, 1984 is especially revealing:
> "Open your hearts to me, come close. Say in a loud voice your intentions and your prayers." Our Lady was very attentive to the prayers of the visionaries. While praying for Bishop Zanic of Mostar, Her eyes welled up with tears and She says: "You are my little flowers. Continue to pray; my task is lighter because of it." She then blessed the visionaries and the people with a crucifix and ascended back to Heaven crying.

7. Very significant also is the fact that the visionaries have sometimes received messages from the Gospa that the Franciscans were unwilling to publicize - resulting in tension between the Franciscans and the visionaries. An example is the Gospa's message of a special blessing that can be received in Medjugorje - this is a message that the visionaries maintain as coming directly from the Gospa and which the Franciscans have tried to downplay (historically speaking, this

message cannot be considered an anomaly: in other apparitions, the Virgin has spoken of special graces coming from the Miraculous Medal, the Scapular, the Rosary, the healing spring in Lourdes, etc.).

Polemic aside, as pointed out at the outset, the papally appointed Vatican Commission now recognizes the authenticity of the first seven apparitions in Medjugorje without making any judgment on subsequent claims. Further, the Church has not only acknowledged Medjugorje's status as a Marian shrine but has placed it under the leadership of a papally appointed Apostolic Visitor. This is "certification" of a very high degree.

Returning to the encounter itself, the Gospa has said that each of the visionaries will receive ten secrets and when the six of them have received all ten secrets, the apparitions will cease and the apocalyptic events revealed in the secrets will begin to unfold. Among the ten secrets is the promise that, at the end of the apparitions, Medjugorje itself will be the site of a lasting "Great Sign" that will convince the skeptics. To date, three of the visionaries (Mirjana, Ivanka and Jackov) have received all ten secrets and the other three have received nine. The three who have received the ten secrets no longer have daily apparitions. On the 25th of every month, the Gospa gives the visionaries a message that is intended for the world. (About the concept of secrets, we read this in St. Paul: "But I will move on to the visions and revelations I have had from the Lord. I know a man in Christ who, fourteen years ago, was caught up - whether still in the body or out of the body, I do not know; God knows - right into the third heaven. I do know, however, that this same person - whether in the body or out of the body, I do not know; God knows - was caught up into paradise and heard things which must not and cannot be put into human language." 2 *Corinthians* 12: 1-4.).

In his book *Heaven Wants to Be Heard*, the British scholar Dudley Plunkett lists the following spiritual appeals of the Medjugorje messages as Heaven's message to the modern world:

- ○ attend daily Mass (30 March 1984)
- ○ offer three hours of prayer a day (4 July 1983)
- ○ pray three rosaries each day (14 August 1984) as well as 7 Paters, Aves and Glorias for peace
- ○ go to monthly confession (6 August 1982)

- give time for adoration of the Blessed Sacrament (15 March 1984)
- read the Scriptures daily (18 October 1994)
- pray before the cross (12 September 1985)
- observe family prayer (20 October 1983)
- make an act of consecration to the Sacred Heart of Jesus and to the Immaculate Heart of Mary (25 October 1988)
- undertake pilgrimages, penance, sacrifices, and fast on bread and water twice a week (27 June 1981).

In the final analysis this is what Medjugorje is all about. This is why it has attracted tens of thousands of priests and religious and converted millions of men, women and children. Herein is set forth the banquet of Grace to which the Mother of God who is the Mother of Humanity invites all her children - especially those most in need of the Divine Mercy.

The choice is stark: Heaven or Hell:

"Today many persons go to Hell. God allows His children to suffer in Hell due to the fact that they have committed grave, unpardonable sins.... People who commit grave sins live in Hell while here on earth and continue this Hell in eternity. They actually go to Hell because they chose it in life and at the moment of death." (July 25, 1982)

"I want to bring you to Heaven with God. I want you to comprehend that this life is very short in comparison with that in Heaven. Therefore, dear children, today decide anew for God. Only in that way can I show you how much you are beloved by me and how much I want all of you to be saved and be with me in Heaven." (November 27, 1986).

Four of the visionaries were, in fact, taken to Heaven, Hell and Purgatory. Asked about their journey to Hell, this is what Vicka and Marija said:

> Vicka: "We saw many people in hell. Many are there already, and many more will go there when they die... The Blessed Mother says that those people who are in hell are there because they chose to go there. They wanted to go to hell... We all know that there are persons on this earth who simply don't admit that God exists, even though He helps them, gives them life and sun and rain and food. He always tries to nudge them onto the path of holiness. They

just say they don't believe, and they deny Him. They deny Him, even when it is time to die. And they continue to deny Him, after they are dead. It is their choice. It is their will that they go to hell. They choose hell.

Question: "Describe hell as you remember it.

Vicka: "In the center of this place is a great fire, like an ocean of raging flames. We could see people before they went into the fire, and then we could see them coming out of the fire. Before they go into the fire, they look like normal people. The more they are against God's will, the deeper they enter into the fire, and the deeper they go, the more they rage against Him. When they come out of the fire, they don't have human shape anymore; they are more like grotesque animals, but unlike anything on earth. It's as if they were never human beings before...They were horrible. Ugly. Angry. And each was different; no two looked alike...When they came out, they were raging and smashing everything around and hissing and gnashing and screeching.

Question: "Has seeing hell changed how you pray?

Vicka: ""Oh, yes! Now I pray for the conversion of sinners! I know what awaits them if they refuse to convert."

Vicka: "People turn away from God by choices they make. In this way they choose to enter the fire of hell where they burn away all connection to God. That's why they can never get back to God. It takes God's mercy to get back to Him. In hell, they no longer have access to God's mercy...They choose to destroy their beauty and goodness. They choose to be ugly and horrible. People do this all the time. Each choice that is against God, God's Commandments, God's Will, singes God's image in us...They become one with hell even while they have their body. At death they go on as they were when they had a body."

Question: "Marija, have you ever seen hell?

Marija: "Yes, it's a large space with a big sea of fire in the middle. There are many people there. I particularly noticed a beautiful young girl. But when she came near the fire, she was no longer beautiful. She came out of the fire like an animal; she was no longer human. The Blessed Mother told me that God gives us all choices.

Everyone responds to these choices. Everyone can choose if he wants to go to hell or not. Anyone who goes to hell chooses hell.

Question: "Marija, how and why does a soul choose hell for himself for all eternity?

Marija: "In the moment of death, God gives us the light to see ourselves as we really are. God gives freedom of choice to everybody during his life on earth. The one who lives in sin on earth can see what he has done and recognize himself as he really is. When he sees himself and his life, the only possible place for him is hell. He chooses hell, because that is what he is. That is where he fits. It is his own wish. God does not make the choice. God condemns no one. We condemn ourselves. Every individual has free choice. God gave us freedom.

Question: "Marija, what about people who grow up spiritually deceived, people who have been told that God does not exist, that there is no God?

Marija: "People, as they grow up, can think. Everyone knows and can recognize what is good and what is bad by the time they grow up. God gives us freedom of choice. We can choose good or bad. Everybody chooses here in this life whether he goes to Heaven or hell.

Question: "How do we choose Heaven or hell or Purgatory for ourselves?

Marija: "At the moment of death, God gives everyone the grace to see his whole life, to see what he has done, to recognize the results of his choices on earth. And each person, when he sees himself in the divine light of reality, chooses for himself where he belongs. Every individual chooses for himself what he personally deserves for all eternity.[2]

THE MEDJUGORJE PROGRAM- A FORMULA FOR THE HAPPINESS OF HEAVEN

Medjugorje is essentially a divinely designed Program of Conversion and Consecration, Purification and Protection, Sanctification and Salvation, and finally human participation in the divine Plan. The hundreds of messages received at Medjugorje form a blueprint for becoming and being a Christian in the modern world. Moreover each component of the Program in one sense is identical with every other component because they are all simply different ways of looking at the same fundamental reality of union/reconciliation/peace with God. Thus conversion = consecration = purification = protection = sanctification = salvation = participation in the plans of God.

It is quite apparent that the possibility of living a truly Christian life has never been as difficult– in terms of the temptations of the world, the flesh and the Devil – in any era as it is today. Evil, packaged in a thousand attractive and instantly gratifying incarnations, is all but irresistible, even to the very elect. The intellect, the will and every one of the senses have been seduced and subjugated by the most ingeniously invasive vehicles of sin (from global cable television to widely-used hallucinogens) imaginable. Never has the soul been in such peril as it is today.

But just as she came "out of the blue" to the seat of the Enlightenment (Paris, France, in 1830) and the heart of the pagan New World (Tepeyac, Mexico, 1531), the Virgin initiated an innocuous but instantly effective counter-attack against all that is evil in modernity in the country which triggered off the first great wave of destruction of the modern world (the First World War).

The Medjugorje messages can be classified under the categories that form its basic Program: conversion, which literally means ripping out the root of evil in us implanted by Original Sin and hardened by the modern world; consecration, the complete surrender of all that we are and have to God, a letting-go that is as unsettling as it is comforting; purification, the eradication of the "habits" of sin and the allure of temptations through fasting and penance; protection from the world, the flesh and the devil through prayer from the heart and the use of all the aids given us by God; sanctification through the sacraments and again prayer; salvation, with graphic portrayals of the consequences of our present choices in the life to come; and human participation in the divine Plan, an unveiling of the impact of our actions and our prayers on God's scheme of salvation for the human race. In practical terms, the Program calls us to daily Mass, monthly confession, daily prayer of three hours (this includes the time spent at Mass and praying the Rosary) and fasting on bread and water on Wednesdays and Fridays. The Medjugorje Program is the divine Physician's life-support system for the patients who lie comatose in the intensive care units of the inferno of modern life; it is a formula for both sanity and sanctity in a world that knows neither.

In sum, the Medjugorje Program if whole-heartedly embraced and applied, will set us on the path of salvation - and its sanctifying fruits will soon become evident in our personal experience (as millions can testify). But, warns the Program Director, any departure, any deviation from the Program, no matter how slight or innocuous, can be disastrous, exposing us to the full fury of the world, the flesh and the Devil. We dare not make any exception lest we be defiled. "Satisfaction" is guaranteed but only if the conditions are met.

Of these conditions, the one emphasized in almost every one of the messages is prayer, prayer that is all but constant, prayer from the heart. The heart is very important in everything about Medjugorje: it is a Program of the heart from the Queen of hearts: she leads our hearts to her Immaculate Heart and through that to the Sacred Heart of her Son. There can be no earthly way to communicate the joy that comes from entering the life of prayer from the heart - it is so easy to enter and yet so easy to overlook for years and years and even throughout one's life. Hence the Gospa's constant reminder to "Pray! Pray! Pray!". But prayer to be fruitful must be undergirded by three other conditions that are again consistently taught at Medjugorje: utter humility, reconciliation with all our brothers and sisters and total consecration to Jesus through Mary. Humility is fundamental: we can do nothing by ourselves: we have to let God do everything and be humble instruments in His Hands. This means we should not have any trust in our own abilities or our own spiritual strength: we must recognize that all we are and have comes from God and God has to continually sustain these (and the one good that God brings about from our falling into sin is this recognition). Then there is reconciliation: complete forgiveness of all those who may have hurt or insulted us is essential for us to start on the path to Heaven. Jesus' warnings about God not forgiving those who cannot forgive their brothers have to be taken seriously - and they are at Medjugorje. Finally, we have to be totally consecrated to Jesus through Mary. We must be consciously and constantly aware that we have entrusted our entire being to God through the hands of the Blessed Mother. There is no alternative to total surrender of the self in its entirety. No part of us can be our own - because anything we own or control inevitably falls under the world, the flesh or the Devil. Once we make this consecration, once we give all that we own materially or spiritually, most especially the spiritual merits of any of our actions, to Jesus through Mary, we can be fully protected from our enemies.

NOTES

[1] https://www.vaticannews.va/en/church/news/2018-07/archbishop-hoser-envoy-medjugorje-st-james-apparition-mary.html

[2] https://www.medjugorje.com/medjugorje/heaven-purgatory-hell/description-of-hell.html

REFERENCE

The New Eve in History and Today

Yes

The odyssey of the Blessed Virgin Mary is one of the most astonishing tales in the history of humanity. But it is so familiar we take it for granted. And so we fail to realize its utterly remarkable nature. Here was a human person whose Son was God incarnate – and whose mother she remains for all eternity. A person who entered into the most intimate union possible union for a human person with God the Holy Spirit. A person specially chosen and prepared by God the Father to be not just the Mother of his only begotten Son (*Luke* 1:30) but of all who bear witness to the Son and keep the divine commandments (*Revelation* 12:17). Most important, the Incarnation of God the Son was contingent on her consent – a consent she granted from the depths of her being. She was called to share totally in the sorrow that was to be his life (*Luke* 2:30) – a participation she whole-heartedly offered up. The earliest apprehension of her by the faithful was, in fact, in her role as Sorrowful Mother.

Our salvation comes from Christ Jesus. But the salvific coming of Christ was made possible by his Mother's free act of obedience to the divine Will. She was not a puppet, not a mindless vessel chosen by a super-human puppet-master to achieve his aims as some critics of Marian devotion have said. Such critics are ideologists who deny the plain words of Scripture and devalue both the dignity of the human person and the gift of freewill given by our Maker. But the followers of Christ from the beginning recognized that she was not simply chosen by God but that Mary herself chose God in the most important choice ever made by a human person. Therein lies her blessedness through all generations. "Blessed are *you who believed* that what was spoken to you by the Lord would be fulfilled." (*Luke* 1:45).

Holy Virgin Mother – the Historic Christian Consensus

Any study of the Virgin Mary begins with her Son. Historically, the recognition of Jesus as God incarnate was accompanied by an awareness of the role of his Mother in his mission. And like the truths specific to the Incarnation of God in Christ, there emerged a historic Christian consensus on affirmations about the Mother of the Messiah. This consensus sprang from the rendezvous of five different streams of thought and practice.

There was, first, the faith of the early Christian communities that predated the consolidation of the canon of Scripture. This consolidation of the canon took place only in the fourth century and was, in fact, guided by this very faith that came before it. As we have said, the catacombs of the Christian martyrs of the second and third centuries not only show images representing the scriptural stories but also images of the Virgin in which her mediation is invoked for protection and defense.

Another interesting, though startling, resource pool is the set of second century apocryphal gospels and third century *transitus mariae* narratives. Now these were obviously fantasies with no basis in historical fact but they do show us something important. The idea that the Blessed Virgin was the most important participant in salvation history after her Son was so rooted in the minds and hearts of the faithful that some of them felt compelled to invent stories about Jesus and Mary that paid homage to their exalted status. What is important here is not the story but the state of mind that led to the invention of the story: these stories were written by and for people who already took the adoration of the Lord and the veneration of the Virgin for granted.

Secondly, there was the testimony of canonical Scripture. Every word uttered by Mary the Mother of Jesus – and these were numerically few in number – had momentous consequences in the divine plan of salvation. When she said to the angel Gabriel, "Let what you have said be done to me," the Holy Spirit "came upon" her and she became the Mother of the

Redeemer of humanity. When she greeted her cousin Elizabeth, the Holy Spirit himself spoke to her through Elizabeth saying that at the sound of Mary's voice, "the child in my womb leaped for joy" - an event that has historically been regarded as the sanctification of John the Baptist in the womb. When the inspired Elizabeth praised her for the act of faith and obedience that caused her to be "blessed," Mary responded with the proclamation of praise we call the Magnificat. Two things should be noted about this hymn: first, Mary attributes her glorification to God and, second, she says "all generations will call her blessed" because of what God has done for her (and God bestowed this blessing, we find from Elizabeth's statement just before, because Mary "believed").

Finally, in the most famous wedding in history, her Son changes his own timeline for his ministry in response to her words, "They have no wine." Mary already knows he will do what she requested and tells the servants, "Do whatever he tells you." The miracle that follows not only begins the public ministry of Jesus but also causes his disciples "to believe in him."

The significance that the Virgin's words have in Scripture are matched by the importance attributed to her at key events in the biblical narrative: at the presentation in the Temple, the Holy Spirit inspires Simeon to say to her that, when her Son is rejected, "you yourself a sword will pierce;" at Calvary, her Son establishes her as mother of all believers, "This is your mother"; at the birth of the Church, the author of Acts notes that "the mother of Jesus" is present when the Holy Spirit descends on all the believers gathered in prayer; and in *Revelation* 12 we are given the glorious vision of her as the mother of all those "who obey God's commandments and bear witness for Jesus."

The strategy of dissecting Marian doctrines with scriptural proof-texts is historically and logically wrong-headed because the Church that selected the canon of Scripture was previously already committed to the veneration of the Virgin. If the early Church was wrong in its teaching about the Virgin Mary, then there is no reason to believe it was authoritative in its teachings about what constituted Scripture.

Thirdly, there was the witness of the Eastern and Western Fathers. These are the great and ancient interpreters of Scripture whose interpretations have been taken as normative by generations of Christians, Protestant,

Catholic and Orthodox. Any doctrine taught unanimously by the Fathers of East and West is generally considered authoritative by that very fact. These are the same holy thinkers whose teachings and interpretations helped guide the Councils to their conclusions. The writings of all of the Church Fathers, the Teachers of the earliest Christian communities who interpreted Scripture for the faithful, bear eloquent testimony to Marian veneration. In their scripturally derived understanding of Mary as the New Eve and the New Ark of Covenant, the Fathers established an unassailable basis for Marian veneration that was accepted for centuries by the Christians of East and West.

Fourth, there was the voice of the liturgy. Perhaps the truest witness to the faith of the believing community is the language of their prayer and liturgical celebration. All of the ancient liturgies, even those before the Council of Ephesus, testify to the firm belief of the Christian faithful in the veneration of the Virgin Mary and the invocation of her intercession. The Eastern liturgies, the most ancient of them all since Christianity sprang in the East, resonate with hymns, odes and prayers to the Virgin.

Thousands of the canons in the Byzantine liturgy are written in honor of the Virgin: "While we sing the glories of thy Son, we praise thee, too, O Mother of God, living Temple of the Godhead. O purest One, do not despise the petitions of the sinner." "Hail, Mother of God, Virgin full of grace, Refuge and Protection of the human race." The Alexandrian liturgy is also replete with Marian veneration and invocation: "Hail to thee, O Virgin, the very and true Queen; hail glory of our race." "Hail Mary! We beseech thee, holy one, full of glory, ever Mother of God, Mother of Christ, lift up our prayers to thy beloved Son, that He may forgive us our sins." The Antiochene liturgy, perhaps the oldest of the ancient liturgies, includes the liturgy of St. James. The Marian invocations in this latter liturgy, such as the following recited during the breaking of the Host, "My blessed Lady Mary, beseech with thine only Begotten that he be appeased through thy prayers and perform mercy on us all," are profoundly moving. In the Western liturgies, Marian veneration and invocation appears in the liturgy of the Mass and also forms a prominent part of regular prayers (offices) and feasts. These liturgies celebrate all of the privileges of the Virgin ranging from her Divine Maternity to her Virginity, Sanctity, Assumption and Mediation.

Fifth, and finally, there was the teaching of the Councils. The great Councils of the undivided Church proclaim the convictions held in common by all Christians for the first fifteen centuries about the role of Mary in salvation history. No Christian can reject these Councils since to reject them would ipso facto mean rejecting the teachings of the Councils about such articles of faith as the Holy Trinity. The Trinity is not a word used in the Bible but it is an interpretation of certain biblical passages ratified by the Councils of the Church. To believe in the Trinity is implicitly to accept the authority of the Councils that taught the doctrine of the Trinity. If one accepts the doctrine of the Trinity then one has also to accept the Marian doctrines taught by the Councils - since both doctrines are ultimately accepted on the authority of the bodies that taught them.

Among the Councils, the Third Ecumenical Council at Ephesus (431), which taught that Mary was Theotokos, Mother of God, gave a new doctrinal momentum to the great wave of Marian veneration and invocation that had been building up in previous centuries. After this Council, more churches were named after her, new prayers were addressed to her, and great feasts in her honor were introduced into the Church's calendar. The language of the first seven Ecumenical Councils, accepted as authoritative by Protestants, Catholics and Orthodox alike, gives some idea of the reverence that Christians had for their Mother: the Fifth Ecumenical Council (Second Council of Constantinople, 553) describes her as "the holy, glorious and ever-Virgin Mary." "The Virgin Mary" was "really and truly the Mother of God" says the Third Council of Constantinople (680). Finally, and most significantly, the Seventh Ecumenical Council (the Second Council of Nicaea, 787) proclaims, "The Lord, the apostles and the prophets have taught us that we must venerate in the first place the Holy Mother of God, who is above all the heavenly powers. If any one does not confess that the holy, ever virgin Mary, really and truly the Mother of God, is higher than all creatures visible and invisible, and does not implore with a sincere faith, her intercession, given her powerful access to our God born of her, let him be anathema."

New Eve

That Mary's "Yes" was the pivotal act of her life was recognized from the start. This is precisely why the first, unanimous and single most important teaching of the Fathers of the Christian Church about Mary, starting with Justin the Martyr, 100-165 A.D., is that Mary is the New Eve. The contrast between Eve and Mary, Adam and Christ, the evil angel in Eden and the good angel at the Annunciation, and the Tree of the Knowledge of Good and Evil and the Tree of the Cross, lies at the heart of the history of salvation.

This is the hidden and yet obvious truth in Scripture that became foundational to the theology and devotional life of the first Christians. Scholars today point out that Justin's understanding of the Virgin Mary is taken exclusively from Scripture (which is not to say that tradition handed down, of which Paul speaks, has no value). The distinguished Lutheran church historian Jaroslav Pelikan notes that Fathers like Irenaeus, when writing about Mary as the New Eve, do not even try to argue for this interpretation since it was already considered a part of the basic body of Christian belief.

The history of salvation in the Judeo-Christian revelation is built around covenants between God and humanity. The idea of a covenant entails an agreement freely entered into by two parties, on the one side God and on the other humanity. Pelikan tells us that, in the Christian vision, two of the key players on the human side were Eve and Mary. This is the consistent message that begins with the first Fathers:

> Justin Martyr: "He became man by the Virgin in order that the disobedience which proceeded from the serpent might receive its destruction in the same manner in which it derived its origin. For Eve, who was a virgin and undefiled, having conceived by the word of the serpent brought forth disobedience and death. But the Virgin Mary received faith and joy, when the angel Gabriel announced the good tidings to her that the Spirit of the Lord would come upon her, and the power of the Most High would overshadow her, wherefore also the Holy One begotten of her is the Son of God, and she replied, 'Be it done unto me according to your word.'" (*Dialogue with Trypho*).

> Irenaeus of Lyons (140-202): "[Eve] having become disobedient, was made the cause of death, both to herself and to the entire human race; so also did Mary, having a man betrothed [to her],

and being nevertheless a virgin, by yielding obedience, become the cause of salvation, both to herself and the whole human race." (*Against Heresies III*). "And just as it was through a virgin who disobeyed that man was stricken and fell and died, so too it was through the Virgin, who obeyed the word of God, that man resuscitated by life received life. ... Adam was necessarily to be restored in Christ, that mortality be absorbed in immortality, and Eve in Mary, that a virgin, become the advocate of a virgin, should undo and destroy virginal disobedience by virginal obedience." (*Proof of the Apostolic Teaching*).

Tertullian (155-240): "God recovered His image and likeness in a procedure similar to that in which He had been robbed of it by the devil. For it was while Eve was still a virgin that the word of the devil crept in to erect an edifice of death. Likewise, through a Virgin, the Word of God was introduced to set up a structure of life." "As Eve had believed the serpent, so Mary believed the angel. The delinquency which the one occasioned by believing, the other by believing effaced." (*The Flesh of Christ*).[1]

The Mary-Eve typology was not just a theological metaphor but entered into the liturgical celebrations and devotion of the early Christians and became a part of all the ancient liturgies. It was in effect a fundamental teaching of the Church and underlies all the doctrines that we call Marian - for instance, she who would begin the process of reversing the consequences of Original Sin could not be subject to these consequences (conception in sin, corruption of the grave).

Moreover, the importance of the Annunciation - of Mary's Yes - for human salvation was not highlighted simply by theologians and pastors. It served as one of the central and persistent themes of artistic creation inspired by the Christian story. Almost all the greatest artists of Christendom have made their own contributions to the depiction of the Annunciation.

But Mary's role in salvation history did not end with the Annunciation. On the one hand, she is permanently the New Eve just as her Son will always be the New Adam. On the other, we see that she is mysteriously present with the New Adam at precisely the times most crucial to the accomplishment of Redemption. When she offers up her infant Son at the

Temple, it is prophesied that a sword will pierce her soul. This prophecy was fulfilled, said the Fathers and the faithful, when her offering came to a climax on Calvary and she became for all time the Sorrowful Mother. The consent given at the Annunciation extended through the Presentation at the Temple to the Sacrifice on Calvary.

As Eve was associated with Adam at all stages of the Fall, so also the New Eve was associated with the New Adam at every step of the road to Redemption. The Fathers recognized that the Incarnation cannot be separated from the Cross and Redemption and in calling Mary the New Eve they drew our attention to the singular role she played in the Redemptive Mission of God Incarnate. Referring to the ancient Church's understanding of Mary as the New Eve, the Anglican theologian Eric Mascall observed that Mary can be "described as coredemptrix in order to bring out the fact that, while Mary has a real part in the redemptive process, because she is morally and physically associated in it with her Son, yet her part is, and must be, essentially subordinate and ancillary to his." "Co" is taken from the Latin term "cum" meaning "with" and, as "The force of the prefix co is to indicate not equality but subordination, as when St Paul tells his Corinthian disciples that 'we are God's fellow-workers', his synergoi, his co-operators."[2]

More recently (in his *Mary for All Christians*), another great Anglican thinker, John Macquarrie, noted that Mary symbolizes the "perfect harmony between the divine will and the human response, so that it is she who gives meaning to the expression Corredemptrix."[3] To the extent that any Christian shares in the redeeming work of Christ, he or she is a coredeemer and the classic statement of this truth comes from St. Paul's epistle to the Colossians, "It makes me happy to suffer for you, as I am suffering now, and in my own body to do what I can to make up all that has still to be undergone by Christ for the sake of his body, the Church." (Colossians 1:24). Macquarrie notes that Mary's coredemptive "contribution was unique" because through her willing acceptance she became the Mother of the Redeemer.

Also, Mary's co-redemptive role does not eliminate the fact that she herself had to be redeemed; it is believed that her redemption took place at conception through the redemptive effects of her Son's death, which could go backward and forward in time, so that she was not affected by Original Sin; no other satisfactory explanation can be given of the term *kecharitomene* used of her, by the angel Gabriel, which meant that she had already been transformed by grace before the birth of her Son.

The great teaching of Irenaeus and all subsequent Church Fathers is that history - under divine direction - repeats itself but in an equal and opposite manner! This is the gist of his teaching about recapitulation and recirculation. This inverse parallelism shows itself first in the contrast between Adam and Eve and Jesus and Mary: as the evil angel seduces Eve to disobey God and Eve in turn persuades Adam to open the doors of damnation, so a good angel comes to Mary with a divine command that she obeys and thus gives birth to the Jesus Who opens the doors to redemption. She is the New Eve and Jesus the New Adam.

But the parallelism of Adam and Eve and Christ and Mary does not cease with their individual acts of obedience and disobedience. These acts had cosmic effects. With the Original Sin of Adam (caused by Eve) the human race and all of creation were thrown into decay and destruction. With the redemptive death of Christ (in which His Mother sorrowfully participated as Simeon had described), the human race and all of creation were called to enter a new splendor even greater than the perfection present before the Fall when everything is brought together "under Christ, as head, everything in the heavens and everything on earth." (*Ephesians* 1:10).

The Christian message is that God does not lose, that his plans always bear fruit. If humanity fell through a man and a woman, humanity would be saved through a man and a woman. If Adam and Eve left the Eden that God had planned for them and their progeny, then the new Adam and the new Eve would take their offspring into a new Eden infinitely more joyous than the first Eden for here all of creation is transformed by the very life of God. In the Christian dispensation, all of human history is moving inexorably toward this great climactic consummation when "all things [are] to be reconciled through him [Christ] and for him, everything in heaven and everything on earth." (*Colossians* 1:19-20). And as the Virgin Mary brought Christ into the world in his first coming and suffered with him to the end, she likewise, in her Contact as the Queen-

Mother, prepares the way for his coming Reign as King when the divine Will is to be done on earth as it is in Heaven.

Prophecy of the Virgin Birth

As a footnote, we consider the prophecy, in *Isaiah* (7:14), of a virgin giving birth to a son who shall be named Emmanuel. Critics have said that the Hebrew word "almah" used here refers to "young woman" and not "virgin." But *Genesis* 24:43 and *Exodus* 2:8 use this same word when referring to an "unmarried woman" of marriageable age – someone who, at least in biblical times, was thought of as a virgin. The text also says the birth is given by the Lord as a "sign." A young woman giving birth to a son is not in itself a sign.

More to the point, "virgin" was the word used in the Greek translation of the Old Testament used by Jews in the pre-Christian era.

As one commentator points out, in the

> Septuagint, which is the Greek translation of the Old Testament, the word almah is translated by the Greek word parthenos which means virgin and is unambiguous. Now this might not seem like such a big deal until you realise that the Septuagint was completed over 130 years before Christ came. It is a pre-Christian, Jewish translation of the OT. And when the 70 Jewish scholars who did this translation saw the Hebrew word almah in Isaiah 7:14, they translated it with the Greek word that means virgin and is the very same word (parthenos) that was later used by the evangelists in Matthew 1:23 and Luke 1:27 where there is no doubt that it means virgin. This is clearly not a matter of Christians trying to force the OT to say something. Matthew and Luke were simply translating the verse the same way it had been translated by the Jews up until that time. We have the clear testimony from the very Bible (the Septuagint) that was used all over the Hellenistic world of Judaism at the time of Jesus' birth that the word, according to the 70 Jewish scholars who did the translation, means virgin in Isaiah 7:14.[4]

A New Recognition of the Virgin Among All Christians

The Virgin's identity as the New Eve, with its attendant and ancillary implications, was accepted by all Christians for the first 1500 years of Christianity. Although it has been in eclipse in certain parts of the Christian world for the last 500 years, we cannot reject this truth without throwing into question a whole host of other fundamental truths. For instance, the doctrine of the Incarnation, the teaching that Jesus of Nazareth is fully God and fully man, is an interpretation of Scripture that is accepted as authoritative because it emerged over centuries in the writings of the Fathers, the teaching of the Councils and the worship of the liturgy. If we reject the authority of these three pillars, then we cannot teach the doctrine of the Incarnation as an authoritative Christian doctrine. But if we accept their authority, then we cannot reject the doctrine of the New Eve.

Despite the mutual polemics that followed the Reformation, many Protestant Christians today have a new appreciation for the role of the Virgin.

Prominent theologians from mainstream Protestant denominations now accept some of the Marian titles celebrated by Catholics (for instance, Mother of God) while giving qualified assent to various Marian doctrines (for instance, the Immaculate Conception). These include theologians from the Anglican/Episcopalian, Presbyterian, Lutheran and Methodist denominations.

Some Evangelical Protestant theologians now admit that Protestants have failed to notice, let alone honor, the Virgin Mary and should rectify this oversight. They are quick to add that any attention to Mary must be tempered by the content of Scripture.

These trends were highlighted in a *Time* magazine cover story titled, "Hail, Mary: Catholics have long revered her, but now Protestants are finding their own reasons to celebrate the mother of Jesus" (March 21, 2005), in an article in the *Economist* called "A Mary for All" (December 18, 2003), and in cover stories in various Protestant publications ranging from the Evangelical *Christianity Today* ("The Blessed Evangelical Mary") to the liberal *Christian Century* ("St Mary for Protestants").

R.A. Varghese

"Hail Mary", *Time*, March 21, 2005

In a shift whose ideological breadth is unusual in the fragmented Protestant world, a long-standing wall around Mary appears to be eroding. It is not that Protestants are converting to Catholicism's dramatic exaltation: the singing of Salve Regina, the Rosary's Marian Mysteries, the entreaty to her in the Hail Mary to "pray for us sinners now and at the hour of our death." Rather, a growing number of Christian thinkers who are neither Catholic nor Eastern Orthodox (another branch of faith to which Mary is central) have concluded that their various traditions have shortchanged her in the very arena in which Protestantism most prides itself: the careful and full reading of Scripture.

Arguments on the Virgin's behalf have appeared in a flurry of scholarly essays and popular articles, on the covers of the usually conservative *Christianity Today* (headline: The Blessed Evangelical Mary) and the usually liberal *Christian Century* (St. Mary for Protestants). They are being preached, if not yet in many churches then in a denominational cross section--and not just at modest addresses ... but also from mighty pulpits like that at Chicago's Fourth Presbyterian Church, where longtime senior pastor John Buchanan recently delivered a major message on the Virgin ending with the words "Hail Mary ... Blessed are you among us all."

This could probably not have happened at some other time. Robert Jenson, author of the respected text Systematic Theology, chuckles when asked whether the pastor of his Lutheran youth would have approved of his (fairly extreme) position that Protestants, like Catholics, should pray for Mary's intercession.... A growing interest, on both the Protestant right and left, in practices and texts from Christianity's first 1,500 years has led to immersion in the habitual Marianism of the early and medieval church....

[Princeton Scripture specialist] Beverly Gaventa ...She approached her Mary work in "a Protestant sort of way. We pride ourselves on reading Scripture, so let's read Scripture and see what we find."

What she read--and what Protestants had been more or less skimming for centuries--was a skein of appearances longer and more strategically placed than those of any other character in the Gospels except Jesus....

Gaventa's conclusion was that although Mary's appearances can be brief and frustratingly devoid of anecdote, "there isn't a figure comparable to her." No major player appears earlier in the story, and none, she notes, "is present in all these key situations: at Jesus' birth, at his death, in the upper room." Protestant treatments, Gaventa asserted, tended to limit themselves to what God does through Mary rather than talk about Mary herself.

"Protestants and Marian Devotion – What about Mary?", Jason Byassee, *Christian Century*, December 14, 2004

Much of what being Protestant has historically meant has involved a protest against the Catholic devotion to Mary.... But recently there has been a flurry of publications by Protestants on Mary, works that suggest she could be an ecumenical bridge -- or at least that the Protestant aversion to Marian devotion is eroding....

Church historians of all stripes have long granted that Marian teaching and devotion dates from the earliest days of the church. And they grant that devotion to Mary was not discarded even by the leading Reformation figures Luther, Calvin and Zwingli....

The most important contribution of these recent reflections is to give fresh attention to the incarnation....

What she lacks in quantity of appearance in scripture she makes up for in quality. Luke's telling of the gospel begins with her, and her *fiat* ("let it be' in Latin) to Gabriel's announcement of God's incarnational intent opens the way for a new eruption of grace into the world. She is present at and indeed an instigator of Jesus' first miracle at Cana in Galilee (John 2: 1-11). She and other women are present at the cross, when the male disciples flee. Depending on how one reads the resurrection narratives, she is present there too (Mark 15:40; 47).

It is striking that Mary is in the upper room at Pentecost -- the only woman present there who is named -- to receive the outpouring of God's Spirit at the birth of the church (Acts 1:14). When Paul makes his one oblique mention of Jesus' mother it is to point to her as a sign that he was indeed born, and so was genuinely human (Gal. 4:4). To cite a more contested passage, her image in Revelation 12:17 as a woman clothed with the sun with a crown of stars in the agony of giving birth to a son who will rule the nations is, at the very least, impressive. Mary's appearances in scripture are indeed limited, but they are tied to crucial moments in salvation history, without which there would be no church.

Scripture presents Mary as an important agent in her own right, not just as the mother of her son. If her Magnificat is any indication, she is an extraordinary reader of the Bible, lyrically weaving together Jewish scripture into a new song that is perhaps the most frequently sung canticle in church history. We are twice told that she "treasures" the words entrusted to her by angels and shepherds and that she "ponders these things" in her heart (Luke 2:19, 51). Aged Simeon promises her that her child's destiny to be for the "falling and rising of many in Israel" will cause a "sword to pierce" her own soul too -- suggesting that Mary's importance continues in the saga of salvation long after her child's birth. (Luke 2:34-35)....

Her womb was the physical site of the enfleshment of God. This leads Robert Jenson to a conclusion that may sting Protestant sensibilities -- we ought to ask Mary to pray for us.

Jenson argues that death does not sever the bonds of the body of Christ -- as even most Protestant eucharistic prayers make clear. To ask for a departed saint's prayer, then, is not in principle different from asking another Christian for her prayers. We hold that the saints are not simply gone but are ever alive to God, and so we ought also consider them to be available as intercessors, and powerful ones at that.

This is precisely the point at which Protestant theologians get most nervous. Such a request of prayer from Mary smacks of an effort to gain divine favor by some route other than Christ -- the height of idolatry. To prop the door open here even an inch threatens to bring back the medieval system of veneration of scores of saints in an effort to earn the favor of a distant and foreboding Jesus. Hence we slam the door shut. To honor Christ, the saints must be excluded.

Yet this needn't be so. Jenson insists that "the saints are not our way to Christ; he is our way to them." Each saint's particular graces can be seen as reflections of the grace of Christ, whose greatness grows in our eyes as we attend to the saints' individual stories. The strengthening of the bonds of the body of Christ, stretching as they do across the divide between earthly life and death, should bring tribute to Christ rather than discredit

"The Blessed Evangelical Mary", Timothy George, *Christianity Today*, December 5, 2003

Honoring Mary certainly doesn't come naturally to Protestants. For complex historical reasons, to be a Protestant has meant not to be a Roman Catholic. To worship Jesus means not to honor Mary, even if such honor is biblically grounded and theologically sound. But, as the Reformers were quick to point out, Mary is the embodiment of grace alone and faith alone, and thus contemporary Protestants, along with the Reformers, should highly extol Mary in our theology and worship.

Other developments include the founding of the Ecumenical Society of the Blessed Virgin Mary in the United Kingdom in 1967. The ESBVM has brought together Christians from diverse denominations to explore their common interest in the Mother of Jesus through conferences, books and other publications. Notable anthologies produced by the ESBVM include *Mary's Place in Christian Dialogue, Mary and the Churches, Mary in Doctrine and Devotion, Mary for Everyone* and *Mary for Earth and Heaven*.

In parallel with the operation of the ESBVM, the last three decades of the 20th century saw the publication of three of the most powerful books on Marian doctrine and devotion – all from Protestants. These were Evangelical John de Satge's *Down to Earth: The New Protestant View of the Virgin Mary* (1976), Methodist Neville Ward's *Five for Sorrow, Ten for*

Joy: A Consideration of the Rosary (1973) and Anglican John Macquarrie's *Mary for all Christians* (1991).

Fast Forward

The ecumenical emphasis on viewing the Virgin from the perspective of the Incarnation is of enduring importance. The incarnation of God in Christ took place in and through a family: he was the virginal child of a married couple. The participation of the family went beyond the Incarnation and extended to the Son's redemptive mission. In the case of the Mother, she was told she would be pierced with a sword as she participated in her Son's mission. The redemption of humanity was achieved not as a solitary act but an act begotten in solidarity because it was an act into which the Redeemer drew his family. The father and the mother played a supporting role in the lifework of the Son of God-made-man in a manner that was completely distinct from the part played by his Apostles and other followers. They belonged to an "order" of action in salvation history that radically transcended the role played by all other human persons – *they were participants in the mission of Jesus even before his birth*! As we have seen, the first Christians recognized from the very beginning that Mary was the New Eve just as Jesus was the New Adam. At the center of Incarnation, Redemption and Mediation is the incarnate Word of God who is Redeemer and infinite Mediator. But united with him, GIVEN by him and working with him in a unique and irrevocable mode is his mother, the New Eve and the Mother of all Christians.

The gate of Heaven is open. But there is no guarantee of entry. No matter what some theologies say, the teaching of Jesus in the Gospels is unequivocal: we have to say "Yes" to him and "Yes" on a continuous basis (see the last section of this work or just read the Gospels). In grasping the role of the Virgin's "Yes" in the divine Plan of salvation, we come to see the urgency of saying "Yes" to God ourselves. We will realize too that the Mother of Jesus is our Mother who helps us with our own continuing "Yes" to God.

NOTES

[1]Citations from Bertrand Buby's *The Marian Heritage of the Early Church* (New York: Alba House, 1997):

[2]Eric L. Mascall, "Theotokos: The Place of Mary in the Work of Salvation," in *The Blessed Virgin Mary: Essays by Anglican Writers*, E.L. Mascall and H.S. Box, eds. (London: Darton, Longman & Todd Ltd, 1963), 19.

[3]John MacQuarrie, *Mary for all Christians*, (London: Collins, 1990), 112.

[4]https://www.crpchalifax.ca/almah-virgin-or-young-woman.html

Faith and Works, Mediation and Intercession

The Contact is all about the mediation and intercession of the Virgin, of a Mother for her children. Maternal mediation.

But the ancient affirmation of Marian mediation has created a yawning chasm between the historic Christian consensus and certain later theories. The Protestant Reformers, who accepted Mary's attributes of Mother of God, rejected any kind of Marian mediation. Quite obviously, abuses and excesses in popular Marian devotion need to be corrected. But this wholesale rejection of the Virgin's continuing role in the history of salvation flies in the face of the Christianity of the Apostles, martyrs, catacombs, Fathers and Councils. Further, many of today's Protestant Fundamentalists seem to reject even the Marian doctrines accepted by the Reformers. Fortunately, other Protestant Christians – Evangelicals, Methodists, Episcopalians, Lutherans, Presbyterians, Pentecostals, Baptists – are re-discovering the inextricable presence of the Virgin Mother at the heart of salvation history.

We should note, however, that dissension over Marian mediation takes us to a more fundamental issue. More controversial than the role of Mary in Christian belief is the question of salvation itself. It is no exaggeration to say that wars have been fought over this issue since it was the single most important disagreement that led to the Protestant Reformation and the subsequent division of Christian Europe. But in the present day, numerous conferences and ecumenical groups have created a friendlier climate. For instance, there are Anglican-Catholic, Lutheran-Catholic and Evangelical-Catholic dialogues and other such initiatives studying areas of agreement and disagreement. The joint statements from these dialogues have at least created a better understanding of the conflicting positions.

It is commonly agreed by Catholics and Protestants that salvation was given by Jesus Christ and accepted in faith by the believer, that God's grace takes primacy over every human initiative and that we are able to live as the children of God only because of the gift of the Holy Spirit. Disagreement begins over the question of whether or not our freedom plays a role in our salvation. But this is not a disagreement between Catholics and Orthodox, on the one side, and Protestants on the other. Its roots reach down to two entirely different views of God and humankind and subsequently two different understandings of a wide range of biblical verses. On the one side you have the Calvinists and other determinists and on the other you have Catholics, Orthodox, Protestants from various denominations (like the Methodists) and movements (Pentecostals) and all those who believe in human freedom. Calvinism is not the standard position even among Protestant Evangelicals as illustrated by the anthology of Evangelical scholars titled *The Grace of God, The Will of Man*.

The parting of the ways centers on an issue that is central to this book, namely the question of whether or not we can say "yes" or "no" to God. To the Calvinists "No" was never an option for those whom God has decided to save and when he offers them his grace, his offer is irresistible. The human response is entirely a divinely ordained action and so no merit attaches to it. This means that those whom God has not foreordained for salvation have been foreordained for damnation.

Unlike the Calvinist position, the historic Christian consensus is that God is an infinite Lover who thirsts for every human soul, that he moves Heaven and Earth to make salvation available to his creatures, that he gives every person sufficient grace to say *fiat*, "yes", to him. We can say "yes" to God because of the grace he gives us to say "yes." But we can also say "no" – and this is a free act. The power to say "no" is a negative power we have: one we own. All positive powers are from God. To say "yes" is the greatest, most praiseworthy decision of our lives – one which will bring us endless joy. We look to all those who have said 'yes' as models who motivate us and the greatest of these models is the maiden whose "yes" made her mother of her Savior.

The historic Christian insight into the importance of this "one thing about Mary" is the understanding of biblical teaching that we find professed and proclaimed by the Church Fathers and Councils.

At this point, we will consider in some detail the questions relating to freedom, salvation, mediation and intercession.

1. Predestination to Salvation and Damnation vs. Freedom of the Human Person
The Calvinist, determinist view was well summarized by John Calvin himself in his "Predestination of Some to Salvation and Others to Destruction": "All things being at God's disposal, and the decision of salvation or death belonging to him, he orders all things by his counsel and decree in such a manner, that some men are born devoted from the womb to certain death, that his name may be glorified in their destruction.... No one can deny that God foreknew the future final fate of man before he created him, and that he did foreknow it because it was appointed by his own decree."[1] "The wicked themselves have been created for this very end – that they may perish."[2]

Martin Luther adopted the Calvinist view although he was clearly troubled by it: "Doubtless it gives the greatest possible offence to common sense or natural reason, that God, Who is proclaimed as being full of mercy and goodness, and so on, should of His own mere will abandon, harden, and damn men, as though He delighted in the sins and great eternal torments of such wretches.... I have stumbled at it myself more than once, down to the deepest pit of despair."[3]

The historic Christian response to this line of thought was well summed up by John Wesley in his "Predestination Calmly Considered," the most extraordinary extant refutation of Calvinism, "Now if man be capable of choosing good or evil, then is he a proper object of the justice of God, acquitting or condemning, rewarding or punishing. But otherwise he is not. A mere machine is not capable of being either acquitted or condemned. Justice cannot punish a stone for falling to the ground.... And shall this man, for not doing what he never could do, and for doing what he never could avoid, be sentenced to depart into everlasting fire, prepared for the devil and his angels (cf. Mt. 25:41)? 'Yes, because it is the sovereign will of God.' Then you either found a new God, or made one! This is not the God of the Christians. Our God is just in all his ways.... He requireth only according to what he hath given; and where he hath given little, little is required. The glory of his justice is this, to 'reward every man according to his works.' (cf. Tm 4:14)."[4]

The Council of Orange had declared in 529 "We not only do not believe that any are foreordained to evil by the power of God, but even state with utter abhorrence that if there are those who want to believe so evil a thing, they are anathema."

As long as you take the Calvinist view of the matter, which Luther did, there can be no further progression on mediation. But, as John Macquarrie points out, this view is at odds of both human experience and Christian doctrine and experience because it treats "human beings like sheep or cattle or even marionettes, not as the unique beings that they are, spiritual beings made in the image of God and entrusted with a measure of freedom and responsibility."[5]

The main foundation for the doctrine that our free decisions determine our eternal destiny is the teaching of Jesus:

> "And there was a man who came to him and asked, 'Master, what good deed must I do to possess eternal life?' Jesus said to him, '... If you wish to enter into life, keep the commandments. ... If you wish to be perfect, go and sell what you own and give the money to the poor, and you will have treasure in heaven; then come, follow me.'" (*Matthew* 19:16-22).

> "For every unfounded word men utter they will answer on Judgment day, since it is by your words you will be acquitted, and by your words condemned." (*Matthew* 12:37)

> "In his anger the master handed him over to the torturers till he should pay all his debt. And that is how my heavenly Father will deal with you unless you each forgive your brother from your heart." (*Matthew* 18:34-5).

> "You will be hated by all men on account of my name; but the man who stands firm to the end will be saved." (*Matthew* 10:22).

> "For the Son of Man is going to come in the glory of his Father with his angels, and, when he does, he will reward each one according to his behavior." (*Matthew* 16:27)

> "I tell you solemnly, in so far as you neglected to do this to one of the least of these, you neglected to do it to me.' And they will

go away to eternal punishment, and the virtuous to eternal life." (*Matthew* 25:45-6).

"The hour is coming when the dead will leave their graves at the sound of his voice; those who did good will rise again for life; and those who did evil, to condemnation." (*John* 5:28-8).

In the *Book of Revelation*, Jesus says, "Very soon now, I shall be with you again, bringing the reward to be given to every man according to what he deserves." (*Revelation* 22:12).

Some have said that any attempt to focus on being good and holy is a deception of the Devil who tries to make us rely on our own good works for our salvation instead of focusing only on the all-sufficient atonement of Jesus. While affirming that salvation is possible only because of the redemptive death of Jesus and that we cannot be saved unless he draws us to him and gives us the grace to accept him, we could just as plausibly say that any attempt to downplay the need for holiness and for turning away from sin is a deception of the Devil who wants to lead us from trivial sins to the terrible fate of which we are warned in Hebrews: "If, after we have been given knowledge of the truth, we should deliberately commit any sins, then there is no longer any sacrifice for them. There will be left only the dread prospect of judgment and of the raging fire that is to burn rebels. Anyone who disregards the Law of Moses is ruthlessly put to death on the word of two witnesses or three; and you may be sure that anyone who tramples on the Son of God and treats the blood of the covenant which sanctified him as if it were not holy, and who insults the Spirit of grace, will be condemned to a far severer punishment." (Hebrews 10:26-30).

St. Paul has a similar warning: "Your stubborn refusal to repent is only adding to the anger God will have toward you on that day of anger when his just judgments will be made known. He will repay each one as his works deserve. For those who sought renown and honor and immortality by always doing good there will be eternal life; for the unsubmissive who refused to take truth for their guide and took depravity instead, there will be anger and fury." (*Romans* 2:5-8).

Moreover, the followers of Jesus participate in His work of salvation. As St. Paul said, through his bodily suffering, he does what he can "to make up all that has still to be undergone by Christ for the sake of his body, the Church." (*Colossians* 1:24). St. James even says that "Anyone who can bring back a sinner from the wrong way that he has taken will be saving a soul from death and covering up a great number of sins." (*James* 5:20).

To recap what was said earlier, the Virgin is a key participant in God's plan of salvation in human history. She was called to be the Mother of the Savior and to share in his salvific suffering; it was her *fiat* ("Let it be done") to the messenger from God that made the Incarnation possible; she played a key role in the miracle that began his ministry in the world; she was there with him at the end of his life; and she was called to be the Mother of all those who witness to Jesus. As the Witness who is the Mother of all witnesses, she is a human expression of the infinite love of God that seeks the salvation of every soul. When she tells us about coming to her Son and about her maternal protection she is speaking to us as a mother seeking the well-being of her children.

2. Mediators in the Old and New Testaments
Both Old and New Testaments not only show the significance of our free acts but the very real role of mediators in God's scheme of salvation. Adam, Noah, Abraham and Moses, the Prophets, Judges and Kings of the Old Testaments, were all mediators between God and humanity. Their free actions could bring divine blessings on their people. They could cause or avert God's wrath. Things are no different in the New Testament. The Apostles and disciples are chosen and commissioned to spread the Good News, to bring people to salvation, to celebrate the sacred mysteries that "transmit" the grace of God. And we have already mentioned Colossians 1:24.

3. The One Mediator
1 Timothy 2:5 says, "There is only one mediator between God and mankind, himself a man, Christ Jesus, who sacrificed himself as a ransom for them all." Does "one" here mean "exclusively one" or does it mean "the same" and by extension "primary"? Interestingly, the Greek word used for "exclusively one", *monos*, is used in every other instance of "one" in the epistle except in this verse. The word used here is *"heis"* where it means "sameness" of function. In his study of *Timothy* 2:5, "For there is one God, and one mediator between God and men, the man Christ Jesus; Who gave himself a ransom for all,"

Manuel Miguens points out that an accurate translation of this passage is "There is one and the same God [for all], there is also one and the same mediator [for all]." The author is not trying to show that there is one and not a multiplicity of gods or that there is one and not many mediators. His point, rather, is that God's love and providence applies to all not just to a few (the Jews, for instance) just as the redemptive mediation of Jesus is for all. In his epistles, St. Paul, of course, talks of himself as a mediator and even talks of three kinds of mediators: priestly (Aaron, Christ), covenantal (Moses, Jesus) and de facto mediators (Abraham and Paul). The last category comprises those chosen to be vehicles of divine grace.

The mediation of all Christians (as described in Colossians 1:24 and elsewhere) is a participation in the unique and primary mediation of Christ. He alone is the unique Son of God - but all Christians can and must participate in this Sonship as they can and must participate in His unique Priesthood. So also, all are called to participate in the unique mediation of the Primary Mediator. All followers of Jesus participate in his work of salvation. "We are co-workers with God," said St. Paul.

4. Maternal Mediation

Given that Christians are co-workers with Christ and hence mediators of salvation and God's grace, how are we to understand the role of the Mother of the Lord?

We have seen that the Blessed Virgin was always seen as the New Eve.

Macquarrie notes that, "In the glimpses of Mary that we have in the gospels, her standing at the cross beside her Son, and her prayers and intercessions with the apostles, are particularly striking ways in which Mary shared and supported the work of Christ - and even these are ways in which the Church as a whole can have a share in co-redemption. But it is Mary who has come to symbolize that perfect harmony between the divine will and the human response, so that it is she who gives meaning to the expression Corredemptrix. But secondly there is the further context in which Mary has to be considered, the context of the incarnation of the Word. In this context, the language of co-redemption is also appropriate, but in a different way, for in this regard her contribution was unique and by its very nature could not be literally shared with anyone else. We are thinking of her now not just as representative or pre-eminent member of the Church, but as Theotokos or Mother of God. Mary's willing acceptance of her indispensable role in that chain of events which constituted the incarnation and the redemption which it brought about, was necessary for the nurture of the Lord and for the creation of the Church itself."[6]

And just as her coredemptive participation in the work of the One Redeemer is qualitatively different from the participation of other coredeemers in Christ, her maternal mediation is qualitatively different from the way in which other mediators participate in her Son's mediation. Jesus is the unique and unrepeatable Redeemer and Mediator. He is God and man. But all Christians are called to participate in his redemptive activity and his mediation - and the first to do so was the New Eve who was uniquely also *Theotokos* (Mother of God). Her mediation also arises from the biblically recorded uniqueness of her union with the Holy Spirit (*Panagia*) which was acknowledged and celebrated by the Christian community from the beginning.

The mediation of Mary, to repeat, is intrinsically maternal in nature: she is the most perfect created image of the Father because only the Father and Mary have generated the Son and by her cooperation in the Incarnation she "mediates" the Redeemer of fallen humanity; she is also mother of all those who witness to Christ (*Revelation* 12:17) for those who participate in the sonship of Christ (*Galatians* 4:4) are adopted sons and daughters of his eternal Father and his human Mother. Even when she is a mediator of her Son's power at Cana, this mediation is maternal in nature and it is a mediation that inspires faith in the Apostles.

The Presbyterian scholar Ross Mackenzie writes, "To bid Mary stand beside us is to remember that we are already with her in the new creation. She is linked with us, and ministers to us still in the new creation as the Mother of mercy. To invoke her in public and private prayer is to recall that, while the first creation came about by the will of God alone, the new creation involved this woman's will also. She is a minister of God, *synergos theou*, to use one of Paul's daring phrases. Even the least of the apostles considered himself linked with Christ in a glorious cause: 'We entreat you on behalf of Christ,' he says to the Corinthians, 'to be reconciled to God,'

2 Cor 5:20. To speak on behalf of Christ, is therefore to be a mediator of God's saving work in the world."[7]

Intercession

Does Mary continue to intercede for us in Heaven? The larger question here concerns whether or not a person in Heaven can affect events on earth. We can address these issues by consideration of five different issues.

1. Perseverance in prayer is commended in Scripture with the promise that this will achieve results.

"He said, 'There was a judge in a certain town who neither feared God nor respected any human being. And a widow in that town used to come to him and say, 'Render a just decision for me against my adversary.' For a long time the judge was unwilling, but eventually he thought, 'While it is true that I neither fear God nor respect any human being, because this widow keeps bothering me I shall deliver a just decision for her lest she finally come and strike me.' The Lord said, 'Pay attention to what the dishonest judge says. Will not God secure the rights of his chosen ones who call out to him day and night? Will he be slow to answer them? I tell you, he will see to it that justice is done for them speedily.'" (*Luke* 18:2-8).

2. Intercessory prayer from multiple persons will achieve results.

"Peter thus was being kept in prison, but prayer by the church was fervently being made to God on his behalf." *Acts* 12:5.

"First of all, then, I ask that supplications, prayers, petitions, and thanksgivings be offered for everyone, for kings and for all in authority, that we may lead a quiet and tranquil life in all devotion and dignity. This is good and pleasing to God our savior, who wills everyone to be saved and to come to knowledge of the truth." 1 *Timothy* 2:1-5

"As you help us with prayer, so that thanks may be given by many on our behalf for the gift granted us through the prayers of many." 2 *Cor* 1:11.

3. The prayer of a holy person is especially effective

"The fervent prayer of a righteous person is very powerful." *James* 5:16

4. The prayer of the Holy Ones in Heaven has an effect on earthly events.
"When he took it, the four living creatures and the twenty-four elders fell down before the Lamb. Each of the elders held a harp and gold bowls filled with incense, which are the prayers of the holy ones." (Revelation 5:8). The elders in this instance are Christians in Heaven. "The smoke of the incense along with the prayers of the holy ones went up before God from the hand of the angel." (*Revelation* 8:4). "I saw underneath the altar the souls of those who had been slaughtered because of the witness they bore to the word of God. They cried out in a loud voice, 'How long will it be, holy and true master, before you sit in judgment and avenge our blood on the inhabitants of the earth?' Each of them was given a white robe, and they were told to be patient a little while longer until the number was filled of their fellow servants and brothers who were going to be killed as they had been." (*Revelation* 6:9-11).

The Anglican theologian Edward Symonds observes that "There are other considerations however in favour of the view that the saints hear us. There is actual evidence for this belief in the New Testament. Heb 12:1 says: 'Therefore let us also being compassed about with so great a cloud of witnesses ("martyrs", alluding to the heroes of faith in the preceding chapter) run with patience ("endurance") the race which is set before us', where the witnesses, though primarily witnesses to their faith suggest at least, as Westcott points out, 'spectators' looking on at our earthly struggle in running the race appointed for us Christians. This is confirmed by the picture of the heavenly Jerusalem in the same chapter to which Christians on earth are now come, with the solemn assembly of the firstborn and the spirits of just men made perfect. (Verse 23)". [8]

5. The Intercession of the Mother of God
Of all the saints in Heaven, it is the mediation of the Mother of all saints that is the most powerful. She is the daughter who "found favor" with the Father, the New Eve who intercedes with the New Adam whose "hour" has now come, the Spouse of the Spirit of God who said of her "blessed are you who believed." She is the Queen-Mother "clothed with the sun" who intercedes on behalf of "her offspring, those who keep God's commandments and bear witness to Jesus." (Revelation 12).

It was Mary's compassionate request that led to her Son's first miracle at the beginning of his Ministry - and so Mary's intercession especially as it relates to miracles was widely accepted.

Symonds points out that, "Mary is recognized as the mother of all Christian people from at least the time of Origen, who says, 'No one will be able to understand the meaning of St John's Gospel if he has not leaned on the breast of Jesus and received from Jesus the one who has become his mother also. Because Christ lives in him, the words are said to Mary of him, "Behold thy Son the Christ".' This motherhood is perpetual, for the Incarnation is a permanent reality not a merely past event. Our Lord retains his human Nature in Heaven. Therefore Mary is still his Mother, but also the Mother of the Church which is his Body, the living organism of Christ's glorified human Nature and of each of its members, who are made her adopted, not her natural children, by their baptismal incorporation into the human Nature of her Son. But a further question is, how does our Lady exercise this motherhood? The answer is by love, and by intercession. There can be no doubt that the saints exercise charity, the crown of Christian virtues, in Heaven. And that charity which is primarily directed towards God is, as the New Testament teaches, empty and worthless if it does not include the love of man, specially of our fellow-members in the Body of Christ. And this love finds its chief (though not its only) expression, in the case of the saints in Heaven, in intercession."[9]

This is the historic Christian consensus about Marian mediation that echoes through ancient prayers and liturgies, councils and creeds, doctrines and devotions. To the question of why we cannot pray directly to God, the reply is that we can and do – but also that prayers to the saints ultimately results in prayers that go directly to God from them. If we can legitimately ask our friends to pray for us why can we not ask the Holy Ones in Heaven to pray for us? We remember that "The fervent prayer of a righteous person is very powerful," that the "the spirits of righteous men made perfect" are in Heaven (*Hebrews* 12:23), and these spirits are very much alive since our God is "not the God of the dead but of the living." (*Matthew* 22:32).

Admittedly these approaches to mediation and intercession are incompatible with a strict reading of the Reformation writings. Nevertheless, much progress has been made on justification, the major theological issue of the Reformation.

In their landmark 1999 Joint Declaration on the Doctrine of Justification, the Lutheran World Federation and the Catholic Church concluded, "The understanding of the doctrine of justification set forth in this Declaration shows that a consensus in basic truths of the doctrine of justification exists between Lutherans and Catholics." Professor Tadeusz Zielinksy of the Baptist World Alliance noted on December 5, 2003, that the doctrine of justification in the Joint Declaration (nn.14-18) "can be … endorsed by all Baptists without hesitation. Those paragraphs [nn.19,22,31,34,37] showing the Lutheran-Catholic consensus [deserve] full Baptist support."

Ongoing dialogues between Catholics and Lutherans, Methodists, Anglicans and other denominations on the subject of mediation, and in particular Marian mediation, have helped eliminate some misconceptions. The 2005 declaration from the Anglican-Catholic dialogue (ARCIC) titled *Mary: Grace and Hope in Christ* is of particular importance: "Affirming together unambiguously Christ's unique mediation, which bears fruit in the life of the Church, we do not consider the practice of asking Mary and the saints to pray for us as communion-dividing. Since obstacles of the past have been removed by clarification of doctrine, by liturgical reform and practical norms in keeping with it, we believe that there is no continuing theological reason for ecclesial division on these matters."

On the way forward, Methodist David Butler's recommendations seem to be specially relevant: "Protestants need to receive what they already have espoused theologically, in terms of Mary as a type of the true believer, one who offered her 'let it be' to God in faith and thereby becomes an example of how we must act. They need to unpack for themselves the implications of the title offered at Ephesus 431 of *Theotokos*, or Mother of God, for Marian devotion. After all, Protestants acknowledge the fundamental principles of the historic creeds, and the Council of Ephesus 431 safeguards the humanity of Christ. Perhaps this preliminary work, which is devotional as much as it is doctrinal, will enable them to see the value of the definitions of 1854 and 1950."[10]

The significance of the Virgin is above all as a link to her Son. The fundamental driving force of all Marian doctrine and devotion is the perception that it is only through her we can fully accept and appreciate both his divinity and his humanity. Her divine maternity – human mother of God the Son

– is the most telling testimony to his true humanity. Her special status – immaculately conceived, perpetually virgin, assumed into Heaven, New Eve – presupposes and confirms his divinity. We know too that in the entire Bible, only two human persons beheld God in his Supernatural Splendor: Moses on Mount Sinai and Mary who was "overshadowed" by the Holy Spirit. Both said "Yes" to God with respect to their specific missions. But whereas Moses, like Abraham, was tasked with "forming" the People of God, Mary was called to become the Mother of God.

NOTES

[1] John Calvin, *Institutes of the Christian Religion*, Volume II, Philadelphia: Presbyterian Board of Christian Education.

[2] Citation in John Murray, *Calvin on Scripture and Divine Sovereignty* (Michigan: Baker Book House, 1960, 61

[3] Martin Luther, *Bondage of the Will*, translated J.I. Packer and O.R. Johnston (Revell: 1957), 217.

[4] John Wesley, "Predestination Calmly Considered," in Albert C. Outler, ed. *John Wesley* (New York: Oxford University Press, 1964), 451.

[5] John MacQuarrie, *Mary for all Christians*, op. cit.,104.

[6] Ibid., 113-4.

[7] Ross Mackenzie

[8] H. Edward Symonds, "The Blessed Virgin Mary," in *The Blessed Virgin Mary: Essays by Anglican Writers*, E.L. Mascall and H.S. Box, eds. (London: Darton, Longman & Todd Ltd, 1963), 6-7.

[9] Ibid., 6.

[10] David Butler in *Mary for Everyone* edited by William McLoughlin and Jill Pinnock (Herefordshire: Gracewing, 1997, 65.

Divine Directive or Diabolic Deception?
Idols or Icons?

Is the Contact "authorized" by God? Are the encounters with the Virgin from God or the Devil? Are the images and statues associated with her instances of idolatry and therefore diabolic?

Paradoxically, these same kinds of questions were raised about her Son both in the Gospel accounts and in later history. And the same irrefutable answers made to such critics apply as much to the Mother as they did to her Son.

The enemies of Jesus did not deny that he performed signs and wonders. But they attributed these to Beelzebub! They crucified him because they did not accept his claim to be sent by God. And non-Christian monotheists have said that the proclamation of Jesus as God incarnate was idolatry.

With respect to the Beelzebub question, Jesus said in response: "Every kingdom divided against itself will be laid waste, and no town or house divided against itself will stand. And if Satan drives out Satan, he is divided against himself; how, then, will his kingdom stand?" (*Matthew* 12:25-26.) This means that the only person who would benefit from hindering Jesus by calling him an agent of Satan would be Satan himself because Jesus was toppling his kingdom.

Jesus' claim to be sent by God could be verified at two levels: his life and actions conformed to the prophecies made about the coming of the Messiah in the Hebrew Scriptures. Of course, the scriptures, like any written document, could be interpreted in alternate ways but there certainly were enough passages in these scriptures that were fulfilled only in Jesus (Isaiah 53 for instance). Secondly, and most importantly, the Resurrection of Jesus and his presence to millions of his followers throughout history was the ultimate vindication of his claims. We know the resurrection took place because the transformation of Jesus' demoralized followers cannot be explained in any other fashion.

The proclamation that Jesus was God incarnate can be considered idolatrous only if you have an idolatrous view of God. This is because before and after Jesus, even monotheists have seen God as quasi-physical. It was Jesus who revealed that God is pure spirit. Only in recognizing God as infinite Spirit can we come to see the Trinity of Persons in God as well as the possibility of one of the Three divine Persons acting through a human body and soul.

If we ask whether the Contact made by the Virgin is divinely "authorized," we simply have to see how the Scriptures and the earliest Christians understood her. She was always seen as the New Eve, as the Mother. The Gospel of John and the *Book of Revelation* show her as the mother of all Christians. All Christians from the beginning understood her to be their Mother active in their lives and well-being. Were they wrong? Who is more likely to be wrong: people who make their own personal arbitrary interpretations 2000 years after the origin of the new Faith or the entire community of Christians for the first 1500 years of their existence? If this community was wrong on such a fundamental matter, then why should we believe them on anything else? The choice comes down to this: accept what Christians have always believed or create your own religion with only your own authority to back it. What cannot be denied is this: all Christians considered Mary, the Mother of Jesus, as their Mother, active in their lives for the first millennium and a half and most Christians continue to do so.

Next question: are the signs and wonders associated with the Contact made by the Virgin from God or the Devil? Remember signs and wonders were part of Christianity from the very beginning and continued wherever there was widespread growth of the Faith. These signs and wonders sustained Christians in the face of hostility and led to conversions and spiritual fruits. *"Many signs and wonders were done among the people at the hands of the apostles. They were all together in Solomon's portico.... Thus they even carried the sick out into the streets and laid them on cots and mats so that when Peter came by, at least his shadow might fall on one or another of them."* (Acts 5:12, 15)

But given the finality of the revelation of Jesus, why should we expect any further supernatural intervention such as that associated with the Contact? *There is no passage in Scripture that states that supernatural communication ceases after the fixing of the canon; in fact, the principle that there will be no further supernatural communication is non-scriptural.* For instance, 1 *Thessalonians* 5:21 and 1 *John* 4:1 tell us the very opposite: these verses assume that both the Spirit and good spirits will be communicating with us and that, in the case of communication from spirits, we should test them to see if they are divinely-directed: "Never try to suppress the Spirit or treat the gift of prophecy with contempt; think before you do anything - hold on to what is good and avoid every form of evil." (1 *Thessalonians* 5:21); "It is not every spirit, my dear people, that you can trust; test them, to see if they come from God; ... you can tell the spirits that come from God by this: every spirit which acknowledges that Jesus the Christ has come in the flesh is from God." (1 *John* 4:1-3). Just from these verses, we see that claims of a supernatural communication do not necessarily have a diabolic source and that we should instead expect there to be such communications from a divinely authorized source and should exercise discernment when studying these communications.

Plainly nothing Jesus could have said or done in response to the critics who said he cast out demons through Beelzebub would have proved sufficient for them because of the mental framework in which they were trapped. Any miracle he performed or magnificent doctrine he preached would be dismissed as a deception of the Devil since (they would reason) the Devil is more ingenious than men and could easily deceive them through such means. The critics' mistake was to leave no room for divinely directed activity in their minds - as a result they could not discern any such activity even if it took place before them. So it is with the critics of the Marian encounters. Their mental frameworks have locked out the possibility of such divinely directed encounters and so every such encounter has to be attributed to the Devil no matter how good the doctrine or how real the miracle. But if the Holy Spirit acts through his Spouse, the Virgin Mary, in such a manner as to make it unmistakable that he was thus active, then we should be cautious about peremptorily dismissing these phenomena as diabolic deceptions for the reasons given in *Matthew* 12.

The right model or paradigm in responding to supernatural phenomena is laid out in 1 *Thessalonians* 5:21 and 1 *John* 4:1. We are asked to expect and welcome phenomena such as the encounters with the Virgin – not to reject them wholesale. We are told to "test" each claim of a supernatural nature and then hold on to what is good. For the Holy Spirit does indeed continue to act through his chosen Messenger and good spirits do communicate with us.

The next question is how do we "test" a claim of an apparition or appearance of the Virgin for we are also warned that we cannot trust every spirit. Historically, Church authorities have taken the attitude of "testers". And we must admit that they, like any of us, cannot simply accept every claim of a supernatural nature at face value. Essentially, any "test" of an apparition should consider the facts of the phenomenon itself (the ecstasy, the visionary), the doctrine that emerges and the spiritual and other fruits.

These three central criteria have been systematized by Church authorities into a rigorous framework (as noted by Blackbourn and Pelikan) that has been traditionally utilized in assessing and approving the authenticity of the claim of a supernatural encounter. Once the three criteria of facts, doctrine and fruits are accepted as sound starting points, this framework itself should be acceptable to most Christians. Moreover, since the Church was instrumental in assembling and authorizing the content of the public revelation – namely, the books of the Bible that we have today – its historical criteria for assessing claims of private revelation should be given serious consideration.

Finally, what about statues and images?

The Incarnation of God in Jesus of Nazareth tells us definitively that the physical can be a vehicle of the divine presence as was already apparent to the Israelites in their encounters with the living God. Since God is incarnate in Jesus, to see him is to see the Infinite-Eternal in finite terms: "Jesus said to him, 'Have I been with you for so long a time and you still do not know me, Philip? Whoever has seen me has seen the Father. How can you say, 'Show us the Father'?" (*John* 14:9).

Now it is one thing to profess that Jesus is the image of the invisible God and to acknowledge that this image itself can potentially be imaged literally as with the Shroud of Turin. But what about humanly created images of God incarnate and his Mother and of angels and those who have lived lives of heroic holiness (the "saints")? Do they fall under the biblical prohibition against idolatry?

In addressing this let us start with a few indisputable principles:

- The same biblical texts that prohibit the worship of graven images also command the creation of holy images (the Cherubim) and even images of creatures like lions and oxen to celebrate and proclaim the presence of the invisible Holy of Holies
- Likewise, these texts describe the presence and action of God in and through physical media: the burning bush, the glory of God covering the Ark
- Jesus, the image of the invisible God, reveals that God is a spirit and is to be worshipped as such while also proclaiming that whoever has seen him has seen the Father
- The incarnation of God in Jesus of Nazareth liberates us from the two extremes of Transcendent/vertical and Immanent/horizontal that eventually lead to atheism
- The Incarnation, because it is a tangible act of the wholly spiritual God in the physical world, shows us that the physical can serve to represent the spiritual without reducing the spiritual to the physical
- We are created as flesh and blood creatures and we are "meant" to communicate our non-physical powers (knowing, loving) through the physical
- Just as exposure to evil images (e.g., child pornography) can lead to evil thoughts and acts, an environment of holy images encourages holiness
- We treasure photographic images and videos of those dear to us, alive and dead, because we love them and want to be reminded of them
- We communicate our non-physical thoughts among each other through physical media such as speech, writing, gestures, etc.
- The biblical texts themselves, including those concerned with the non-physical, are communicated through physical media such as printed or electronic books, oral proclamations or videos.

As Marshall Mcluhan, the prophet of the Internet said, "the medium is the message": the power of a message is magnified by the medium used.

With these principles in mind, it should become obvious that images of holy persons, whether they be icons, statues or simple pictures, should be encouraged for those who wish to draw closer to God.

Here we are not talking of the worship of graven images or idolatry. In idolatry, an image of a non-human, non-angelic being is worshipped as a god or deity. This is expressly prohibited because worship, adoration and glorification can only be directed to infinite-eternal God. Graven images are lifeless and finite and to direct to them the adoration due to the Creator is destructive to the soul.

Images of holy persons (God incarnate, angels, humans who have fought the good fight), on the other hand, are simply vehicles for drawing us closer to God. They are themselves lifeless and finite and can never be an object of worship. But they are vehicles of communication and, above all, of love. They direct our minds and hearts, thoughts and feelings, to the realities they represent. They influence and mold our behavior. "The medium is the message." An icon or statue of the Blessed Virgin turns our hearts and minds to the Mother of Jesus whose intercession with God we seek. Or it fills us with love for this mother whose heart was pierced by the death of her beloved Son. This is hardly different from a photo or video of our earthly mothers which fills us with thoughts and feelings of affection for them; and, of course, we can ask our mothers to pray (intercede with God) for us.

"We become what we eat." Likewise, our souls "become" what we see and hear and think. We were created by God as flesh-and-blood beings with spiritual powers of communication, perception and interaction embedded in the physical. To deny this is to deny our humanity. We are not angels who are pure spirits. Of course, God is wholly spiritual. We know this because this was revealed to us *by God incarnate*. The All-Holy infinite-eternal Spirit, who created all things visible and invisible, manifests Its glory and love through both the sensory and the spiritual, the physical and the non-physical. To the extent we are flesh-and-blood creatures, our communication and interaction with spiritual realities has to use the physical as a vehicle. And to the extent that our physical environment affects our behavior, an environment of physical representations of the holy, will be "good for our souls."

If we try to restrict our interaction with God and the spiritual realm to the wholly non-physical, we end up with vague mental representations and speculative abstractions that eventually dissolve into a dense fog of unknowing. At that point, we simply focus on actions in this world. God ends up as a remote, impersonal force. Practically speaking we will not be very different from atheists. Interestingly, at times some who believe in the incarnation of God in Jesus Christ also choose to restrict themselves to the non-physical. In such cases, Jesus becomes wholly human or a superman and God is thought of as semi-physical. The revelation that the infinite-eternal Spirit has chosen a physical locus to manifest his glory to the fullest degree possible in human terms is lost.

At the other extreme, those who worship idols and think of everything around us as a part of God restrict God to the wholly physical. God becomes synonymous with the physical world. Some of these pantheists might say that everything is a part of God but that God also has an additional spiritual dimension. Interestingly this approach is also taken by certain monotheisms. The problem with this is that you no longer believe in the infinite-eternal Spirit that is God. To have a physical component is to be limited and finite. We wonder inevitably how this whole arrangement came into being: a spirit that has the world as its body and is trapped in time: who created it?

The only approach that is true to our everyday experience and the revelation of God in history is the incarnational path. We note first that the wholly spiritual infinite-eternal Creator of all manifests his glory to us through the physical world. We can apprehend this glory only because we are spiritual creatures with sensory capacities. God's glory is manifested by the physical somewhat as a mirror reflects the sun. The mirror is not in the sun nor is it the sun. This simile is imperfect because God brought the world into being out of nothing and keeps it in being. Nevertheless, the creation necessarily reflects the Creator. God's revelation of himself to the human race proceeded through the path of divine incarnation described in the Hebrew Bible that came to completion with the redemptive life, death and resurrection of the Man of Sorrows whose very name signified his salvific mission. The incarnational God is neither vertical nor horizontal: it is God present here and now AS GOD: not as part of the world but as a wholly transcendent and yet wholly personal Being communicating with that dimension of our being which is also non-physical. At the heart of the matter, we are concerned with communication and love and the personal.

With the Incarnation of God in Jesus of Nazareth, the true role of the physical became apparent:

> "If anyone says, 'I love God,' but hates his brother, he is a liar; for whoever does not love a brother whom he has seen cannot love God whom he has not seen." 1 *John* 4:20. "What you did not do for one of these least ones, you did not do for me." *Matthew* 25:45. The physical became a vehicle of the spiritual and the salvific: "Jesus answered, "Amen, amen, I say to you, no one can enter the kingdom of God without being born of water and Spirit." *John* 3:5. "Jesus said to them, 'Amen, amen, I say to you, unless you eat the flesh of the Son of Man and drink his blood, you do not have life within you.'" *John* 6:53.

Moreover, it was confirmed that human beings will be embodied forever through the resurrection of the body after death. The physical, albeit a radically transformed version of the physical, will always be a part of us. "It is sown a natural body; it is raised a spiritual body. If there is a natural body, there is also a spiritual one.... The first man was from the earth, earthly; the second man, from heaven.... Just as we have borne the image of the earthly one, we shall also bear the image of the heavenly one." (1 *Corinthians* 15:44,47,49).

In this context, the role of images should be obvious. As physical beings, we need physical "signs" to remind us of the non-physical and point us to the spiritual. But the "signs" must be of the right kind. Only signs that are related to God incarnate are permissible for "spiritual use." Images of the Sacred Heart or of the Virgin Mother or of the saints of God are vitally important because through them our minds and hearts turn to the divinely revealed realm they represent.

At a psychological level, someone who prays before a statue of the Virgin is not praying to the statue: they are not "serving" the statue or bowing down before a deity: they are *speaking to the person represented by the statue* and can continue doing so whether or not there is a statue before them. This is no different from a person kneeling in prayer with an open Bible in hand.

The statue is made of wood or plaster, the book of paper. Neither of them have any power in themselves: they perform the same role at a mental level as an automobile in getting us from Point A to B: they are not objects of worship: to bow before them is to show respect to the person addressed just as Joseph's brothers bowed before him. Those who reject the role of images in turning our minds to Jesus seem to have no problem watching and promoting movies about Jesus. But a movie is nothing more than a series of moving images! Whether we are talking of statues or videos, the objective is to turn our hearts to God. Images inspired by the Incarnation call us to God and holiness and love and empower us against evil. Above all they are testaments to the presence of God in our midst.

The early Church recognized all this as documented in the decrees of the Second Council of Nicea (787 A.D.), one of the Seven Ecumenical Councils accepted by Protestants, Orthodox and Catholics. The veneration of the Virgin extends to veneration of her images. The Ecumenical Council taught that:

"We decree with full precision and care that,
like the figure of the honoured and life-giving cross,
the revered and holy images,
whether painted or
made of mosaic
or of other suitable material,
are to be exposed
in the holy churches of God,
on sacred instruments and vestments,
on walls and panels,
in houses and by public ways,
these are the images of
our Lord, God and saviour, Jesus Christ, and of
our Lady without blemish, the holy God-bearer, and of
the revered angels and of
any of the saintly holy men.

The more frequently they are seen in representational art, the more are those who see them drawn to remember and long for those who serve as models, and to pay these images the tribute of salutation and respectful veneration. Certainly this is not the full adoration {latria} in accordance with our faith, which is properly paid only to the divine nature ... he who venerates the image, venerates the person represented in that image."

Martin Luther's interpretation of Old Testament passages on idolatry is helpful, "Nothing else can be drawn from the words: 'Thou shalt have no strange gods before me' except what relates to idolatry. But where pictures or sculptures are made without idolatry, the making of such things is not forbidden." Luther also said, "If I have a painted picture on the wall and I look upon it without idolatry, that is not forbidden to me and should not be taken away from me."[1]

Also relevant here is that curious incident in *Numbers* 21:7-9: "'Intercede for us with Yahweh to save us from these serpents.' Moses interceded for the people, and Yahweh answered him, 'Make a fiery serpent and put it on a standard. If anyone is bitten and looks at it, he shall live.' So Moses fashioned a bronze serpent which he put on a standard, and if anyone was bitten by a serpent, he looked at the bronze serpent and lived."' This event was important enough for Jesus to refer to it in the context of His own mission ("as Moses lifted up the serpent in the desert," *John* 3:14)

A Lutheran writer explains the relevance of the Incarnation for images: "After the incarnation, through Christ's taking upon himself our humanity, this lowly nature of ours, even the entire creation is hallowed, redeemed. With the incarnation everything has changed and become new.... Even this material world can now be seen as 'holy' and can provide the starting point for our journey home. Iconophobia reveals a lack of appreciation for the new world God has created in the coming of Jesus Christ in the flesh."[2]

NOTES

[1]William Cole. "Was Luther a Devotee of Mary?" (*Marian Studies*, Volume XXI, 1970, p.131).

[2]Karlfried Froehlich, "The Libri Carolini and the Lessons of the Iconoclastic Controversy," in *The One Mediator, The Saints and Mary*, H. George Anderson, J. Francis Stafford, Joseph A. Burgess eds. (Minneapolis: Augsburg Fortress, 1992), 208.

Church Criteria for Evaluating the Authenticity of Apparitions

(includes the author's interview with Joseph Cardinal Ratzinger, the future Pope Benedict XVI)

When it comes to claims of a supernatural phenomenon, the Church's default position is skepticism. Consequently, the Church's standard response to such claims is to examine and deploy all natural models and mechanisms within which the phenomenon can be explained. Scientists and other specialists are invited to study the phenomenon and to consider all known natural explanations for it.

For instance, before an exorcism is considered, psychiatrists and other medical personnel have to certify that the subject is not suffering from some medical or mental affliction as opposed to an intrusion from an external agent that requires an exorcism. But when the subject displays superhuman strength or levitates or exhibits some other kind of behavior that cannot be naturally explained, then the Church considers the possibility of an exorcism. The Church then reviews the behavior against the history of other verified exorcisms and if it fits the model, then it authorizes an exorcism. If the behavior ends after an exorcism, this is further evidence of an external agent at work. Some irrational skeptics will continue to say, well, in the future science will come up with an explanation for the behavior and the efficacy of the exorcism. This kind of dogmatic thinking represents a refusal to take the evidence as it stands and to make the kind of inferences demanded by this evidence. It takes blind faith to believe that an infringement of the law of gravity (levitation) in the case of certain disturbed individuals can somehow be explained later by the existence of an entirely new set of undiscovered natural laws. And it is hard to argue with blind faith.

The Church adopts the same default skeptical position in other claims of supernatural phenomena whether it be an alleged miracle cure, an apparition of the Virgin Mary or a Eucharistic miracle. But it also lets the evidence render the final verdict. This is why the Church acknowledges very few of the claimed cures from Lourdes. Medical specialists have to first evaluate all the scientific studies and diagnoses relating to the claim of a cure before they reluctantly reach a conclusion as to supernaturality. In claims of apparitions, the witnesses first have to be judged psychologically normal and not delusional or deceptive. In many famous apparitions, there are tangible items belying the ordinary operation of the laws of nature that serve as physical evidence supporting the claim, for instance, the Tilma of Guadalupe.

In claims of Eucharistic miracles where the elements transform into flesh or blood, the Church first asks the scientists to evaluate these elements so as to rule out bacterial growth or some other natural agency as the cause of discoloration. But if, as in the case of Lanciano, the elements date back to 700 A.D. and were scientifically shown to manifest the properties of muscular tissue from the heart and fresh blood, then the skeptic's refusal to take the evidence as it stands moves from blind faith to sheer superstition – given that the elements have retained the properties of flesh and blood for over a thousand years, something that does not comport with any known law of nature! Add to this the fact that this phenomenon is not isolated but fits within a pattern of a wide variety of Eucharistic miracles taking place across continents and centuries.

Can the Transcendent Source of our space-time continuum and its laws operate within it in such a fashion as to manifest Its transcending these laws? If you take all the evidence as it stands, the answer is Yes.

Claims of Apparitions

When it comes to claims of apparitions, we have seen earlier that the Church performs the role of "tester" when "testing" the "spirits" and its starting points are facts, doctrine and fruits.

These starting points were systematically organized into a framework of positive and negative criteria by the Sacred Congregation for the Doctrine of the Faith which replaced the guidelines drawn up at the Fifth Lateran Council in 1516. This is the framework utilized by the Church in its evaluation of apparitions past and present:

Positive Criteria
1. Moral certitude or a high probability that the facts are consistent with what has been claimed.
2. The persons involved are psychologically balanced, honest, living a good moral life, sincere, respectful toward church authority.
3. Immunity from error in theological and spiritual doctrine.
4. That there be sound devotion and spiritual fruits, such as the spirit of prayer, testimony of charity and true conversion.

Negative Criteria
1. That there be no manifest error regarding the facts of the event.
2. That there be no doctrinal errors attributed to God, Mary or a saint.
3. That there be no evidence of material or financial motives connected with the event.
4. That there be no gravely immoral acts by the person on the occasion of the revelations or apparitions.
5. That there be no psychopathic tendency in the person which might enter into the alleged supernatural event; no psychosis or collective hysteria of some type.

These criteria have been applied in evaluating the claims of apparitions described in this book - and have been judged to be successfully fulfilled in all of the approved apparitions. To the charge of diabolic deception, we should also ask how the fruits listed below are to be evaluated. Here are some of the things that happen to visionaries at apparitions and to those influenced by the apparitions: total conversion; increasing holiness; prayer; aversion to sin and Satan; evangelization. Physical healings and miracles are also associated with most of these apparitions but are less important than the spiritual and moral transformation that takes place. We would be well within our rights to ask whether Satan would bring about any of these spiritual changes. In point of fact, it cannot be denied that each one of these changes is fundamentally inimical to Satan and can only be attributed to him by someone who is lost without a compass in the moral universe.

A survey of the major apparitions will show that the ecclesiastical authorities who investigated them tended to be hostile and often alleged that the phenomenon was diabolic in nature. The approved apparitions, then, were only accepted after rigorous scrutiny by hostile prosecutors.

Although the apparitions cited in this volume can easily meet the criteria laid out above, there are still some Christians who remain unhappy with claims of apparitions for yet other reasons. Their argument can be summarized as follows:

1. Those who are apparition enthusiasts tend to give more importance to messages from apparitions than to the Gospel message.
2. Apparitions have an unhealthy eschatological or apocalyptic side to them that can whip up hysteria in the mobs.
3. Because they receive messages from a supernatural source, visionaries have a temptation to ignore or disobey those who have legitimate authority.
4. If an apparition message simply comes from a this-worldly and not a heavenly source, then those who are followers of the apparition will be focused on messages that have no external validation.
5. If an apparition comes from a diabolic source, the followers will eventually be enslaved by Satan.

Each one of these concerns can be appropriately addressed when we are dealing with authentic apparitions:

1. The accredited apparitions actually center our attention on the Gospel message and remind us forcefully of its truth and current applicability.
2. The apocalyptic and eschatological dimensions of apparitions are also found in many biblical passages. These dimensions are simply illustrations of the hard fact that violations of the laws of the spiritual universe have consequences of a cause-and-effect nature: every evil act calls forth punishments and chastisements. But the apocalyptic and eschatological dimensions are usually conditional in nature: they are requests from a loving mother to her children to avoid putting their hands in flames or playing on a busy highway.
3. Disobedience to authority is almost always a sign that an apparition is either human or diabolic in origin – since disobedience is the original sin of both Satan and the human race. None of the visionaries of the approved apparitions were guilty of such disobedience.
4. Before we accept the claims of an apparition, we must first be satisfied that it comes from a divinely directed supernatural source. That is why

it is important to "test" the spirits to see if they are from God – but we cannot reject them automatically without violating a scriptural command.

5. We have seen that it is possible to ensure that an apparition claim does not originate from Satan. Once we are sure that there is no satanic root in a given apparition, then we are not in any danger of being enslaved by Satan if we adopt the recommendations of the apparition. In fact all of the approved apparitions help liberate us from the slavery of Satan.

With all this, it still remains true that every apparition claim must be rigorously evaluated and should be accepted only if it meets all the relevant criteria. The dangers of human fraud and diabolic deception are ever present as are the human tendencies to gullibility and an unhealthy obsession with signs and wonders. We cannot let down our guard in these areas. But neither should we be on guard to such an irrational extent as to close our eyes and ears to the Messenger and Message sent to us by God. This latter is as much a danger as the former as we see in the Gospel accounts of the charges against Jesus.

Author Interview with Joseph Cardinal Ratzinger, Prefect of the Vatican's Sacred Congregation for the Doctrine of the Faith and the future Pope Benedict XVI, on the Evaluation of Apparitions

Q *Is it the case that the Church pronounces on the doctrinal soundness of the messages coming from an apparition but not on the validity as such of the apparition.*

The Church cannot and will not decide with absolute certainty if it was an apparition or not. [It deals] only with the "symptoms" and concludes this must come from another source but these are conclusions from the indications we have.

There can clearly be situations where we can say that "this is not an apparition." This is possible because indications can be so clear that it is possible to give this judgment. But it's not possible with absolute certainty to say this was an apparition.

It's spiritual and pastoral guidance that we must give in the light of authentic revelation. We will not give an absolute judgment about what is in this person. But we can and must give pastoral guidance in the light of the authentic revelation of Christ.

Q *That would mean determining whether the message is compatible with orthodox doctrine*

This is the essential criterion but there are other criteria. The essential criterion is coherence with authentic revelation.

Q *What role do the bishops' conferences and bishops play? Is the final decision on the authenticity of an apparition from the Vatican?*

It depends a little on the importance of a phenomenon. If we have only a local phenomenon it's not necessary that the Vatican intervene. If the bishops have sufficient evidence about the situation it's sufficient if the bishops give guidance to the people. Only if we [have something] of universal importance I think it's useful that the Vatican approves and confirms [it]; studies and, after study, confirms the decision of the bishops.

Q *But does the bishop's pronouncement have the authority of the Church as such if it is only an empirical judgment.*

I would distinguish. As pastoral guidance it has the authority of government in the Church. It is not a doctrinal authority in the strict sense but it has the authority of the pastors of the Church who give disciplinary guidance to the people.

Q *The Church does not validate or invalidate apparitions (although it could invalidate some). But it will not proclaim apparitions as a matter of public faith.*

The Church is charged by Our Lord to interpret official revelation and she is not charged to interpret with the same authority and authenticity other events. But this includes [the fact] that apparitions are never required for salvation. The Old and New Testament revelation have all that is necessary for salvation. So it is not necessary that the Church have a special, definitive charisma about these things because they are not necessary for salvation.

ACKNOWLEDGEMENTS

I am grateful first to my wife, Anila, and my family for the many sacrifices they have had to make in the course of my working on this book.

I am grateful also to many of the students and authorities on Marian apparitions who have provided direct assistance for this work and in particular the following:

Paul Massell for his numerous critical reviews and invaluable recommendations particularly the title!

Dwight Agor for all his copyediting and graphical work on the book

Ann Phillips, Mary Wilson and Janine Peake for their invaluable feedback

Dr. Thomas Petrisko, for photographs used in this volume and for the information in his many works on Marian apparitions.

Dr. Courtenay Bartholomew, for the use of his fine collection of photographs and for the information in his two books on the subject.

Dudley Plunkett for his kind and thorough reviews of previous versions of this volume and for the information in his books on Marian apparitions.

Mr. Robert Schaeffer, for photographs used in this volume.

Mrs. Rocilda Oliveria of Campo Grande, Brazil for the information on the Black Madonna of Brazil.

Mrs. Patrizia de Ferrari of Cordoba, Argentina for information on Our Lady of San Nicolas and the use of photographs.

Mrs. Monica Acquaviva for information on Our Lady of Buen Suceso and the use of photographs.

Mr. Mark Alder of London, England for information on Our Lady of Walshingham.

Mrs. Loreto Mary Whelton of London, England for information on Our Lady of Walsingham.

Ms. Ann Ball of Houston for the use of photographs and for valuable information from her book on Marian shrines.

Mrs. Miriam A. Weglian and Mr. Stephen M. Weglian for information on Our Lady of Cuapa from their book *Let Heaven and Earth Unite*.

The copyright on the image of Our Lady of La Vang reprinted here belongs to the Blue Army of Vietnam.

CPSIA information can be obtained
at www.ICGtesting.com
Printed in the USA
LVHW070015230222
711710LV00010B/472